IRELAND AND THE IRISH
A Short History

IRELAND AND THE IRISH

A Short History

KARL S. BOTTIGHEIMER

COLUMBIA UNIVERSITY PRESS
NEW YORK

Library of Congress Cataloging in Publication Data

Bottigheimer, Karl S.
Ireland and the Irish.

Bibliography: p.
Includes index.
1. Ireland—History. 2. Ireland—
Civilization. I. Title.
DA910.B67   941.5   82-4160
ISBN 0-231-04610-3   AACR2
ISBN 0-231-04611-1   (paper)

Columbia University Press
New York   Guildford, Surrey

p 10 9 8 7 6 5 4 3 2
c 10 9 8 7 6 5 4 3 2

To Edgar and Katherine,
Nat and Hannah, and Sue

CONTENTS

ILLUSTRATIONS

IRELAND AND THE IRISH
A Short History

1

THE INSULAR CONDITION
AND EARLY HABITATION

THIS IS a book about Ireland and its inhabitants. It is
meant to make comprehensible the basic contours of a
rich and complex past. It builds on the work of other
historians who, in earlier ages as well as our own, have
sought to preserve or recover the fleeting moment. Each
historian addresses the subject with an attitude which is an
amalgam of the distinctive interests and the pressing issues
of that historian's day. *My* concern is to provide in brief
and summary form an account of the sweep of Irish history
that renders less mysterious and arcane the enduring problems associated with Ireland in *my* time.

I have sought to separate fact from fiction, not necessarily rejecting the apocryphal, but always indicating the danger of building an elaborate hypothesis on it as a base. But
my principal concern has been not merely to relate the
past, but in so far as possible, explain it. Here, the danger
of error rudely reenters, for no matter how careful one has
been in banishing myth and embroidery from the relation,
the stringing together of undoubted fact into an explana-
tory structure requires assumptions and assertions which
may prove manifestly false. Without cause and effect a history is no more than a listing of notable events, but once
events, notable and otherwise, have been related to one another in terms of agency, an interpretative hypothesis ex-
ists which begs to be challenged.

Thus, no more than my predecessors, can I hold up *this* history of Ireland as *the* history. It is one synthesis at one moment in time; one effort to pull together diverse bits of knowledge and fashion them into an intelligible and satisfying explanation.

THE ISLAND SETTING

Ireland is the second largest of Europe's islands. With a land mass of 32,000 square miles, it is three-fifths the size of England, four times the size of Wales, and just a little larger than Scotland. In American terms it is four times the size of Massachusetts, and about the same size as Maine. Located in the North Atlantic between approximately 52 and 55 degrees north latitude, and 6 and 10 degrees west longitude, it is effectively screened from the European mainland by the island of Britain, nearly three times its size. Until the age of air travel, the shortest route to the European continent was the sea-lane from Cork to westernmost Brittany, a distance of nearly 300 miles. To cross the Bay of Biscay to the northern coast of Spain was 300 sea miles further.

Britain and Ireland, by contrast, are almost contiguous. Two million years ago the islands were still joined, and if one looks at their geographic forms from a distance, they still appear as an inverted V, sprung like a wishbone off the coast of northwest Europe. Between their respective midlands the melting ice of our interglacial period has pushed a watery gap sixty to seventy miles wide at its narrowest points, but in the north of Ireland, where the mountains of Antrim reach across the North Channel to the southward jutting peninsulas of Galloway and Kintyre, the old juncture is nearly intact, the water narrowing to a mere ten miles. In some ways, the closeness is illusory, for after the short sea passage, a traveler would find himself on a circuitous and difficult route through the Highlands and Islands, and would undergo the wildest areas of Scotland before reaching the north of England.

England and Ireland are not as distant from one another as, in the history of the two islands, it sometimes seems, but they adjoin inconveniently at their most rugged extremities in a way particularly hostile to intercourse between the cradles of their respective civilizations. The principal link is between northeast Ireland and southwest Scotland, and this geographical fact has had crucial consequences for the societies that developed in the two islands.

We have mentioned two islands, as if they existed alone, but in fact they are part of an archipelago of some 400 islands, approximately 200 of them inhabited today. One seldom thinks of the British Isles as an archipelago, because they are so dominated by Britain and Ireland, but these smaller islands have proved an important part of the physical environment, affording refuges, stepping stones, and occasional citadels to centuries of inhabitants. Many of the less remote islands are associated with the heavily indented coastlines of both western Ireland and western Scotland. Though the longest straight-line distance in Ireland is about 350 miles, the coastline stretches 2,200 miles, and is nearly as long as that of England and Wales (2,400 miles), despite their much greater area.

The physical environment is composed entirely of changeable elements. What differentiates them, for historical purposes, is their *rate* of change. Climate may alter rapidly with important consequences for flora and fauna. Geological features, for the most part, change too slowly to be perceptible within a mere four or five thousand years, and we can talk, therefore, about Ireland's geomorphology with reasonable confidence that it is today, as it was when the first humans arrived.

The size of the island has not changed. Neither has its basic topography, which is a confusing mixture of upland and lowland. The interior is "essentially a lowland and lies mainly around 200 feet, rising gently to 400 feet and varied by a number of low hills 600–1000 feet high."[1] The mountains tend to lie near the coasts. The highest peak, Carrauntoohil (3,414 feet), is in Kerry near Killarney, and there are a number of high peaks in this celebrated and picturesque, but agriculturally barren, area. The southwest has no monopoly of high country, for there are mountainous districts in each of the four provinces, and they constitute an almost ubiquitous presence in the life of every region. Despite the prominence of the central lowland which dominates Leinster and extends fingers into each of the adjacent provinces, the geography of Ireland is a complex assortment of levels. The regions are not naturally divided into neat compartments of plain and mountain.

The river system is equally complex. Although the Shannon, longest river in the British Isles, flows 240 miles down the western length of Ireland, it is not the heart of a great river system, but merely the largest of dozens of streams that run in virtually every direction from the highlands to the sea. As in England, the most advantageous ports and natural harbors lie in the south and west. Cork is the analogue of Plymouth or Portsmouth. Limerick, at the mouth of the Shannon, resembles Bristol's position on the Severn. Ireland's inland waters also include several hundred square miles of freshwater loughs (or lakes). Lough Neagh near Belfast (147 square miles) is the largest freshwater body in the British Isles, but there are many others especially along the Shannon and in Connacht. Still, the effect is one of miscellany. As there are no sizable mountain districts, neither is there a concentrated region of lakes. There are storied rivers: the Lagan, Liffey, Lee, Boyne, Suir, and Blackwater, but with the exception of the Shannon, none constitutes the heart of a sizable valley. The political particularism so notable a part of the history of Ireland is related to its topographical variety and the absence of a single large and easily inhabited area that could have served as the cradle of a dominant civilization.

The mountains and valleys are relatively stable. Soil and vegetation, however, are interrelated (together with climate), and highly changeable. Today, approximately two-thirds of Ireland is improved agricultural land, and more of the remaining third is rough grazing, woods, or forestry plantations.[2] Permanent human settlements are rare above 600 feet,[3] and the upper limit for arable farming is usually 800 feet, with 1,500 feet the limit for cattle.[4] The major areas of arable land are in the central and eastern portions of the country.

Ireland is today the least forested country in Europe with only 3 percent of its area covered with woodlands,[5] but it has been estimated that this percentage was four times greater in 1600.[6] The largest and densest woodlands lie to the northwest of Lough Neagh, in the Erne basin, along the Shannon, in the river valleys of the west and south, and on the eastern slopes of the Wicklow and Wexford Hills.[7] Oak was probably the most common species, and there are nearly 1,600 place-names which contain variations of the Irish word for it, *diabre* (English form: Derry).[8] Ireland may well have been much more heavily wooded in pre-Tudor times, but the almost totally deforested state to which it had evolved by 1800 was basically the result of continuous human exploitation by pre-industrial men, particularly iron-molters working in the seventeenth century.

If Britain screens Ireland from Europe, Ireland protects at least a portion of Britain from the sea. The waters of the Gulf Stream reach the British Isles as the North Atlantic Drift, which divides to pass both north and south of the archipelago. The prevailing westerly winds convey the relative warmth of these waters to an area which would otherwise suffer a climate more like that of frigid Newfoundland, whose northerly latitude it shares. Historical climate is not easily determined, though there have been some highly ingenious hypotheses; but there is no reason to believe that the climate of northern Europe and the British Isles has experienced *major* variations from its current norm in the last ten thousand years. The Roman geographers, two thousand years ago, reported a climate in Ireland very similar to that encountered today: cool, wet, and without extremes of temperature. To Mediterranean peoples it was a salubrious climate, a refuge from the epidemic diseases of the warmer Mediterranean basin.

The rainfall pattern for Ireland vaguely resembles that of Britain, with the wettest regions (over sixty inches per year) in the extreme west, gradually giving way to drier regions in the center and east. But the weather maps document Ireland's tendency to the mean, for nowhere in Ireland are there areas receiving over 100 inches of rainfall such as exist in North Wales, the English Lake District, and the Scottish Highlands, nor is there any area as dry as the less than twenty-five-inch-per-year regions of East Anglia and the eastern English Midlands. The same tendency toward the mean appears in projections of daily temperatures in the British Isles.

Ireland is neither so cold as the coldest parts of Britain in January, nor so warm as the warmest parts of Britain in July; and if this is true of Ireland as a whole, it is even more pronounced around the coasts, particularly the north, west, and south. There (as in western Wales, Cornwall, and parts of Scotland) the mean temperature varies not much more than 20°F. between January and July, that is to say, approximately from the low forties to the low sixties. This is a climate which those accustomed to central heating tend to find uncomfortable, and which even English colonists relocating from their drier, warmer south lamented. But it has not, historically, been regarded by the inhabitants of Ireland as rigorous or hostile to the maintenance of life. There was no need to anticipate with rugged buildings and stock-piled fuel the onslaught of winter, which in some areas could hardly be distinguished from summer except for the shortened days.

The environment I have sketched is, in short, an Atlantic projection of northern Europe and very closely related to that of Britain. There are certain differences particularly in the distribution of mineral resources such as coal, but generally Ireland is an integral part of the British archipelago, divided from it only by narrow seas, and by the much more formidable sense of separateness which has been the legacy of the last 2,000 years.

EARLY HABITATION

The earth is perhaps four billion years old, and man as a species has existed for some two million years, but the earliest reliable traces of human activity in Ireland date from around 6800 B.C.[9] These are the Mesolithic (or Middle Stone Age) remains clustered in Antrim, the most northeasterly county of Ireland and the closest landfall for migrants from southwest Scotland. They take the form of microliths, small stone implements usually of flint that were sharpened to make weapons or tools. Such implements become much more common and widespread in the period after 3500 B.C., by which time they are found as far south as Dublin Bay and as far west as County Sligo in Connacht.

The Neolithic, or New Stone Age, dates in Ireland from about 3700 B.C. and is characterized by the appearance of polished stone implements alongside the more crudely worked flint. Neolithic man kept domesticated animals such as oxen and sheep and planted crops such as barley and wheat. If the 1967–68 excavations at Ballynagilly near Cookstown in County Tyrone are typical, early Neolithic man lived in crude, covered pits, which only gradually gave way to wooden structures.[10] Fragments of pottery were found in the same site, radiocarbon dated to 3675 ± 50 B.C., and are of a turned-out rim type similar to what was being produced in the Yorkshire wolds of England at about the same period.

The most abundant remains of Neolithic man in both Britain and Ireland are the megaliths, or large stones, of which there are about 1,200 examples in Ireland, far more widely scattered than in Britain, where they are concentrated in such areas as Salisbury Plain, the West Country, southwest Wales, and northeast Scotland. These various arrangements of large stones—for an assortment of purposes still only dimly understood—range from the massive and monumental, to less conspicuous constructions of three, four, or five stones. They were built over a very long period of time, probably more than two millennia. Some were for use in religious rites, others for burial or monumental purposes, and yet others for astronomical calculations of a sophisticated order.

The earliest megalithic remains in Ireland are structures called court cairns, mounds of stone heaped over long rectangular stone-built burial chambers fronted by a semicircular open space or court flanked by standing stones. They appear to have served as communal burying places for decades or even centuries and, from the hundreds of tons of stone which had to be moved to construct them, archaeologists have inferred that "the society which built them must have been very well organized and have had considerable manpower at its disposal." But the greatest of the megalithic monuments in Ireland were communal burial places of a different sort. Called "passage graves," they take the form of large round earthen mounds "with a long passage leading from the bottom edge of the mound to a tomb at or near the centre of the mound."[11] About three hundred of them have been discovered, often in clusters, and mostly in the northern part of the country.

By far the most imposing and celebrated is the group located on three neighboring hills of Dowth, Knowth, and Newgrange in a bend of the River Boyne between Drogheda and Slane in County Meath. The existence of a burial chamber in the mound at Newgrange had been known since at least the end of the seventeenth century, but recent excavations have been extremely productive, and work at Knowth in 1968–69 revealed one of the most remarkable passage graves anywhere in Europe.

What distinguishes the Boyne Valley passage graves is not only their size and complexity, but also the presence in them of the earliest recognizable Irish "art" or decoration. Early man communicates to posterity by the physical vestiges of his life: his buildings, graves, implements, bones, and even garbage, tell the archaeologist how, when, and where he lived. But the discovery of his art, whether frivolous or ritualistic, is a leap forward in this process equalled only by the discovery of a written language. The "art" of Newgrange and Knowth takes the form of geometrical engraving upon stone. The motifs are primitive, bold, and simple, but they reappear in diverse and sometimes brilliant forms in the metalwork and manuscript illumination of later Irish civilization. Irish archaeology remains in its infancy, but enough is known to establish Ireland as the area of a remarkable neolithic civilization which flourished between approximately 3700 and 2000 B.C.

The Stone Age ended, strictly speaking, with the development and spread of metal implements, first gold and bronze (a mixture of copper and tin), and later iron. The introduction of metalworking to the British Isles is associated with the migrations from the Continent of the so-called Beaker people, the shards of whose distinctive earthen pottery have provided abundant clues to their whereabouts. It used to be thought that the Beaker people did not reach Ireland in large numbers, but beakers keep coming to light, particularly in the north, making it necessary to revise this assumption. Whether or not the Beaker people were actually the developers and disseminators of metalworking techniques remains to be seen. What can be said with certainty is that they were present at the time—approximately 1800 B.C.—from which the earliest British metalwork dates. Here again, what survives in Ireland is remarkable and among the most sophisticated work of its time. Gold was panned from rivers in County Wicklow, on the east coast, and made into jewelry which traders carried to Britain and the continent. Enough remained at home to be discovered in modern times and provide for the National Museum of Ireland in Dublin one of the finest collections of prehistorical gold anywhere in Europe.

CELTICIZATION

Thus far I have discussed Ireland, and its earliest inhabitants, without mention of the "Celts." The Celticization of Ireland—indeed, of Britain as well—remains a confusing phase of ancient history. Basically, there are three theories, which sometimes, conveniently, coincide to reinforce each other, but elsewhere, more annoyingly, diverge. The first construct is derived from the Greek and Roman writers of antiquity, who encountered and described a widespread European people whom they called *Keltoi* or *Galatae*. The second construct is derived from modern archaeological research and the identification with a particular material culture (and certain arts, artifacts, and metallurgical talents) of those whom the ancients called "Celts." The third construct is a linguistic theory that identifies the Celts with a family of common languages, the evidence of which remains largely in place-names. In other words, one can refer to a particular inhabitant of the ancient world as a Celt either because the ancients themselves did, because one has evidence that he or she had the same skills and possessed the same implements as those the archaeologists call Celts, or because one has evidence that he or she spoke what the linguists term a Celtic language.

From an *archaeological* point of view, Ireland entered the Bronze Age (c.1800 B.C.) without benefit of "the Celts." Indeed the earliest inhabitants of Ireland are sometimes referred to as "pre-Celts," an imprecise but serviceable term. At some time between the Bronze Age and the Iron Age, that is, in the first millennium B.C., Ireland took on a Celtic character as defined by all three theories elaborated above. Archaeologically, this transition is marked by the appearance in Ireland of a decorative style known as La Tène, named after the site on Lake Neuchatel in Switzerland where, in the nineteenth century, a Celtic settlement of the fifth century B.C. was excavated, revealing a treasure of artifacts. So impressive and influential were the finds at La Tène that they became the reference point for determining what was or was not Celtic in the last centuries of the pre-Christian era.

The appearance of La Tène designs in Ireland has thus been interpreted to mean that this central European culture had finally reached Ireland. Celebrated objects in the

La Tène style include the Turoe stone from County Galway and a stunning gold collar (now in the National Museum of Ireland, Dublin) found in a gold hoard at Broighter, County Derry. Both are usually dated from the third century B.C. The same distinctive La Tène style is also found on bronze objects of a similar date such as brooches (used as garment fasteners), horse-bits, spear-butts, and discs, but these objects are without exact parallels outside Ireland.

One archaeologist has concluded that "it was only the art style and not the types of objects which had been introduced into Ireland from outside during the Iron Age." Such an interpretation leads to a more modest view of the impact of La Tène Celtic civilization upon Ireland than has often been advanced. Rather than large-scale migrations of continental Celts to Ireland in the pre-Christian period, perhaps the Bronze Age inhabitants of Ireland were only "intruded upon by small bands of iron-using Celtic chieftains who may have been accompanied by Celtic craftsmen who manufactured objects of Irish type but decorated them in an art style which they had brought with them from Britain or ultimately from the Continent."[12] The present state of archaeological evidence leads to the conclusion that the linguistic Celticization of Ireland occurred prior to the Iron Age, and was not therefore the result of continental La Tène Celts fleeing to Ireland to escape the conquering legions of Rome in the second and first centuries B.C.

Linguistic evidence is sometimes seen to point in another direction, to a somewhat later Celticizing process. Professor David Greene writes:

We have no reason to believe that the Celtic-speaking peoples had been in Britain and Ireland for any very great period before our historical evidence begins, or that the original invaders represented any more than a fairly thinly-spread ruling class, so that we should not regard Irish and Welsh as languages which were imported into their respective countries, but as languages which are really indigenous in the sense that they have grown up as the result of all the linguistic and social influences which have touched Ireland and Wales over more than two thousand years.[13]

Even if the *first* Celts to reach Britain and Ireland were not driven there by the Romans there can be no doubt that the expansionistic Romans both caused and recorded a subsequent exodus in the last two centuries before Christ. The refugees of the second and first centuries B.C. may only have swelled a population already Celtic, or near Celtic in speech, and added to its culture knowledge of La Tène styles.

How much is known about the civilization of Ireland during the nearly five hundred years the Romans occupied Britain? Because there are no written records of that civilization, historians have been forced to project onto Ireland the image of the Celts recorded by the ancients during their encounters with them on the continent and in Britain. Hecataeus of Miletus, about 500 B.C., described Narbonne (on the south coast of France) as a Celtic town, and Marseilles as a Greek city near Celtic territory. Herodotus, Xenophon, and Aristotle all provided further scraps of information, and Polybius, in the second century B.C., recorded the triumphant resistance of the Roman Republic to Celtic expansion into Italy from central Europe. Polybius gave literary form to the classic image—preserved in numerous works of ancient art—of the Celt as a valiant and heroic savage, a courageous warrior and worthy opponent of Greek and Roman arms.

This image was further amplified in the work of Poseidonios, a first-century B.C. historian whose writings have not survived, but were incorporated by several later writers, including Julius Caesar in his chronicle of the conquest of Gaul.[14] Poseidonios endowed the Celts with their classic ethnography, a delineation of their character, culture, and origins which served as the basis for virtually all subsequent accounts. Caesar reduced this ethnography to what might be called social structure:

Everywhere in Gaul there are only two classes of men who are of any account or consideration. The common people are treated almost as slaves, never venture to act on their own initiative, and are not consulted on any subject. Most of them, crushed by debt or heavy taxation or the oppression of more powerful persons, bind themselves to serve men of rank, who exercise over them all the rights that masters have over slaves. The two privileged classes are the Druids and the Knights.[15]

The writers of antiquity left a detailed account of the Celts, their major European adversary, and there is enough consistency in their reports to make them convincing. On the other hand, we do not know how uniform Celtic civilization was in either time or place. What Poseidonios observed of Celtic life in southern Gaul in the first century B.C. may *not* have been true of Celtic Ireland two or three centuries later. One looks for confirmations or conjunctions in which the evidence of ancient authors is corroborated by archaeological evidence from Ireland itself, or literary evidence from the Irish sagas which began to be written down in the twelfth century after Christ.

A good example has to do with eating habits, always a popular subject in ethnography. Diodorus Siculus, drawing on Poseidonios, says of a feast: "Beside them are hearths blazing with fire, with cauldrons and spits containing large pieces of meat. Brave warriors they honour with the finest portions of the meat."[16] But a seventeenth-century antiquary, Geoffrey Keating, described a rather different and more cumbersome Irish way of preparing meat. Pits were dug in moorland clay and filled with water. A great fire was made nearby, and a pile of large stones was thrown into it. When the rocks became red hot, they were shoveled into the pit until the water boiled. The meat, wrapped in straw, was then cooked in this crude, but commodious cauldron.

Numerous pits of this description survive in Ireland, and an archaeologist who attempted to use one in the prescribed manner reported that "the water turned opaque, and the surface was covered with a scum of globules of fat and ashes, but the meat itself was kept free of contamination by the straw covering."[17] One would think that so crude a method of cooking must antedate the metal-age spits and cauldrons described by Diodorus Siculus, but even in the late sixteenth century Englishmen were observing the common Irish practice of boiling flesh in cauldrons improvised from the skins of slain beasts. Perhaps their metalwork was not equal to making cauldrons, or perhaps they simply preferred the portability of skins.[18]

There are great risks in assuming that the classical ethnography of the Celts developed by Poseidonios and his successors provides an adequate description of Celtic Ireland. The ancients did not reach Ireland, so far as we know. Tacitus, the Roman historian who lived from A.D. c.55 to 120, described how his father-in-law, Agricola, the military commander of the Roman forces in Britain, briefly contemplated an invasion of Ireland A.D. 81:

Agricola had given a welcome to an Irish prince, who had been driven from home by a rebellion; nominally a friend, he might be used as a pawn in the game. I have often heard Agricola say that Ireland could be reduced and held by a single legion and a few auxiliaries, and that the conquest would also pay from the point of view of Britain, if Roman arms were in evidence on every side and liberty vanished off the map.[19]

But for reasons not specified, Agricola refrained from attempting an invasion. It is hard to believe that in four hundred years of occupying Britain, not a single Roman reached Ireland, but no written record of such an encounter survives.

Our picture of early Celtic Ireland is therefore inferential. We know that various waves of Celtic migrants reached Ireland in the last millennium before Christ, that they introduced and successfully propagated a Celtic language, Celtic art forms, and certain Celtic customs. But we are not entitled to assume that what was true of the Celts on the continent or in Britain was true of the Celts in Ireland unless or until we find confirmatory evidence in artifacts of unquestioned Irish origin or in the sagas of early Irish literature. The sagas present the additional problem that they telescope historical time in a poetic but perplexing manner, making it difficult to date precisely the practices they describe.

THE ROMAN IMPRINT

Whatever the nature and diversity of Celtic civilization in the British Isles, the advent of the Romans marked a crucial watershed. In a logical extension of his Gallic campaigns of 58–56 B.C., Caesar conducted an exploratory expedition to southern England in 55, and again in 54 B.C. A century later, A.D. 43, the Romans, under Claudius, launched a full-scale effort to invade, conquer, and colonize Celtic Britain. The resulting colony survived for four hundred years, but the legionaries neither replaced the Celtic inhabitants they conquered, nor subdued the intransigent natives, who took refuge in the rough, mountainous country of Wales and Scotland. In the southeast, Roman towns, camps, and villas were held together by a prodigious network of highways. Romanized Celts were gradually assimilated into both civilian and military administration and, in turn, adopted (at least in part) Roman religion and culture. In the north and west, and even more so, in Ireland and the Isle of Man, Celtic civilization survived without concessions to Rome or Roman ways. No doubt there was trade between Ireland and Roman Gaul, perhaps with Roman Britain as well, but the distinctive patterns of Roman life and culture were decisively rejected.

By the time of the Roman advent, the Celts of the British Isles were divided linguistically into what are sometimes called the P Celts and Q Celts, speaking two related languages which scholars call Brythonic and Goidelic or, more simply, British and Irish. The "qu" or "kw" sound in a Latin word like *quattuor* (the number 4) took on a "p" sound in Brythonic (British) to become *petor*, but kept the "qu" sound in Goidelic (Irish) when it became *ceathair*.[20]

No one is certain how early or by what means this linguistic division developed, but the effect of the Roman occupation in Britain was to make the distinction essentially one between Irish and Welsh, because Wales was the principal refuge of the Brythonic Celts. Scotland was a more complicated case because of the flux of populations be-

tween it and northern Ireland. In the fifth century, if not
before, its language was heavily influenced by the migration of Goidelic-speaking people from Ireland. No such in-
terchange occurred between Ireland and Wales.

Ireland may not have been the last part of Europe to
have been reached by the Celts—perhaps that honor belongs to Scotland—but it was the one insular and insulated
area where Celtic civilization could survive relatively unaffected by other forces and cultural influences. It became
not the ultimate repository of Celtic civilization *in toto,* but
the one surviving variant. Celtic languages survived also in
Scotland, Wales, Cornwall, and on the continent in that
westernmost part of France called "Brittany," after the
Brythonic (or British) Celts who fled there from England
and Wales in the fifth and sixth centuries.

When the legions retreated from Britain in the first decades of the fifth century they left the Romanized Celts of
the southeast defenseless and exposed to their uncivilized
brethren of the north and west, as well as to the depredations of seaborne Germanic invaders. Caesar had found the
Germans almost exclusively east of the Rhine and north of
the Danube. Everything to the west and south of that great
river border was regarded as essentially Celtic. Despite
their heroic resistance, the Celts succumbed to the Roman
advance like grass before the scythe. Where the Celts had
established themselves, the Romans soon followed. Once
the Romans discovered the key to military supremacy, the
exploitation of the tribal particularism with which Celtic
society was ridden, they used it to subjugate every Celtic
area, until only Ireland remained untouched. The Germans
were a different matter, and in the fourth and fifth centuries began to spill into a western Europe that no longer
possessed either the vigor of pre-Christian Celtic society or
the orderly superstructure of a healthy Roman empire. Like
the Romans, the early Germanic invaders did not reach Ireland, but their arrival (as the "Anglo-Saxons") in southern
England provoked the emigration of Celtic peoples to
Brittany.

When the Romans first arrived, the British Isles shared a common Celtic character even if there were important regional differences. That common cultural character was shattered when first the Romans and then the Germans included Britain, but not Ireland, in their conquests. The impact of the Romans upon Britain remains debatable. Beyond the survival of place-names, certain roads, and a number of towns, it is not easy to demonstrate that the Romans left an enduring imprint upon the part of Britain that was to become England. The migrations of the Angles, Saxons, Jutes, and other Germanic peoples had a much more substantial effect. They introduced to England a numerous population and a language which eventually became (in English) the vernacular everywhere save the "Celtic fringe." They gave rise to settlement patterns, legal systems, and widespread customs which provided the most basic fabric of English civilization. England as an entity was the creation of the Germanic invasions, and the British Celts were either assimilated, or fled to Brittany, Cornwall, Wales, and Scotland. Ireland was unaffected, and an ethnic gulf was thus created in an archipelagic civilization which had previously been culturally related, if politically unorganized.

THE CHRISTIAN LEGACY

I cannot leave the Roman contribution without mentioning its crucial postscript. Christianity first reached the British Isles through the Romans. Rome overwhelmed the Celts from without, but Christianity exploited Rome from within. It was a religious and social movement which grew out of, and was adapted to, the urban and commercial civilization of the Mediterranean world. Its apostles carried the faith along the excellent highways and propagated the word in Romanized towns to Romanized soldiers and bureaucrats. In the fourth century the Emperor Constantine saw the light, and Christianity replaced paganism as the official religion of the empire. Just how deep an impact Roman Christianity made upon Britain remains to be seen. We know that when the Romans left, Christianity in England all but disappeared, along with other elements of Roman culture. But at the very moment in the fifth century when this was happening, the seeds of Christianity were being planted in a nearby land where they would survive, and flourish.

The probable agent of this rescue was a Romanized Celt named Patrick, who grew up somewhere on the west coast of England. In his spiritual testament, called the *Confessio* and written in rude Latin, not Celtic, he tells the remarkable story of how at the age of sixteen he was kidnapped near his home by pirates and sold into slavery in Ireland. After six years' captivity he escaped and determined to prepare himself exhaustively for the great mission of propagating the gospel among his former captors. According to tradition he returned to Ireland A.D. 432 and was successful in converting to Christianity the rulers of the north. Whether he was actually the first Christian missionary to Ireland is doubtful, but he is, in any event, the most celebrated and best remembered for reasons which will be discussed below.

The Christianity Patrick brought to Ireland was not entirely "Roman" in its content, a fact which is hardly surprising given the embryonic state of the Roman papacy in the early fifth century. During his lengthy preparation for the return to Ireland Patrick had acquired, probably in France, a number of doctrines which would soon be rejected by Rome, but which—thanks to Patrick—would linger in Ireland. But if Patrick's theology was more Asian and "Eastern Mediterranean" than Roman, he himself was a product of Roman civilization in Britain, and his return to Ireland forged a crucial link between the insular Celts and the Mediterranean civilization from which their ancestors had been driven. Ireland was excluded from *Roman* Europe, but in *Christian* Europe it was to play a vital if sometimes dissonant role.

It is no easy task to discover what the conversion of the Irish actually signified. In the first place, there were probably already some Christian communities in the south, for

in 431 Pope Celestine sent a priest named "Palladius" as
the first bishop to "the Irish believing in Christ." Palladius
may have been a genuine predecessor of Patrick, or he may
have been Patrick himself under another name, but in
either event Celestine thought that there were already some
believers in Ireland. In the second place, it is not clear how
substantial a change Christianity effected in Irish culture
and society. Later writers in the eighth century tended to
maximize and probably exaggerate Patrick's impact. *The
Catalogue of the Saints of Ireland* relates:

The first order of Catholic saints was in the time of Patrick; and
then they were all bishops, distinguished and holy, and full of the
Holy Ghost, 350 in number, founders of churches. They had one
head, Christ, and one chief, Patrick. They had one Mass, one lit-
urgy, one tonsure from ear to ear. They celebrated one Easter, on
the fourteenth moon after the vernal equinox, and what was excommunicated by one church all excommunicated.[21]

The Christianization of Ireland can hardly have been so
complete or dramatic. Pagan ceremonies lingered for decades or even centuries. Patrick's influence was clearly limited to the north, and both his qualifications and means of
proceeding were criticized by influential sections of the
continental Church. He established what later became the
primatial archdiocese of Ireland at Armagh, just two miles
from Emain Macha, a royal fort of the kings of Ulster, but
he did not regard it as a permanent administrative center.
Indeed, Patrick was itinerant and "travelled with a retinue
of the sons of princes, rather as any important Irishman
might have travelled with a retinue suited to his rank."
Bribery was one of his most commonly used means of persuasion. "An ill-educated, itinerant bishop, travelling with
a paid retinue of young nobles, distributing largesse to
petty kings, may well have been regarded with misgivings
by unimaginative churchmen in Gaul and Britain. Patrick's
mission demonstrates that from the beginning the peculiar
conditions of an extra-imperial, heroic society compelled
unconventional measures of evangelization."[22] But every-

where in northern Europe the Church encountered, and
eventually overwhelmed, heroic societies, and the pattern
which emerged in Ireland was similar to that emerging on
the continent and that would soon emerge in Britain as
well. By the sixth century, or the seventh at the latest, the
Church in Ireland was "under the rule of Bishops."

"Each bishop held authority within his own *paruchia* [lit-
erally, parish], and could not exercise his functions in the
paruchia of another bishop without his brother's permis-
sion. No priest might say mass in a church he had built until the bishop of his *paruchia* had consecrated it; no
stranger might minister in the *paruchia* without the bishop's
authority".[23] Each *paruchia* seems to have been the land inhabited by a particular tribe (*tuath*) or one of its subdivi-
sions. The point is that the earliest church structure in Ireland was rational, episcopal, and territorial. There was not,
at the outset, any evidence of that propensity for monasticism and monastic life which was soon to set the Irish
Church apart from every other in Europe.

Nowhere else, however, had the Church attempted the
conversion of un-Romanized Celts, and the un-urbanized,
un-commercial, semi-nomadic Irish seem to have been un-
suited to an episcopal and parochial system which was bu-
reaucratic and urbane at its heart. The consequence was
that monasticism, which in most of Christendom evolved
as a parallel, sometimes rival, system of ecclesiastical authority, in Ireland evolved as predominant and very nearly
exclusive. Armagh had become a monastery by the end of
the century (fifth) in which Patrick established it as a religious center. St. Brigid had founded at Kildare monasteries
for both men and women by the same time. In the early
sixth century St. Finnian transformed the Patrician church
at Clonard (Meath) into what became a monastery of great
renown, and monastic foundations followed throughout
Ireland, but especially in central Leinster. Most were located in the interior, despite the choice for a few of spectacular insular and coastal places.

The Irish annals provide statistical corroboration for the

sixth-century growth of monasticism. For the period prior to 549 they name 28 clerics of whom 25 are described as bishops, one as an abbot, leaving two unidentified. But for the period between 549 and 600 the annals name 33 clerics of whom only 13 are called bishops, while 17 are described as abbots or priests. From 601 to 664 the annals name 97 clerics, of whom 24 are bishops and 48 are abbots. The annals are not altogether reliable on such matters, but they provide a persuasive and largely unchallenged picture of the appeal and rapid spread of monasticism in late sixth- and seventh-century Ireland.[24]

By the end of the sixth century, monasticism was flourishing in Ireland and extending tentacles into western Scotland and northeastern England. Although this efflorescence of religious life is abundantly recorded in hagiography (the literature concerning saints' lives), archaeological evidence is slight. Some dozen of the early monastic sites have been excavated, but even below ground, nothing of the earliest period seems to survive. The first structures were probably of perishable wood, or the small wood lattice work filled with plaster called wattle and daub.

In the west there are numerous stone remains of eremitic dwellings from what scholars believe is a later period, probably the eighth and ninth centuries. The most famous of these is the wind and wave-swept island-monastery of Skellig Michael, but just to the north, County Kerry's Dingle peninsula contains remains of more than 40 small monasteries, each enclosed by a round or oval monastic wall, some with the round "beehive huts" (called *clochans*) which were built of dry stone on the corbeled principle used in the passage graves at Knowth and Newgrange in the 3d millennium B.C. Such tiny and isolated establishments suggest an austere monasticism struggling to escape "community" even in an ecclesiastical form. But elsewhere as at Clonmacnoise and Glendalough, monasteries developed the institutional and collective character which, in the eleventh century, reached its fullest expression under continental influence in ornate and elaborate houses such as the Cistercian Abbey of Mellifont, in County Louth. There, monasticism does not so much escape from the world as re-create it, re-ordered within the walls, cloisters, and courtyards, of a veritable ecclesiastical city.

Early Irish monasticism must have had an appeal beyond the spiritual benefits of an ascetic life. As one scholar has asked: "Why was the endowment of monasteries more attractive to Irishmen [in the sixth century] than the endowment of tribal bishops?" In Wales, too, in the same period there is evidence that monastic organization prevailed in un-Romanized areas in contrast to the episcopal structure elsewhere.[25]

Monasticism seems to have been more compatible with the Irish system of tribal organization and property. "Families built churches on their own lands with their own kin as abbots, or they retained interests in the monastery" established by the family. "The property of such a church would belong, by hereditary right, to the family of the founding saint (or patron), and succeeding abbots would be heirs to the founder." "Succession to the abbacy rested with the family of the donor when the line of the patron saint failed to produce a suitable candidate."[26]

By contrast with the abbots, the bishops tried to separate the land from the control of the laity, creating the Church as a state within a state, endowed with its own inalienable wealth, and administered by its own, independent hierarchy. It is one of the ironies of Irish history that the society which, soon after its conversion, vigorously and successfully resisted the growth of an autonomous church, in modern times permitted the most powerful and independent church in Christendom. It is a salutary reminder that the Irish have *become* what they are and that the character of their culture is an ephemeral and changing attribute. Whatever the source of its strength, monasticism was woven into the fabric of Irish society at this very early period, and through its growth Irish Christianity made its great impact upon Britain and Europe.

The Irish had been innocent of Christianity until the middle of the fifth century, but a century later they were among its active propagators. The most celebrated of the missionaries was Columba (or Colmcille), who founded monasteries at Derry in the north, and Durrow on the central plain, before he crossed the sea (c.563) to begin a monastic colony at Iona, a tiny island off southwest Scotland. Iona became the base for the evangelization of Pictish Scotland, and was the religious component of a secular expansion which saw the fifth- and sixth-century invasion of southern and western Scotland by warriors from the north of Ireland (the Ui Neill), and the establishment of an Irish (as opposed to Pictish) kingdom in Scotland (Dál Riata). Columba was apparently attached to the court of the king of Dál Riata, Aedan mac Gabrain, a great power in the last quarter of the sixth century.

Columba's disciple, Saint Aidan, went from Iona to the Anglo-Saxon kingdom of Northumbria in northern England where he established, about 640, another great island monastery at Lindisfarne, just off the Northumberland coast. Oswald, Anglo-Saxon king of Northumbria, had himself been converted to Christianity at Iona in the early seventh century, and appealed for missionaries to help the propagation of the gospel among his people. Thus the influence of Irish Christianity, embodied in the monastic movement of the sixth century, extended crescent-like into Scotland, and thence southward into northeastern England. This was by no means the limit of its influence. St. Columbanus, a disciple of Columba, traveled from the monastery of Bangor in County Down to the continent in about 590 to establish monasteries at Luxeuil in France and Bobbio in northern Italy. His companion, St. Gall, settled near Lake Constance in what is today Switzerland, and provided the inspiration for a monastery built in his memory and given his name in the following century. St. Brendan allegedly voyaged in the opposite direction, braving the Atlantic for faraway places whose exact identity has long been disputed.[27]

Thus the Irish who had been so late to receive the Christian message, in the sixth and seventh centuries propagated

it back into Europe and, most consequentially, into Anglo-
Saxon England. The progress of their work, particularly in
the north of England, was told by the early eighth-century
Northumbrian scholar, Bede, in his *History of the English
Church and People*. The drama in this Latin classic of early
English historiography is the conflict between Rome and
Ireland for the allegiance of the Anglo-Saxon settlers of
England. Roman Christianity, now represented by the papacy rather than the emperor, made its triumphal reentry
to Britain in 597 when Pope Gregory I sent an expedition
headed by Augustine which landed in the southeastern corner of the country, the Anglo-Saxon kingdom of Kent. Augustine had little difficulty converting the pagan king, Eth-
elbert, and establishing an archepiscopal see at Canterbury,
but in the north of England his successors encountered
Anglo-Saxons who had already been converted to Christianity by Irish ecclesiastics and who were in no hurry to de-
fer to the authority of Rome. Although the matter on which
Rome and Ireland most palpably differed was the method
for calculating the correct date of Easter, this dispute
merely symbolized the independence of Irish Christianity
from a continental faith that was increasingly hierarchical
and institutional. According to Bede, the confrontation between the two traditions occurred in 664 during the reign
of King Oswy of Northumbria, an event remembered as the
Synod of Whitby. Oswy wished to be sure that he was on
the right track to salvation and asked his own Irish-leaning
bishop, Colman, to debate with Wilfrid, a monk of Ripon
who had been Romanized in his views by a period of study
in France and Rome:

Our Easter customs are those that we have seen universally observed in Rome [Wilfrid began], where the blessed Apostles Peter
and Paul lived, taught, suffered, and are buried. We have also
seen the same customs generally observed throughout Italy and
Gaul when we travelled through these countries for study and
prayer. Furthermore, we have found them to be observed in
many different countries and languages at the same time, in Africa, Asia, Egypt, Greece, and throughout the world wherever the

Church of Christ has spread. The only people who are stupid
enough to disagree with the whole world are these Scots [mean-
ing Irish] and their obstinate adherents the Picts and Britons,
who inhabit only a portion of these two islands in the remote
ocean.[28]

Oswy chose Rome, and the later seventh century saw the
replacement of the Irish example by the Roman order in
Anglo-Saxon England. Although English students continued for a time to gravitate to Irish monasteries, by 704
most of the Irish themselves adopted the Roman dating of
Easter, though they did not quickly accede to Roman
claims of hegemony. It is perhaps a mistake to see the two
traditions as antipodal, for Irish Christianity was not so insular as Wilfrid claimed. It was eccentric, however, in its
predominantly monastic organization and it was also distant from the discipline of the emerging papacy. Toleration
of divergent practices seem to have been the Irish custom
in liturgical matters in this period. "Let each of us do what
he believes, and as seems to him right" are the words im-
puted to another spokesman for the Celtic reckoning of
Easter.[29]

EARLY CHRISTIAN IRISH ART

In the next chapter I will take up the assimilation of the
Irish Church to the Roman order, and the displacement of
monasticism from its nearly exclusive position of authority.
But in the three and a half centuries between St. Patrick
and the coming of the Northmen to Ireland, the monasteries were the backbone of Irish culture, the seats of learning
and literacy, and finally, both consumers and producers of
the most brilliantly successful art of the Middle Ages. I
could, of course, discuss early Irish Christianity without
reference to art history, and if a few more art-objects had
perished in the long, damp centuries we should have no
choice. Once seen, however, the art of the eighth and ninth
centuries demands our attention, just as Stonehenge, in
England, forbids us to dismiss the prehistoric inhabitants

of England without considering their extraordinary talents. The Church, in general, and the monasteries, in particular, provided a new demand and a new rationale for the beautification of objects sacred to the Christian faith. Ancient styles, forms, and motifs were adapted and employed.

The Celts of antiquity were famous for their metalwork and, in particular, their weaponry. The oldest examples of Irish metalwork are early Bronze Age items from about 1200 B.C., but in the seventh and eighth centuries after Christ, Irish metalwork reached a beauty and perfection which few civilizations have rivaled.

The outstanding example is the Ardagh Chalice, named from the place in County Limerick where in 1868 a boy digging potatoes discovered it buried in the roots of a thorn tree. Basically, it is a beaten silver bowl resting on a hemispherical base, both of which are ornamented with gold filigree and elaborate enamel. Barely visible, except on close examination, are the names of the twelve apostles in angular lettering running in a band around the middle of the chalice. The chalice is usually dated to the first half of the eighth century, and must be seen (and compared to other medieval metalwork) to be fully appreciated. Though it would require two hands to drink from it comfortably, the chalice is not large, perhaps eight inches across. It was never intended to overawe by size. The shape is simple and pleasing, and the areas of elaborate decoration are sparse. But the eye returns to them with growing wonder, for the detail is microscopic, and almost incredible in its precision. Perhaps what is most impressive is the absence of *horror vacui*. As the "doodler," given sufficient time, fills his page, so the skilled hand tends to run on, doing what it knows how to do until the empty spaces are filled. But on the Ardagh Chalice the ornamenter's capacity is restrained. The graceful shape of the bowl itself is not overwhelmed with riotous and fussy detail. An inspired balance is achieved. An object frequently paired with the chalice as representative of the pinnacle of the Irish metalworker's genius is the Tara Brooch, which dates from the same period.

In February 1980 a treasure-hunter with a metal detector turned up a very similar chalice, along with other liturgical objects, at the monastic site of Derrynaflan in County Tipperary. Within a matter of weeks the hoard was acclaimed as "undoubtedly the most exciting addition to the corpus of early Christian art to come to light in Ireland in this century."[30] Exactly when and where the objects found at Derrynaflan were produced, and why and when they were buried there are questions likely to occupy archaeologists in the future, but the Derrynaflan hoard is already contributing to the fame and importance of early medieval Irish art.

It is instructive to compare these objects with the similar products of Germanic (or Saxon) workmanship dating from about the same period. A rich hoard of Saxon work was discovered at Sutton Hoo, in East Anglia in England just before the second world war. Dr. Françoise Henry has examined both the Irish and Saxon objects closely and attempted an explanation of the similarities. On the whole, she sees the Irish as imitators and refiners of designs and styles which originated on the continent and were brought to England by the Anglo-Saxons.

The omnipresent influence of Saxon objects so manifest in these works can easily be explained by the contacts which existed in the seventh century between England and Ireland. Some Saxon objects may have reached Ireland by trade, or through travellers whilst England was still pagan. Later the Irish missions in England were an obvious means of transmission of patterns and objects.[31]

But the level of workmanship and esthetic sense found in the Ardagh Chalice and Tara Brooch represents a distinct advance of the art. The Irish work, compared to the Saxon, is of "incredible delicacy."

There is obvious imitation, but never a copy. We are faced with constant adaptations, where different techniques are used to give a similar effect and a few motifs are chosen carefully and completely incorporated into the current of Irish repertory. The Irish artist is never overwhelmed by what confronts him. He assimilates what he borrows and submits it to the inner rhythm of his ornament.[32]

Dr. Henry has used the term "pagan decoration masquerading under the guise of an ecclesiastical art" to describe the art of seventh- and eighth-century Ireland. Nowhere is it more true than in the most celebrated of all the art objects of this period, illuminated manuscripts. Illumination (which is no more than drawing or coloring with various substances on paper) was the only form of painting to survive from antiquity into the Middle Ages. It was put to ecclesiastical purposes to honor and embellish the sacred texts of the new faith. The earliest Irish manuscript, called the Cathach of St. Columba, may actually have been written by that saint toward the end of the sixth century. Cathach means "Battler," a name derived from the fact that it was subsequently treated as a relic and used as a talisman or charm by generations of O'Donnell warriors. The manuscript, though early, is an only slightly illuminated fragment of a psalter, an arrangement and translation of the Psalms, in this case, into Latin.

The characteristic features of Irish illumination first appear clearly in manuscripts executed in the early seventh century at Bobbio, the monastery founded by St. Columbanus in northern Italy. These features were "chiefly the tendency to turn initials into curvilinear patterns, whilst surrounding them with dots, and the adoption of the scheme which consists of putting in the beginning of each section of a book a decorative page on the left and an introductory page with large initial on the right."[33] In all, there are only fifteen surviving illuminated manuscripts in the Irish style from the fertile period, 650–800, and most of them are copies of the Gospels. Not all were produced in Ireland, but all were products of Irish scriptoria, studios or workshops where manuscripts were copied and illuminated.

The Book of Durrow is a particularly apt illustration of "pagan decoration masquerading under the guise of an ecclesiastical art." In this colorful copy of the Gospels, probably produced in the latter half of the seventh century, and

preserved since the seventeenth century in the library of
Trinity College, Dublin, the highly geometrical and abstract motifs familiar from the metalwork of the Ardagh
Chalice are adapted to allow the portrayal of the symbols
for the four evangelists: the man for Matthew, the lion for
Mark, the bull for Luke, and the eagle for John. An art
which had shied consistently from the representation of human or animal forms is, in the *Book of Durrow*, hesitantly,
almost childishly, put to their service. The figure of St.
Matthew is unabashedly drawn without arms. The cartoon-
like head is utterly symmetrical, the face virtually circular,
the eyes, ears, and mouth rendered in neat, elliptical lines.
But Matthew's coat is a mosaic of brilliant colors reminis-
cent of the enamel studs on the Ardagh Chalice or the Tara
Brooch. The border is an elaborate network of interlace.
Just as the apostles were named below the band of the
chalice, here the art form is making way, almost grudgingly, for an iconographic necessity. The idols of the new
faith must be identifiable, one from the other. In the solution to this dilemma, the synthesis of Christianity and the
pagan Celtic decorative tradition was artfully expressed.

The culmination of this synthesis is the early ninth century *Book of Kells*. It is the richest and most elaborate of all
the Irish manuscripts, and analysis shows it to be the work
of at least several different illuminators. Here, the traditional geometrical art, in its most ornate manifestation, is
stretched to allow didactic biblical scenes, such as the
temptation of Christ, or the Nativity. Real objects and crea-
tures are depicted recognizably in various arrangements
and poses, but the vitality of the art is its exuberant, im-
aginative, and sometimes whimsical decoration, its utter
preoccupation with line, color, and form. Photographs
rarely do justice to these manuscripts, and even the traveler fortunate enough to confront them in Dublin will find
that they can only be examined through thick glass, and at
the pedestrian pace of one page a day!

Despite their muteness and relative inaccessibility (in
contrast to literary epic like the *Iliad*), the great art objects
of early medieval Ireland preserve and express the fact of a

remarkable transformation. Within eight centuries of the birth of Christ, one of the most remote and isolated areas of Europe, almost altogether innocent of Rome and the civilization of the ancient Mediterranean, had not only been brought within Christianity, but had infused it with immense energy and creativity. The Irish monastic movement involved a small portion of the population of a sparsely populated island. We should not imagine a monastic illuminator under every eighth-century bush. Nevertheless Irish monasticism made a major impact upon early medieval European culture. It brought literacy and learning to Ireland and propagated it back into Britain and the continent from which it had come. It created vital links with Scotland and Anglo-Saxon England, and imparted to pagan art forms a purposefulness and dedication which alone can explain the achievements of the seventh, eighth, and ninth centuries.

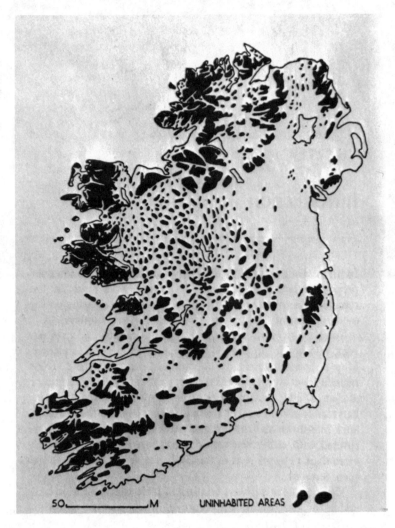

1. Uninhabited areas, bog and upland.

The map suggests that the most hospitable areas for agricultural Man lay in a reversed "L" running from eastern Ulster down through eastern Leinster, and then running westward through Munster.

from *Ireland, Its Physical, Historical, Social, and Economic Geography,* by T. A. Freeman; this version from Eileen McCracken, *The Irish Woods since Tudor Times* (Newton Abbot, Eng.: David and Charles, 1971), p. 16.

2. *Carved stone in front of tomb at Newgrange, County Meath, probably third millennium B.C.*

Megalithic remains are, by and large, distressingly mute. Few include painting, inscription, or sculpture, other than what is strictly architectural. The carved stone at Newgrange is an exception, and its incised spirals suggest a pre-Celtic taste for forms not unlike those brought to Ireland several thousand years later by La Tène Celts.

from Harbison, *The Archaeology of Ireland,* p. 34.

3. *Early Bronze Age gold earrings above, c.1200 B.C.; later Bronze Age gold ring, pendant, and bracelet below, c.700 B.C. At the National Library of Ireland, Dublin.*

Irish goldwork dates from as early as 2000–1800 B.C. and came to be influenced by eastern Mediterranean models, either because samples of it were imported to Ireland, or because immigrants brought with them the knowledge of eastern Mediterranean styles and techniques. Brilliant examples of metal work existed in Ireland long before the Celtic migrations.

from Harbison, *The Archaeology of Ireland,* p. 48.

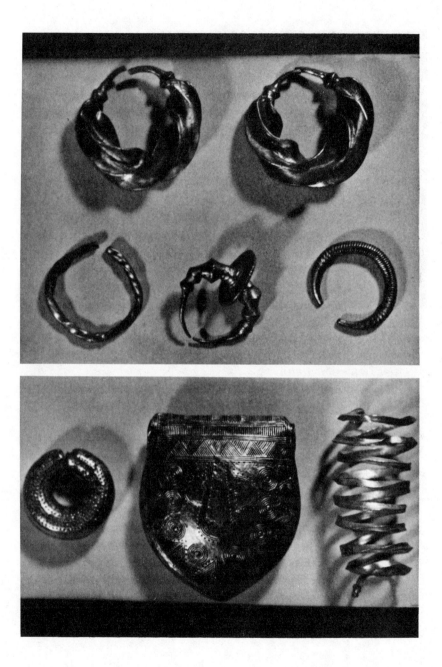

4. *Gold torque from the Broighter hoard, County Derry, first century*
B.C. *An example of the insular La Tène style. At the National Museum of Ireland, Dublin.*

The magnificent torque, or collar, from Broighter illustrates the
confluence of the pre-Celtic metalworking tradition with the La Tène
style of the Celts. The torque is tubular, not solid, and the curvilinear
designs are more complex and organic than the spirals on the
Newgrange stone in figure 2.

from Harbison, *The Archaeology of Ireland*, p. 58.

5. *A schematic of the Ogam alphabet.*
   The alphabet is exhibited on several hundred surviving so-called Ogam stones in the British Isles. They are dated from approximately the fourth to the seventh centuries A.D., *and generally contain brief commemorative inscriptions rendered into Ogam from Celtic or Latin originals.*

from De Paor and De Paor, *Early Christian Ireland*, p. 62.

6. *The Ardagh Chalice, early eighth century, found in nineteenth century near Ardagh, County Limerick. National Museum of Ireland, Dublin.*

The chalice is a mere six inches high, and yet it is one of the world's great treasures. Made of silver, bronze, and gold, with glass and rock crystals added to make the gems of the bosses, the chalice was accidentally discovered in the mid-nineteenth century by a boy digging potatoes. The names of the apostles inscribed (though barely visible in the photo) below the rim establish that the chalice was the work of a Christian artist or workshop. Clearly it was part of a monastic hoard buried for safekeeping in the Middle Ages.

from F. Henri, *Irish Art in the Early Christian Period.*

7. *Detail of handle of the Ardagh Chalice.*

It is not easy, through photographs, to obtain a sense of the artistry of eighth-century Irish metalwork. One must somehow grasp the relative smallness and simplicity of the basic object before one can be impressed by the profuse and microscopic detail which has been lavished upon it. In this view of a handle, from below, one gets an intimation of the thought and workmanship which went into the creation of a few square centimeters of surface.

from F. Henri, *Irish Art in the Early Christian Period.*

8. Detail from the side of handle of Ardagh Chalice.

In this partial side-view of a handle, one sees how the elaborate treatment of surface combines with the sculpture of volume to create an elegant whole. Although large portions of the chalice are left undecorated by conscious choice, those portions decorated exhibit an almost relentless determination to beautify.

from National Museum of Ireland

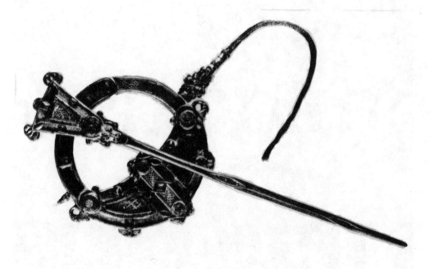

9. *The Tara Brooch, eighth century, found near Bettystown, County Meath (and* not *at Tara!). National Museum of Ireland.*

The famous brooch is the companion piece to the Ardagh Chalice, although it was found in a different location. Unlike the chalice, it has no undecorated surfaces, probably because the tunic or garment which it closed would with its fabric provide a background of un-decorated color, against which the brooch could radiate. In any event, the brooch is as fine and elegant as the chalice, and with it represents the ultimate artistry achieved by the metalworking tradi-tion in medieval Ireland.

from F. Henri, *Irish Art in the Early Christian Period.*

10. *An example of text from the* Book of Kells, *associated with St. Columba's monastery at Kells, County Antrim, dated mid-to-late eighth century. Library of Trinity College, Dublin.*

The fanciful imagination of the illuminators of the Book of Kells *appears not only in the glorious "carpet pages" (see figure 11), but also in the text itself. Here the careful calligraphy of the sacred word suggests the flowing vertical strokes of cursive writing which in turn give rise to a whimsical lionlike beast with flowing tail. The animal, as it were, grows out of the geometry of the writing.*

from F. Henri, *Irish Art in the Early Christian Era.*

11. The Page of Eight Circles, from the Book of Kells.

The photograph shows only a portion of the page (folio 33r), one in which abstract design reigns supreme. In other fully illuminated pages, such as folio 32v, a portrait of Christ, or 114r, the arrest of Christ, the abstract ornamentation gives way, reluctantly, one feels, to the rendering of the human figure, albeit in a highly stylized, geometrical form. In such pages the Book *of Kells embodies and illustrates the fusion of early Celtic civilization with the humanistic religion of Christianity brought from the eastern Mediterranean.*

from F. Henri, *Irish Art in the Early Christian Era.*

12. *Muiredach's Cross, Monasterboice, County Louth, early tenth century.*

As an art object, Muiredach's Cross is both more public, and more didactic, than the Book of Kells. *With sculptured scenes central to the faith, such as the arrest and crucifixion of Christ, the High Cross is, vulgarly speaking, the tenth century's counterpart of the modern highway billboard. In France and England this function was later to be performed in stained glass windows, as well as sculpture.*

42

2

A HEROIC AGE: THE CELTIC, VIKING, AND NORMAN INHERITANCE

CHRISTIANITY OVERLAID, rather than transformed, the civilization already established in Ireland by the Celts and their predecessors. The central feature of that civilization was its decentralization and regionalism, a characteristic which accorded well with the dispersed nature of habitable living space in the island. When St. Patrick came to Ireland in the mid-fifth century he found the population divided into as many as 150 *tuatha*, a word most nearly translated as "tribes" or "clans." These were kin groups with a recognized leader, or chief, and collective claims to the wealth of, and authority over, specified territories. The early history of Europe saw many areas inhabited in a similar fashion and a general, long-term tendency for these units to grow larger and less numerous as a consequence of generations of struggle and consolidation. Thus the Anglo-Saxon invaders of England crystallized between the fifth and seventh centuries into a handful of "kingdoms," and the kingdoms were, in turn, consolidated into a single Anglo-Saxon kingdom in the ninth century.

A similar process was at work in Ireland, and by the twelfth century the number of these tribal units (which by then existed within the framework of the Anglo-Norman "Lordship") had shrunk to something on the order of thirty. But the process proceeded much more slowly in Ireland than in England and the result was a patchwork of competing and clashing political units that endured virtually up to the Tudor conquest in the sixteenth century. By the sixth century a few of the most powerful *tuatha* were struggling to build themselves into regional kingdoms by the use of diplomacy, marriage alliances, and warfare.

The four modern provinces of Leinster, Ulster, Munster, and Connacht existed in embryo, although a large chunk of modern-day Leinster north of the river Liffey constituted for some time a separate kingdom of Meath. Ulster too was split among contending dynasties. In the south and the west matters were relatively simpler. By the second half of the sixth century Munster was dominated by the Eóganacht (descendants of Eogan), ruling from a rocky citadel at Cashel in what came to be County Tipperary. West of the Shannon, it was the descendants of Conn, or the Connachta, who gave their name to the province and formed the ruling power within it. Leinster was divided between a dynasty called the Laigin in the south, and the southern Ui Neill in what became Meath. Ulster was split between the northern Ui Neill in the center and west, the Dál Riata in the northeast (with an extension in western Scotland), and the Airgialla in the southeast. None of these kingdoms was stable or enduring in the form described, and all contended with other *tuatha* for supremacy.

Such a society left wide scope for warriors and warfare. The survival and expansion of any single tuath, or collection of *tuatha* in a petty kingdom or kingdom (there is no precise way to distinguish between them) often turned on the exploits and reputation of a single great fighter or commander, and tales of such prowess were early formalized and transmitted as part of an oral tradition.

The very earliest writing in Ireland is that found engraved on certain burial or memorial stones which date from approximately the fourth to the seventh centuries. The writing takes the form of series of horizontal strokes cut on either side of, or across, a stem line. This cypher is known as Ogam, and the stones as Ogam stones. The strokes represent letters in the Roman alphabet, and when decoded they reveal what seem for the most part to be funeral inscriptions in Irish, such as "Ronan the priest son of Comgall."[1]

Some of the Ogam stones contain hints of Christian influence; others do not. Most are laconic, cryptic, and uncommunicative. For more discursive writing one must await the Christian era. St. Patrick brought to Ireland not only the knowledge of Latin writing, but also the immense emphasis Christianity put upon its "scriptures." Reading and writing flourished in the monasteries, as the magnificent illuminated manuscripts attest, but it was reading and writing of Latin, not Irish.

The vernacular, the language people spoke in their everyday affairs, remained almost exclusively oral until the twelfth and thirteenth centuries when some of its greatest works came to the ambit of Monkish interest and began to be copied down. Up until that time much lore and literature had been preserved by oral transmission, and the society had developed prodigious means of storing and propagating this knowledge. Writing is but one of many ways of storing and distributing information, and the potential of the oral tradition for performing this function should not be underestimated. When Irish monks began to write down what had become the classics of the Irish oral tradition they froze in a permanent form stories, legends, descriptions, and parables which had been passing, orally, from generation to generation for hundreds of years, sometimes since well before the birth of Christ.

The monks made compilations that are now famous. One, for instance, is called the Book of the Dun Cow, and was written at the monastery of Clonmacnoise on the Shannon. Others include the Book of Leinster, the Yellow Book of Lecan, and a manuscript preserved in the Bodleian Library at Oxford called by its catalogue number of "Rawlinson B502." These manuscripts contain the current (twelfth to fourteenth century) versions of a rich heroic literature. Like archaeological sites they represent strata of historical evidence, some of which can be quite recent (deriving from the lifetime of the monkist copyist) and some of which can be ancient beyond all reckoning: pre-Christian or even pre-Celtic. They combine references to real people, real places, and real events with extravagant flights of fancy and wholesale alteration of historical fact. But all of them provide valuable clues to the nature and character of heroic society as a continuum from the Celtic migrations to at least the advent of the Normans.

The surviving sagas are roughly divided into four "cycles." The mythological cycle is a collection of stories relating to the tribes of the Danann, a supposedly pre-Celtic population. The Fenian cycle tells of Finn mac Cumaill, his son Oisin, and the warriors associated with them in the pre-Christian period. The cycle of the kings (sometimes called "the historical cycle") centers on various rulers, many of them fictional, said to have reigned between the third century B.C. and the 8th century after Christ. Finally, the Ulster cycle celebrates a northern king named Conchobor and his great champion, Cuchulainn, in their struggles with the king and queen of the rival kingdom of Connacht. It is this last cycle which contains the most enduring epic of the Irish heroic past, *Tain Bo Cuailnge* (The Cattle Raid at Cooley). The *Tain* may have something to do with real events in Ireland in the first century A.D.; but then again it may not.

The plot of the *Tain* is simple to the point of childishness. Alil and Maeve, king and queen of Connacht, have a spat over which of them is wealthier. Alil taunts Maeve with lacking a great bull such as is the pride of *his* herds. Maeve determines to acquire an animal which will excel her husband's and learns that the greatest bull in all Ireland is in Ulster at Cooley (the modern day Carlingford peninsula of County Armagh). When her efforts to borrow the bull for a year go awry she resolves to take it by force, and she and her husband (now reunited) march across Ireland with their warriors. En route to Cooley the men of Connacht encounter Cuchulainn, the superhuman champion of King

Conchobor of Ulster, and most of the *Tain* is taken up with descriptions of Cuchulainn's extraordinary feats. A short passage will illustrate Cuchulainn's style. At one point he is challenged in private combat by a young hothead from Connacht named Etarcomol. Cuchulainn endures his taunts briefly because of an obligation he is under to Etarcomol's comrade, Fergus, but Cuchulainn's patience begins to wear thin.

"It's you who want this," Cuchulainn said to Etarcomol.
"It isn't my wish."
"You have no choice," Etarcomol said.
Cuchulainn cut the sod from under his feet. He fell flat, with the
    sod on his belly.
"Go away now," Cuchulainn said. "I don't want to wash my
    hands after you. I'd have cut you to pieces long ago but for
    Fergus."
"I won't leave it like this," Etarcomol said. "I'll have your head,
    or leave you mine."
"It will be the latter for sure."
Cuchulainn poked at the two armpits with his sword and the
    clothes fell down leaving the skin untouched.
"Now clear off!" Cuchulainn said.
"No," Etarcomol said.
Then Cuchulainn sheared off his hair with the sword-edge as
    neat as a razor, leaving the skin unscratched. But the fool
    stubbornly persisted and Cuchulainn struck down through the
    crown of his head and split him to the navel.[2]

Cuchulainn is not a lovable hero. His outstanding virtue is murderous strength, and it is this quality along with loyalty which recommends him to the king of Ulster. These are the most esteemed qualities in a warfare state, but in an ordered polity they are a liability and a menace.

    The cult of the warrior-hero and his celebration in epic literature both grew out of, and contributed to, the protracted strife of medieval Ireland. The theme of The Cattle Raid at Cooley reflects a fundamental element in the early Irish economy—the centrality of livestock. Evidence survives of considerable crop-raising by the seventh and

eighth centuries, the fencing of fertile land, and the tillage
of wheat, oats, and rye; but herding remained the predominant agricultural activity. It differs from crop raising in
that it does not tie the herdsmen to precisely defined lands.
Four-footed property is highly mobile. One may drive it
wherever there are grasses to sustain it, fleeing (or pursu-
ing) one's enemies, making a seasonal circuit, or simply
wandering the land. By the same token, four-footed property is immensely vulnerable to the depredations of others,
and agricultural economies based on livestock are disposed
to very different kinds of squabbles from those that char-
acterize economies based on crops. A man must stay with
his planted fields, or lose their harvest. His land cannot be
taken away from him unless he is physically forced away
from it. But the *tuatha* of the heroic period often had the
mobility which only a pastoral economy can provide.

At the same time we must beware of envisaging an early
Ireland of political formlessness. We know that more or less
fixed centers of power emerged at Emain Macha in Ulster,
or Cashel in Munster; that ecclesiastical centers such as Armagh (near Emain Macha) or monasteries like Clonmacnoise were of almost uninterrupted importance, and that
Ireland was not simply a bubbling cauldron of nomadic
wandering. Archaeological excavation of the sites of early
forts and churches provides the most informative evidence
about more or less permanent areas of habitation, but the
Irish were not great house or town builders. Much of their
construction was of perishable wood, and their stone and
masonry work was rudimentary up until the advent of the
Normans.

Prior to the end of the eighth century the civilization of
Ireland was a compound of only two major elements: the
civilization of the Celts, and the influence of Mediterranean
Christianity. Neither the Romans, who had occupied Britain from the first to the fifth centuries, nor the Anglo-Saxons, who had invaded and settled it from the fifth century
onward, had a significant impact upon life in Ireland. This
relative insularity was rudely shattered in A.D. 795 when

Viking raiders fell upon the island of Lambay, a few miles northeast of present-day Dublin. In the same year they also plundered Inismurray (in Donegal Bay) and Inisbofin (off western Galway). A new and disruptive era had begun in which the internecine strife of the Celtic *tuatha* and kingdoms was joined by the savage attacks of strangers from across the sea.

The Viking diaspora originated in Scandinavia, but by the mid-eighth century, at the latest, there were Norse fishing and farming settlements in the Orkneys and Hebrides, the islands which flank the northern and northwestern coasts of Scotland. From such bases the marauders fanned out to launch attacks against both Britain and Ireland. They were drawn to the wealth of the ecclesiastical centers, especially the monasteries, and literate monks who were fortunate enough to survive recorded in bitter detail the terrible punishment suffered by the faithful. St. Columba's great monastery at Iona (off the Scottish coast) was attacked in 795, and again in 802 and 806. On the last occasion eighty-six members of the settlement were killed, and in the following year at least some of the survivors withdrew to central Ireland, where they founded a new monastery at Kells. The Vikings' first targets were islands and coastal locations, or sites on the lower reaches of navigable rivers, but by the second quarter of the ninth century they were reaching into the hinterland. Seemingly only the elements could stop them. "An Irish monk . . . listening thankfully to the howling of a storm one night, wrote in the margin of his manuscript:

> The wind is rough tonight
> tossing the white-combed ocean;
> I need not dread fierce Vikings
> crossing the Irish Sea"[3]

Recent writers have endeavored to put the Viking depredations in a broader perspective, pointing out that the monasteries were by no means immune from violence before the Vikings. They had been raided on numerous occa-

sions by their own Christian kings, and had even resorted
to waging war on one another. In 764, more than thirty
years before the Vikings burst upon the scene, a battle took
place between the monasteries of Clonmacnoise and Durrow in which more than two hundred people were report-
edly killed. The monasteries were in many cases no longer
simply religious houses. They had become centers of wealth
and population, ecclesiastical towns of a sort, and their
treasures, stores, and livestock were envied by Irish kings
and Viking raiders alike.[4]

From about 830 onwards the Viking raids became more
intense and intrusive. Large fleets pushed up the Shannon,
Boyne, Liffey, and Erne, reaching and ravaging inland
areas. In 838 a Viking fleet established itself on Ulster's
landbound Lough Neagh, and a contingent wintered there
in 840–41. The following winter saw Vikings established at
the site of modern-day Dublin (a Scandinavian name meaning "dark pool"), and gradually their presence became permanent instead of seasonal. Land replaced movables as
their objective, and by 842 there are references to military
cooperation between certain Irish and Viking leaders. Conflict no longer occurred exclusively across the ethnic gulf,
for as the Vikings became permanent inhabitants they were
slowly assimillated into Irish society. Their settlements
were chiefly along the coasts and provided the origins of
the modern port cities of Limerick, Cork, Waterford, and
Wexford, in addition to Dublin. Even as permanent settlers,
the Vikings retained the maritime mobility which made
them voyagers and traders. Viking Dublin is still revealing
its secrets to archaeologists, but it seems clear that the urban and mercantile tradition came to Ireland from the
North, and not, as was the case in so much of Western Europe, from Mediterranean antiquity.

By the middle of the ninth century the Vikings were at
war with each other as new waves of Scandinavians fell
upon earlier waves that were partially domesticated. In
851, for instance, Viking Dublin was attacked by a fleet of
Danes, probably from England. When in 852 a fleet of 160

Norse vessels attacked some Danish Vikings established at Carlingford Lough, the Norse were heavily defeated by an alliance of Celts and Danes. In similar fashion, the Irish began to ally with Vikings against *their* particular Irish enemies, as in 860–62 when the northern Ui Neill allied with the Dublin Vikings to catch their rivals, the southern Ui Neill, in a pincer movement. The Vikings established themselves as unejectable members of the island community, much as the Danes thrust themselves upon the Anglo-Saxons in neighboring England. Intermarriage between Irish and Vikings became common, and the newcomers were slowly drawn to Christianity. The process of absorption was interrupted in the early tenth century when yet another wave of pagan Vikings from Scotland and the Orkneys descended upon Ireland, raiding and pillaging in the style of their forebears.

According to tradition the Viking threat to Ireland was finally ended by the heroic and fatal exertions of King Brian Boru of Munster at the battle of Clontarf (just outside Dublin) in 1014. Brian's twelfth-century biographer cast him in the mold of England's King Alfred, vanquisher of the Danes, but modern historians are less convinced that Brian's accomplishment was so significant. That he was a successful and formidable king remains beyond doubt, but his struggles were as much with other Celts, especially the Ui Neill, as with the Vikings. Internal struggles among the Ui Neill in the latter part of the tenth century freed much of the south and west from northern influence. Brian established himself as king of Munster and began to build up an alliance with which to challenge the hegemony of the Ui Neill over the island as a whole. He was quite capable of allying with the Vikings when it served his purposes, and did so in 984 when the Vikings of Waterford joined him in preparing an attack upon Viking Dublin. In 997 the Ui Neill king, Mael Sechnaill II, agreed to recognize Brian's influence in the south in return for recognition of his own claims in the north.

Despite the alliance with Mael Sechnaill, Brian continued to make inroads against the north, and in 1005 he claimed, with some justice, to be king of all Ireland. In that sense he may have been the first unifier of Ireland, but his real accomplishment was the overthrow of the several-centuries-old domination of the island by the north, and his colorful embodiment of "high kingship," as this wider dominion came to be called. The Norse of Limerick, Cork, and Waterford became his subjects, as did the Norse of Dublin, somewhat less reliably. The battle at Clontarf was an anticlimax to these accomplishments, as well as the cause of Brian's death. It was occasioned by the revolt of the Irish king of Leinster, allied with the Dublin Vikings. Brian's campaign to suppress the revolt culminated in the battle on April 23, 1014, in which he was killed, but in which his army triumphed. The Dublin Vikings were defeated, but Brian's ambitious monarchy collapsed at his death, and in the century which followed Ireland was riven with regional struggles.

We should not assume that political consolidation, such as occurred in England during these same critical centuries, was normal, and that its failure to occur in Ireland was eccentric. There were many geographical impediments to unification, and the rural and pastoral nature of Celtic life provided a different political matrix from that which existed in Anglo-Saxon England. Even the Viking settlements were more scattered in Ireland than in England, where a whole large region called the Danelaw emerged, in contrast to the isolated coastal enclaves established by the Vikings in Ireland.

It is inappropriate to place a value judgment on either unification or its opposite, sometimes called "particularism," but it is important to recognize that by the twelfth century, and really long before, a major difference existed in the political organization of the two islands. The whole of the southern part of Britain had been unified, first under the Anglo-Danish monarchy, and then, after 1066, under the Normans. No such unification had occurred within Ireland despite various aborted tendencies in that direction.

This difference meant that once the Normans had consolidated their hold on England, they faced to the west an island which lacked either the incentive or the power to oppose them in a concerted fashion. It does not follow that such a difference attracted the Normans irresistibly to Ireland, any more than it had attracted the Romans to Ireland a thousand years earlier. The Romans had not crossed the water and the Normans showed very little enthusiasm to do so either. But it was probably only a matter of time before they were drawn into the Irish imbroglio, and once engaged, there was no political entity in Ireland capable of restricting their role.

A typical episode of internecine Irish strife opened the way for Norman involvement. By the early twelfth century the O'Connor kings of Connacht had supplanted the descendants of Brian Boru as the great power in the south, but in 1156 the O'Connors suffered a major defeat at the hands of Murchertach MacLochlainn, king of Tir Eoghain, and in 1161 Murchertach recognized one Dermot MacMurrough as king of Leinster. There were other claimants, however, and after five years of setbacks to his own claim, Dermot took ship for England, in the hope of finding a powerful champion for his cause. In Bristol he enjoyed the hospitality of the Augustinian canons, some of whose sister houses he had patronized in Ireland. The monks sent Dermot in search of King Henry II who was, as often, away campaigning in France. Dermot caught up with the king in Aquitaine and won his sympathy but no substantial support. Like most of his successors, the first Angevin king was too preoccupied with his continental possessions to be lightly drawn into Irish adventures. Dermot returned to Bristol, and there succeeded in awakening the interest of a powerful Norman, Richard Fitzgilbert de Clare, called "Strongbow."

Pembroke was the westernmost shire of south Wales and a mere sixty miles of water separated it from the excellent Irish harbors in Wexford and Waterford. Like the Roman conquerors a millennium before them, the Normans after 1066 had cut through southern and central England and penetrated southern Wales, following the coast. The Welsh took refuge in the mountainous north, from which they were not to be routed until the campaigns of Edward I in the thirteenth century. South Wales, and especially Pembrokeshire, became a Norman stronghold, fortified with some of the strongest castles in the realm, and governed by a handful of rough and ready "marcher lords" (a march being a zone of critical military importance) to whom great independence and power was granted by the Crown. It was these veterans of the Welsh wars who were first drawn into the Irish imbroglio, and who brought their king and country in behind them, in due course.

Dermot returned to Ireland to await the arrival of his new allies. They began to join him in May 1169, and in August 1170 Strongbow himself crossed the water with a small army of 200 knights and 1,000 other troops. The action centered in the southeast, with the invaders coming ashore in the Wexford-Waterford area and then striking north and west. Dermot soon recovered his throne, only to die in May 1171. Strongbow had taken the precaution of marrying Dermot's daughter and requiring (as the price of his support) that Dermot name Strongbow his heir. Thus, at Dermot's death, Strongbow, in his own view, at least, became king of Leinster.

Here was a disturbing anomaly. King Henry II, now weighed down with the guilt for complicity in the murder in 1170 of his own archbishop of Canterbury, Thomas Becket, had previously taken a casual attitude toward Dermot and his Irish problems. Now one of Henry's vassals, by a bold maneuver and some good fortune, had become an Irish king. Henry rushed to secure and demonstrate Strongbow's subordination to the English Crown, lest a separate and hostile Norman kingdom of Ireland spring up on his western doorstep. By July 1171 Henry had decided upon an expedition to Ireland, but first he summoned Strongbow to return to England and account for his activities. The Norman lord crossed from Ireland and reached Henry as he was assembling a formidable army. He convinced the king of his continuing loyalty, and arranged to keep his Leinster inheritance, no longer as king, but as Henry's Irish vassal.

Henry sailed for Ireland in October 1171 and landed at Waterford. Strongbow formally surrendered the town to him and did homage for his Leinster fief. The king then toured the west and received the homage of various kings and chieftains, some of whom bound themselves to Henry with solemn oaths of loyalty. Many of the Irish leaders welcomed the English king, believing that he alone could keep in check the Norman interlopers, that the English king genuinely shared their desire that Norman power in Ireland be sharply delimited. Certainly this is the role the king played. From November 1171 to February 1172, Henry held court at Dublin, the former Viking capital, which the king now granted by charter to the citizens of Bristol.

Before returning to England in April 1172, he granted the ancient kingdom of Meath to a Norman lord, Hugh de Lacy, as a means of balancing the power of Strongbow in central Ireland. De Lacy was also appointed the king's justiciar (in effect, his deputy) and constables with garrisons were appointed to govern the cities of Dublin, Wexford, Waterford, Cork, and Limerick in the hope that they might remain independent of the Irish lords (both Norman and Gaelic) and loyal to the English sovereign.

The events of 1167–1172 constitute a watershed in Irish history. Invaders had come before, but they were detached and distant from their Danish and Norwegian homelands. No organized kingdom, or powerful state, could come to their assistance. Furthermore, their settlements in Ireland were dispersed and discrete and did not dominate any single portion or section of the island. The Normans were a different kind of presence. Independent adventurers Strongbow and his companions may have been at the outset, but the Angevin monarchy of England was too strong, too close, and too jealous to let them carve up Ireland for their own greater glory. It followed them to Ireland post haste, in the wish to curb their power, but the most enduring accomplishment was the insertion of the English monarchy into the politics of the island.

When Henry II left Ireland in 1172 his Norman vassals began immediately to expand their holdings. Warfare with the Irish kings resumed. At the Treaty of Windsor (near London) in 1175 an effort was made to define two distinct spheres of influence in Ireland: a Norman one to include Meath, Leinster, and the parts around Dublin, Wexford, and Waterford which were still in the king's hands; and an Irish sphere which included everything else, and over which Rory O'Connor was recognized as high-king, under the lordship of Henry II. (The papacy had granted away the sovereignty of Ireland to the English monarchy in 1155 by its bull, *Laudabiliter,* discussed below. It remained to be seen what, if any, practical use would be made of this papal authority.) But the drawing of such a frontier made little difference. The Norman barons were indifferent to, and unrestrained by, the distant authority of the English king. The Irish were far from agreement to accept the high-kingship of Rory, who became suspect as soon as he bore an English stamp of approval. Unable to stop the continual conflict in Ireland, Henry II and his successors tended to take the side of their Norman countrymen, hoping to balance them against one another so that no single baron emerged as king of a united Norman Ireland.

In the closing decades of the twelfth century additional Normans plunged into Ireland in an effort to conquer lands for which they had been given royal grants. This was a betrayal of the many Irish kings whose sovereignty Henry II had sworn to protect, and it laid an enduring curse on future efforts of the monarchy to revive a policy of arbitration in good faith. It initiated a dolorous precedent of "confiscation," the appropriation of a man's lands in response to some alleged crime or disloyalty. It is a drastic remedy which appealed to a monarchy with almost negligible knowledge of, or control over, events in a separate island. If it could not reach with its law and rule the distant, refractory parties, it simply dispatched companions in arms to conquer and displace them.

In 1177 Henry II made his ten-year-old son John lord of Ireland, much as Edward I was to make *his* son Prince of Wales a century later. Under John's lordship the Norman interest experienced dramatic expansion. The Normans had already acquired large holdings in northeast Ulster, Leinster, and eastern and central Munster. Prince John came personally to Ireland in 1185 (at age eighteen) and launched the fortunes of a number of his favored attendants. Theobald Walter, John's butler (from the French, *botteil*, for bottle, literally, the man in charge of John's drink), established the famous Butler family in what is now County Kilkenny. William de Burgo started a dynasty in south Tipperary which, by 1235, had siezed the lion's share of remote Connacht. By 1200 the Fitzgeralds had received grants of land in Kerry and Limerick and were busily building up their wealth at the expense of the native MacCarthys.

Proficient fighters, horsemen, archers, and armorers the Normans were quick to throw up sturdy castles in their newly won areas. These were earth and timber at first, but were soon replaced by ingenious and imposing stonework fortifications. Ireland is still littered with their remains, but perhaps the most famous are the great castle at Trim, in County Meath, and that at Carrickfergus, on Belfast Lough. Though found throughout Ireland, the greatest concentration of Norman fortifications was in the southeast, which remained a bastion and focus of Norman power. The traditional Irish forms of fortification had been the ring fort (a circular area enclosed with low walls of earth, stone, and sometimes wooden palisading), the crannog (a man-made island in a lake), and from about the eighth century the slender, tapering, cone-hatted round towers which remain as landmarks in so many parts of the island. The Norman castle with its high curtain walls of dressed stone and massive rectangular (later polygonal or round) towers or keeps made a far superior citadel, and Irish kings and chiefs soon learned to copy them effectively, as at Ballintober, County

Roscommon, where the O'Connor kings of Connaught built a splendid castle about 1300.

Despite their military prowess the Normans' intervention in Ireland was less than triumphant. Compared to England, Ireland was easier to enter, but harder to conquer. Its political disarray virtually invited foreign meddling, but the same disarray impeded a speedy reduction. There was no counterpart to England's King Harold, a monarch who held the keys to his kingdom and from whom they could be wrested after his defeat in battle. Each part of the island was a law and power unto itself. There was no line of dominoes to fall over at the touch of the first one. The twelfth-century intervention which began so promisingly under Henry II and expanded so vigorously under John, reached its apogee in the mid-thirteenth century and thereafter began a long decline. By that time nearly three-quarters of the territory of Ireland had been brought under Norman authority. A mere quarter remained in native hands. Some time in the long lordship of Henry III's son Edward (1254–1307, as King Edward I, 1272–1307), the tide began to turn.

The reasons for this decline are diverse, and in part, conjectural. A common theory is that too few Normans came, that they were insufficiently thick on the ground to maintain their domination of an entire island and its native inhabitants. Not every historian accepts this contention which, in any event, is impossible to prove. Even if it should be correct, the underlying question of why so few Normans came would remain. Another reason sometime given for the decline of Norman Ireland is the so-called Gaelic Revival of the second half of the thirteen century. In that period the O'Neills and the O'Donnells in Ulster, and the MacCarthys in Munster all showed signs of growing strength and independence, but it is almost impossible to say whether this resurgence was the cause, or the effect, of declining Norman strength and influence.

Both factors may have contributed to the process, but the most persuasive explanation relates to the policies of the

English monarchy itself. By the late thirteenth century Ireland's brief priority had been exhausted. Edward I's chief concerns were Scotland and Wales, and the Norman lordship of Ireland was slighted and exploited in order to help pay the costs of his campaigns within Britain. Between 1278 and 1306 Edward I drained off more than £40,000 from Ireland, an average of more than £1400 per annum in a period when the receipts of the Irish Exchequer (in effect, the treasury) seldom exceeded £5000 per annum. It has been argued that these funds were badly needed *within* Ireland and that their removal undermined the foundations of the Norman state and garrison there. The subjugation of Wales was particularly expensive because it involved the construction of an ambitious chain of castles around the coast, several of them (notably Caenarvon) the unsurpassed masterpieces of Norman military genius. In addition to much needed funds, Ireland provided Edward I with soldiers and supplies which might more prudently have been used to strengthen the royal government of Ireland. Wales was taken and secured, but Ireland, which may have been on the verge of fiscal and political viability as a Norman colony, was sabotaged, perhaps irretrievably.[5]

Whatever was responsible for the defects in Norman Ireland, those defects were glaringly revealed by Edward Bruce's invasion of the north in 1315. Edward was the brother of Robert Bruce, the storied king of Scotland whose armies had defeated the English the previous year at Bannockburn, near Stirling, in central Scotland. Wales might fall to the expansive Anglo-Normans, and Ireland might be in a precarious balance, but the Scots—many of whom, by this time, were partially Gaelicized Normans—would successfully draw the line against English encroachment. A Scottish monarchy emerged which fought for, and maintained, its country's independence until a marital alliance in the sixteenth century lead to a union of the crowns of England and Scotland in 1603.

The Bruce invasion of Ireland occurred at a moment of

great Scottish strength and confidence. Edward Bruce
hoped to rally the Celts of Ireland against their oppressive
Anglo-Norman neighbors, and for a time he was brilliantly
successful. Gaelic chieftains flocked to join his forces, and
within months the Norman earl of Ulster had been defeated, and the Norman presence in Ulster and Connacht
shattered. Bruce's invasion transformed the balance of
power in Ireland and tipped the Norman colony into a defensive posture from which it never fully recovered.

The events of 1314–15 in Scotland and Ireland raised
hopes—not for the last time—that the peoples of the "Celtic
fringe" might unite in victorious resistance to Norman
England. "We and you and our people and your people, free
since ancient time, share the same natural ancestry" Robert Bruce wrote expansively to "all the kings of Ireland" in
his effort to drum up support for his brother's campaign.[6]
But it is probably a mistake to take this Scottish propaganda at face value. The Gaelic Irish remained divided
amongst themselves, particularly with regard to reestab-
lishment of the "high king"; and fourteenth-century Scotland was itself a partly Norman realm, as Bruce's own
origins attest. Edward Bruce died in 1318. His invasion fell
far short of its goals, but it dashed the remnants of the
dream that Ireland might one day be as thoroughly Nor-
manized as England.

Before examining the splintered form of late medieval
Ireland we need to discuss the Church, which we have ignored since the close of its Golden Age (the sixth to the
ninth centuries) with the advent of the Vikings. Without
doubt, the northmen dealt the Church a terrible blow. The
monasteries were obvious targets that were attacked sav-
agely and repeatedly. Many of the smaller houses failed to
recover, and the eastern, coastal locations were particularly hard hit. The great monastery at Armagh, however,
maintained its leadership in the considerable portions of
the north dominated by the Ui Neill kings. Pluralism—the
holding of more than one, and sometimes many, ecclesiastical livings or benefices (we would call them "jobs" or "in-

comes")—appears to have increased as a response to the decline in the value of those livings. Ideally, a "living" was an amount of annual income (in cash or kind) sufficient to enable one man to perform one full-time clerical function, as priest of a parish, for instance. If the value of the living declined, as a result of protracted drought or the kind of spoliation carried out by the Vikings, clerics sought to remedy the resulting pinch by acquiring additional livings. The consequent "pluralism" weakened the Church by giving what were meant to be full-time jobs to churchmen who could, at best, devote only a portion of their time to them. Family influence over ecclesiastical appointments, which was an early characteristic of the Irish Church, remained strong in the Viking period as families, septs, and *tuatha* struggled to retain every economic benefit they could possibly claim from wealth nominally handed over to the Church.

The tenth century was a period of Gaelic consolidations as the Viking presence stabilized, and the power of the great Irish overlords increased. The Church looked for protection and patronage to the royal or quasi-royal families. The early monasteries had often accepted as their abbots the ecclesiastical offshoots of powerful secular families, but this genealogical connection was increasingly reinforced by a political dependence on secular powers. Thus one can speak of the "secularization" of the Irish Church as an indirect consequence of the Viking terror. In some cases, secularization proceeded to the point that the king held the highest ecclesiastical office (sometimes bishop, sometimes abbot) as well. Fewer pilgrimages were made to Continental Europe, and more were made to such nearby shrines as Armagh and Iona.

In the scriptoria of the Irish monasteries much more was written in the vernacular language of Irish. There may have been a growing concern with the propagation of the gospel and the need to render it into a familiar tongue. The Church seems to have been turning *outward* in an effort to convert the heathen northmen who had been intruded into its province. It was not rejecting the ascetic tradition of the sixth and seventh century saints, but trying to build on its spiritual strength. If in the eighth century the Church's central function was the proliferation of saintly, ascetic lives, by the tenth century the emphasis was on conversion of the heathen, even if the conversion was only superficial. The art of the Church, both literary and graphic, rose to the occasion. Tales were told and written popularizing the lives of early saints like Brendan the Voyager. Manuscript illumination continued, but was joined by the much more public art of sculpture. From the tenth and eleventh centuries date most of the thirty odd "high crosses" which survived the ages. The illuminated manuscript, however evangelistic, was an intensely private treasure that could be known by only a privileged few. In contrast, a seventeen-foot-high stone cross, graven with scenes from the life of Christ and planted in a prominent part of a churchyard, was the medieval counterpart of the modern day highway billboard. Here was an assertive display of the chief symbols of the faith, a declaration of evangelical purpose well suited to the struggle to win Viking souls.

The campaign was amazingly successful. Not only did the Vikings succumb to Christianity, but they displayed a zeal to feed from what they perceived as its ultimate source in Rome. A new element of ultramontanism, deference to Roman authority, seems to have resulted from the enthusiasm of at least some of the Viking converts. The Viking king of Dublin, Sitric, made a pilgrimage to Rome in 1028 and probably began the negotiating which led to an episcopal see for Dublin. Dunan, the first bishop (died 1074), was of Irish descent, but may have been trained in England, or on the continent. The episcopal structure so favored by Rome apparently had greater appeal for the commercial, seafaring, and city-dwelling Vikings than it had for the rural and agrarian Irish.

In addition to seeking ecclesiastical links with Rome, the Vikings accepted new links with the Church in England.

The Norman conquest there in 1066 had been carried out with papal blessings despite the antiquity and loyalty of the English Church. Canterbury, the superior archdiocese, was therefore the closest font of approved Roman authority, so it is not surprising that the early bishops of Dublin were consecrated there, rather than at Ireland's own archdiocese of Armagh. The Canterbury–Dublin link also provided a conduit through which English and Norman-trained clergy passed into the Hiberno-Norse Church.

Between a synod (or gathering of the higher clergy) at Cashel in 1101 and one at Kells in 1152 a rational administrative structure was created for the Church in Ireland. A church of saints and their successors was slowly made to give way to a church of structured authority such as existed in England and western Europe. At the synod of Raith Bresail in 1111, Ireland was divided into two archepiscopal provinces: Armagh to serve thirteen sees in the north; Cashel to serve twelve sees in the south. Dublin remained paradoxically under the authority of Canterbury until 1152 when it was made a third Irish archdiocese (to placate its Viking rulers), and Tuam was made a fourth archdiocese, to serve the needs of the west. Because of these "political" considerations Ireland acquired four archbishoprics in contrast to England's spare two.

The Vikings were reaching eastward toward the continental church while the Normans, almost simultaneously, were reaching west to extend their power and influence through England and Wales. Ireland was increasingly bombarded by continental ways. Its insular practices were under attack in the twelfth century as never before. Even native churchmen like Malachy, the great reforming bishop of Armagh, sought to remodel Irish institutions after continental models. During a trip through France, Malachy had fallen under the spell of Bernard of Clairvaux, one of the founders of the new Cistercian order. When Malachy returned to Ireland he helped to found in 1140 the first Cistercian house at Mellifont in County Louth. The order spread rapidly through Ireland despite a certain reluctance of continental monks to come to a distant, unfamiliar island.

The Augustinian Rule as practiced at Arrouaise in Flanders had a similar impact in Ireland at about the same time, and architecture and sculpture as well reveal influential continental models. In the marvelous chapel at Cashel built by Cormac MacCarthy, king of Desmond, between 1127 and 1134, may be seen both the zenith of native Irish stonecraft, and the unmistakable evidence of continental Romanesque decoration. In the words of a recent historian of the Church: "By 1152 the transmutation of the Irish church, though not yet complete, was inevitable. A Roman hierarchy, continental religious orders, and legatine commissions were removing the chief anomalies of the traditional system, while new styles in building and sculpture marked the transformation."[7]

The critical point is that this transformation *preceded* the Norman intervention. The Norman monarchy in England undoubtedly promoted it, but the springs and sources of the reform movement grew out of a European-wide movement which the Irish were not likely to escape under any circumstance.

The *coup de grace* was papal recognition of the claim of the English monarchy to ultimate sovereignty over Ireland. This was given in 1155 to Henry II by Pope Adrian IV in the infamous bull, *Laudabiliter.* Henry's dilatory behavior in 1167 (twelve years later) suggests that he was in no great hurry to press his claim over Ireland, but the anomalous fact that Pope Adrian IV (Nicholas Breakspere) was the one English pope in the entire history of the papacy has long nourished the belief in a nefarious conspiracy. No one can prove the contrary, but after Henry's regal visitation of Ireland in 1171–72, the king petitioned Adrian IV's successor, Alexander III, for authorization of his lordship over Ireland. Alexander confirmed Henry's right, and the confirmation was ratified by a coucil of Irish bishops meeting at Waterford in 1173–74. Some of the Irish bishops welcomed the

English king's advent as likely to accelerate much-needed reform. Others saw it as a cruel but righteous judgment of God upon the wayward Irish.

Pope Alexander III warmly welcomed the English king's new role. He wrote to congratulate Henry for having "wonderfully and magnificently triumphed over the disordered and indisciplined Irish, a people, we have heard, the Roman rulers, conquerors of the world in their time left unapproached, a people unmindful of the fear of God, which as if unbridled indiscriminately turns aside from the straight road for the depths of vice, throws off the religion of Christian faith and virtue, and destroys itself in internecine slaughter."[8]

This was faint regard for the Church and the people of Patrick, Columba Brigid, and Brendan, a Church and people which had helped to keep Christianity alive in its darkest days, long before the papacy emerged into its medieval splendor. But from a Roman point of view what mattered was order, control, the responsiveness of the provinces to the levers of power at the pontifical center. In 1213 Pope Innocent III confirmed the acts of his predecessors when he accepted as a papal fief Ireland—along with England—from the refractory King John, and the papacy never seriously reconsidered its approval of English sovereignty over Ireland until King Henry VIII took his heretical path in the sixteenth century. By its alliance with the Anglo–Normans the papacy succeeded in bringing the insular Irish Church closer within its fold, but at a cost of tainting its reputation among many of the Irish. Rome had conspired to assist the aggression of a foreigner against Ireland, and the stigma arising from that act would never disappear entirely.

The Norman intervention was only one part of a broad continental incursion which included the papacy and the churchmen of France. The result was a bifurcation, or duality, in Irish culture far more enduring and profound than anything which the Vikings had caused. Parts of Ireland remained insular, Irish, traditional, and relatively unaffected by the newcomers, while other parts soon conformed to

Anglo–Norman, or continental ways. Political disunity existed before the Normans came. Cultural disunity was
added to it, and duality became the prevailing mode of the
later Middle Ages in Ireland. French (and later English)
were spoken in the Anglo–Norman enclaves. Irish remained
the language of the natives, and the institutions (such as
certain monasteries) they dominated. The failure of either
the Anglo-Normans to complete their conquest, or of the
Irish to expel them from the island doomed the awkward
duality to endure.

Originally the monarchy had hoped to keep Irish and
Norman forces in rough balance, so that it could rule by
playing one interest off against another. By the fourteenth
century it had virtually come to depend on three formidable Anglo-Norman families: the Fitzgerald earls of Desmond, the Butler earls of Ormonde, and the Fitzgerald earls
of Kildare. Insofar as there was English rule of Ireland it
was rule *through* the power of one of those great families, a
system sometimes known as "native rule." The monarchy
either could not, or would not, maintain an independent
bureaucracy and garrison, probably because of the great
expense, and dependence upon the greatest of the Anglo-
Norman families was the unavoidable alternative.

It was not a happy solution, for it was an implicit admission of the English monarchy's powerlessness in Ireland.
Various efforts were made to save the day by heroic exertions. In 1361, for instance, Edward III sent his son Lionel,
duke of Clarence, to Ireland on a campaign of restoration
and recovery. The expedition accomplished little, partly because Clarence had difficulty distinguishing between the
supposedly loyal Anglo-Normans and the supposedly rebellious Irish. He could hardly be blamed, inasmuch as the
Anglo-Normans were less than enthusiastic about English
assistance. Only when their own fortunes were desperate
did they really welcome their brethren from across the
water. The rest of the time they tended to prefer to be left
alone in their endless quarrels.

One fruit of Clarence's venture was the convening of a

long-remembered Irish Parliament at Kilkenny in 1366. In both England and Ireland the institution of Parliament crystallized in the thirteenth century. There were certain peculiarities about the Irish Parliament, compared with its English counterpart, but the most important was the very limited area it represented, or from which its representatives came. At no time prior to the sixteenth century (When Henry VIII created Celtic peers who could sit in the Irish House of Lords) were there representatives from Celtic areas; and as the Norman sphere of influence contracted the Irish Parliament became increasingly truncated and fragmentary. By the early fifteenth century "only eleven counties [of 32] and ten towns were sending representatives. . . . [and] only the area covered by counties Dublin, Kildare, Louth and Meath were regularly represented, with the town of Waterford."[9]

The Parliament which met at Kilkenny in 1366 at the bidding of the duke of Clarence was thus an Anglo-Norman body summoned to serve royal purposes. Its famous product was the so-called statutes of Kilkenny, laws which addressed themselves to the problem of "degeneracy" in Anglo-Norman society. One group of statutes forbade "alliance by marriage, fosterage, or concubinage; the presentation of Irishmen to cathedral or collegiate churches; the reception of Irish minstrels and other entertainers amongst the English; the acceptance of Irishmen into profession in English religious houses; the use of the Irish language, mode of riding and dress; [even] the giving of pasturage on lands to Irish."[10] The statutes are not nearly so important as an example of Anglo-Norman ethnocentricity and bigotry (though they are that) as they are a revelation of the cultural duality of fourteenth century Ireland and the way that duality was breaking down.

What *we* might regard benignly as "assimilation," the merging of one culture into another, the English monarchy and at least some of the Anglo-Normans in Ireland saw as "degeneracy," the deterioration of a superior culture under the influence of an inferior one. Such an attitude was not novel, but it may have acquired a new importance when the Anglo-Normans ceased their expansion. At that point the eccentricities of Irish culture became a threat rather than a curiosity. The numerical thinness of Norman society was all too apparent, and there was growing concern that the sturdy Anglo-Norman virtues would be eroded and lost. Certainly the two cultures looked at one another across a sizable gap. A loquacious churchman called Gerald of Wales (Giraldus Cambrensis) had accompanied John (later King John) on his late twelfth century expeditions to Ireland and left two long accounts of Ireland and its "conquest," neither of which contained anything but scorn for the native population. By the same token, the Irish annalists had little praise for the Normans.

What distinguishes the late Middle Ages in Ireland is that this cultural polarity, or antipathy, becomes institutionalized. It appears in the statutes of the Anglo-Norman parliament; it even characterizes the fabric of the Church. The impact of the continental reform movement of the twelfth century had all but eliminated the customary Irish rule from the Irish monasteries. Cistercians and Augustinian canons regular were thick on the ground before the Normans arrived, and a second wave of foundations followed with the arrival of the friars: first the Dominicans in 1224 and then the Franciscans a decade later. By 1230 there were about two hundred religious houses for men of which roughly eighty were of Anglo-French foundation. Far fewer new houses were established in Scotland (46) or Wales (33) than in Ireland, and the movement may have been a victim of its own success.[11] French and continental monks would not come in sufficient numbers to fill the burgeoning establishments, and native Irish religious bridled at the discipline and cultural authoritarianism of the mother houses abroad. The first Cistercian house, Mellifont, strayed scandalously from the order to which it belonged. On the whole the two cultures mixed no better in the institutions of the Church than they mixed in secular society. Parishes, bishoprics, and monasteries all tended to be polarized as either Irish or Anglo-Norman.

The friaries fared somewhat better at first. By about 1340, there were 33 Franciscan houses, 25 Dominican, 16 Carmelite, and 11 Augustinian. At first Anglo-Normans and Irish "intermingled in these new international religious militias," but they were eventually to go their separate, inimical ways. Repeated attempts at integration ended in failure and were followed by the kind of stratification adumbrated in the statues of Kilkenny. The fourteenth clause stipulated that "no religious house . . . situated among the English shall for the future receive any Irishmen as professed religious, but may receive Englishmen without regard to whether they were born in England or in Ireland."[12] The representatives gathered at Kilkenny were not seeking reconciliation, but rather preservation of the integrity of the embattled Anglo-Norman sphere. The statutes they passed were almost impossible to enforce, and they stand as a kind of monument to the split—one might say paralyzed—nature of late medieval Ireland in which two cultures were locked together and neither was able to supplant the other.

Anglo-Norman efforts to break the deadlock continued throughout the fourteenth century. The duke of Clarence's campaign was followed, in the 1370s by that of his brother, William of Windsor. When Edward III (father of Clarence and Windsor) died in 1377, Richard II succeeded him and displayed a precocious, unusual, concern with Ireland. Richard made two visits to Ireland, the first in 1394 and the second (contributing to his overthrow by Henry Bolingbroke) in 1399. They were the first royal visits since Henry II and the last until William III in 1689. Richard took a large army with him to Ireland, and had some initial success, but was able to see that mere force could not be an enduring solution. In a letter of analysis to the council in England (written in February 1395) Richard divided the inhabitants of Ireland into three groups: "the wild Irish, our enemies the Irish rebels, and the obedient English." "The wild Irish" he put beyond the possibility of redemption, but "the Irish rebels" were those who had made their submission to the Crown at some point, but were now in re-

bellion. Of those, Richard wrote generously: "[they] are
rebels only because of grievances and wrongs done to them
on one side and lack of remedy on the other. If they are not
wisely trusted and put in good hope of grace they will probably join our enemies."[13] Richard hoped to revive the lordship as a guarantor of the rights and privileges of both the
Gaelic and Anglo-Norman aristocracies, but no force was
strong enough to impose peace on the warring factions
once the king had returned to England.

Late medieval Ireland was an island floating rudderless.
There were powerful lords in both cultures able to defend
their own lands and interests, but there was no single interest behind which they could all unite. English concern
with Ireland was, at best, fitful. France remained the chief
foreign entanglement at least until the mid-fifteenth century when England lost all French possessions except Ca-
lais in the concluding phase of the so-called Hundred Years
War. In the decades which followed England was preoccupied with its own civil war called The War of the Roses.
These were a complex set of struggles revolving around
conflicting claims to the throne by two branches of the
royal house: the house of Lancaster, and the house of York.
An Irish dimension resulted from the fact that Richard, the
"great" duke of York, had been lord lieutenant of Ireland in
the 1440s, before the Wars of the Roses erupted.

When the Lancastrians got the upper hand in the ensuing
struggles, York took refuge in Ireland where he was warmly
supported, especially by the powerful Fitzgeralds. A parliament was convened at Drogheda in 1460, and it pro-
pounded a theory of Irish sovereignty and independence of
England, largely to support York's continuing claim to the
lord lieutenancy. A year later York was killed in battle in
England, but his son came to the throne as Edward IV and
ruled until his natural death in 1483. As the first of the two
Yorkist kings, Edward IV maintained his father's close tie
with Anglo-Norman Ireland, and the Fitzgeralds. The Lancastrians responded by cultivating an alliance with the
Fitzgeralds' great rivals, the Butlers.

Edward IV promoted the Fitzgerald earls of Kildare to a primacy which they maintained for more than fifty years. They drew not only on the wealth of their ancestral lands, mainly in Carlow and Kildare, but also upon the support of the Irish Parliament, and an elaborate system of marriage alliances that extended to the Gaelic Irish and even the rival Butlers. Their power grew so great that they wrested from the monarchy more than it wanted to give, including the power of appointment to, and dismissal from, royal office in Ireland. In 1478 the eighth earl contrived to have himself appointed lord lieutenant by the Irish Council in direct contravention of Edward IV's appointment of an Englishman, Lord Grey, to the post.

Kildare transformed the shrunken Anglo-Norman colony into a vest-pocket state. Claims to independence from England by the Irish Parliament were little more than admissions of its intimidation by Kildare. So strong was the eighth earl's hold on Anglo-Norman Ireland that when Henry Tudor defeated the last Yorkist king, Richard III, in 1485 and ascended the English throne as Henry VII, he was virtually forced to acquiesce in the continuing lord lieutenancy of the Irish magnate. It was a bitter pill to swallow. The Tudors were a Lancastrian offshoot. The Yorkists had been their bitter enemies, as had the Yorkists' allies in Ireland, the Fitzgeralds. And how were the Tudors to satisfy their debts to *their* Irish allies, the Butlers?

The strained relationship between Henry VII and the eighth earl of Kildare was made little easier by the gravitation of two Yorkist pretenders to Ireland. These were young men who claimed to be surviving Yorkists with a far better right to the throne than Henry VII. Both were impostors. The first, whose true name was Lambert Simnel, came to Ireland in 1487 to gather support for his cause in England. In the event, his rebellion was so easily quashed that Henry VII spared his life. The second, Perkin Warbeck, was a more serious menace, and the support he received in Ireland in the 1490s illustrated the danger to the English monarchy of an independent, dissident Ireland. "Native

Rule" was "no rule," or so little as to amount to the same thing. Its only virtue was cheapness. It did not deplete the English exchequer or drain off men and arms needed elsewhere. This was the dilemma in which the Tudor monarchs found themselves.

There was no simple and obvious solution. Imposing "direct rule" on Ireland would entail unforseeable expenses. Unless the tax base could be made more secure and expanded beyond the narrow confines of the Pale, the area near Dublin which responded to Dublin rule, those immense expenses would never be recovered. Instead, a permanent garrison state would become a perpetual burden on English taxpayers. On the other hand, how much was the security of Ireland worth? How great was the risk that Ireland might some day, alone, or as the ally of England's continental enemies, deal England a mortal blow? Could the island be left to run its own unforseeable course? Or conversely, might a major commitment of resources to Ireland eventually produce a handsome return?

Monarchs before the Tudors had pondered all these questions without being moved to decisive action. It was the distinction of the Tudors to act. Not the Normans, but the Tudors "conquered" Ireland. It was they who, at last, put an end to "heroic Ireland," who replaced the independent chief, baron, earl, or king with the awesome power of a reformed and strengthened English State.

3

LATE MEDIEVAL IRELAND
AND THE TUDOR CONQUEST

ARCHBISHOP SWAYNE of Armagh wrote in 1427: "The English ground [i.e., land inhabited by Anglo-Normans] that is obeying to the king's law in this land ... is not so much of quantity as is one shire of England."[1] His was but one of many laments. The area around Dublin which responded to Dublin government was called the Pale, but seldom extended more than twenty miles west or more than forty miles north. The Irish Parliament reflected this feebleness of Anglo-Norman power outside of Dublin. Between 1320 and 1494 the town of Limerick sent a representative only in 1483. Cashel was represented only in 1371, and Cork only in 1382.[2]

If by 1427 Anglo-Norman Ireland had contracted nearly to the point of disappearance, for governmental purposes, imagine how much worse Gaelic Ireland appeared in Tudor eyes. A report back to England in 1515 complained:

there be more than sixty countries, called regions, in Ireland, inhabited with the King's Irish enemies; ... where reigneth more than sixty chief captains ...; and every of the said captains maketh war and peace for himself, and holdeth by the sword, and hath imperial jurisdiction within his room, and obeyeth to no other person, English or Irish, except only to such persons as may subdue him by the sword.[3]

Even if the writer exaggerated, he was close to the mark in seeing the challenge to English government as daunting.

The Tudors' first attempt to improve matters by "direct rule" was both tentative and brief. Henry VII made a loyal English soldier, Edward Poynings, lord deputy in 1494 and sent him to Ireland with a small army of 400 men. This was less an effort to subdue the island than to discourage support for Perkin Warbeck, the Yorkist pretender, and counterbalance the immense influence of the earl of Kildare. Even so, the venture cost Henry £18,000 in two years' time, an amount which persuaded him to recall Poynings and reappoint Kildare lord lieutenant. (Lord deputy and lord lieutenant were different titles for what was, in effect, the same office. Men with aristocratic titles, like Kildare, could hold the lieutenancy. "Commoners," like Poynings, were appointed as deputies.)

Poynings is best remembered for the statute named after him and passed by the Parliament he convened late in 1494. It was one of a whole series of laws aimed at undermining the autonomy of Kildare, or any other Anglo-Irish lord who might eventually supplant him. "Poynings' Law" provided that no parliament was to be held in Ireland until license for it had been procured from the king, and further that all legislation to be submitted to the parliament had first to be approved by the king and his council in England. Though later construed as an act to insure the subordination of Ireland to England, Poynings' Law was born of the monarchy's frustration and impotence, rather than its imperial aspirations.

The immediate effect on the earl of Kildare's power was slight. When the earl died in 1513, Henry VIII granted the lord lieutenancy to his son, the ninth earl, thus leaving Ireland in the dynasty's grasp. Another flirtation with direct rule took place in 1520 when Henry sent Thomas Howard, earl of Surrey, to Ireland as lord lieutenant, but again the effort was short-lived. Henry then tried to stave off Kildare by making a member of the Butler family lord deputy, but by 1524 was forced to relent in Kildare's reappointment. In 1529 Henry appointed his own bastard son, the duke of

Richmond, as lord lieutenant, and it was the beginning of a succession (broken only from 1532–35) of English-born governors. Kildare recovered the position in 1532, but the Tudor monarchy was palpably beginning to flex its muscle in Ireland. Kildare was summoned to London in 1534 and left his son Thomas, Lord Offaly, to govern during his absence. When the earl reached London he was charged with using the king's artillery to defend his own castles, and confined to the Tower. When Lord Offaly (called "silken Thomas") heard of his father's arrest (and the rumor of his execution, which was unfounded, though the earl died later in confinement) he dramatically launched a rebellion against the Crown.

Here was the confrontation toward which the Tudors may have been maneuvering, an opportunity for the demonstration of the new dynasty's strength and ability to intervene in Ireland. "Silken Thomas" was joined in his rebellion by an imposing array of Anglo-Norman and Gaelic lords who saw the detention of the ninth earl of Kildare in England as unwarranted English intervention in an Irish government which they were accustomed to think of as their own. The rebellion collapsed, however, when a newly appointed lord deputy, Sir William Skeffington, appeared on the scene with an army. Lord Offaly's stronghold at Maynooth Castle, just west of Dublin, was attacked and overwhelmed in March 1535. Lord Offaly and five of his uncles were sent to London where they were executed like common criminals at Tyburn two years later. The ninth earl of Kildare died in prison in December 1535, whether by foul means or not is impossible to say. In any event Henry VIII had brandished his famous fist in a way almost unprecedented in Anglo-Irish history. The Fitzgeralds and their allies were far from collapse, and they fought on for five years in what came to be called the war of the Geraldine League, but in retrospect it appears that the die had been cast. The Tudor monarchy had made a fateful decision to dismantle native rule and proceed to implant some meaningful semblance of English government in Ireland. It appears to have been a decision from which there was no turning back.]

[Exactly at this fateful junction of political events the religious question entered Anglo-Irish relations.] There had been nominal unity among Christians in the British Isles at least since the eighth century when the Irish gave up their eccentric manner of determining the date of Easter. That a division in religion now occurred was the result, more than anything else, of the new power and ambition of the Tudor monarchy. That power and ambition, in turn, was partly a consequence of the distinctive personalities of the first two Tudor monarchs, Henry VII (1485–1509) and Henry VIII (1509–1547), but it was related also to forces which favored centralization of power in many European societies in the late Middle Ages. Henry VIII's assertion of his power in Ireland was simply the other side of the coin on which he was asserting the power of his monarchy against Rome.

The famous, or infamous, occasion for Henry VIII's assertion of his (and England's) independence of Rome was his infatuation with Anne Boleyn and his consequent desire to divorce his first wife, Catharine of Aragon. When, in 1529, the attempt of Cardinal Wolsey to obtain a divorce from Rome proved futile, Henry began to explore other alternatives and, in 1532, with the aid and encouragement of his capable secretary, Thomas Cromwell, Henry embarked upon the severance of the English Church from Roman authority. [The king allowed Parliament to recognize him as the "supreme head" of the English Church, thus substituting his own authority for that of the papacy.] This done, Henry instructed his new and sympathetic archbishop of Canterbury, Thomas Cranmer, to grant the divorce he had so long desired. Henry had already put Catharine aside and married Anne, who was pregnant with the child who would eventually become Queen Elizabeth I.

[Henry's matrimonial adventures need not detain us, but what is important is that England's break with Rome did not grow out of doctrinal differences or the zeal of English reformers. Although the nature of the faith would slowly change in a climate filtered of Roman influences, there was no missionary impulse to run to Ireland (or anywhere else) with the Word. Devout Irish, like many devout English, regretted the quarrel between their spiritual and secular lords, but without any conviction that it would endure or that they would eventually have to choose between one and the other. A few of the Geraldines took the position that since both they and the pope were fighting Henry VIII, they and the pope must be allies in a single cause. But the Geraldine League was at heart a political alliance in which religious concerns were probably an afterthought.

The English heresy did not officially reach Ireland until 1536. Henry was faced with the troublesome anomaly that he was legally married to Anne Boleyn in England, but not in Ireland, where the Church was yet under Roman authority. Hence Princess Elizabeth, the child of his second union, was legitimate in England, but a bastard and no rightful heir in Ireland. This was no prudent way to leave the succession in an island only just being reduced to some semblance of obedience. Accordingly, it was necessary to bring the Church in Ireland into conformity with the Church in England, and for that purpose Henry caused an Irish Parliament to be summoned in May 1536.

The Parliament was composed entirely of Anglo-Normans, and if they had any private misgivings over the portentous legislation they passed, little evidence of it has survived. The only recorded resistance came from the clerical proctors, representatives of the lower (or parish) clergy who still sat in the Irish Parliament, though they had long since been removed from the English Parliament to Convocation, the separate assembly of the church. Being more remote from royal authority, the lower clergy tended to be more independent, even refractory, and had they been represented in the English Reformation Parliament they would probably have caused a similar fuss. The Irish authorities were unperturbed. They seized the opportunity to declare the proctors an anachronism and ended their participation

in the Irish Parliament for evermore. Thereupon the reformation statutes passed without serious hindrance.

No doubt, many MP's were eager to demonstrate their
loyalty to the English king and their hostility to the rebel
Geraldines. When parliament assembled for a second session in September 1536 the House of Commons was less
amenable than in May, but it was apparently less dis-
tressed by the threatened changes in the Church than by
the steadily growing wealth and influence of Englishmen
newly inserted into the colony. "Direct Rule" meant nothing if not increasing reliance upon English-born soldiers
and administrators in Ireland. This implied the displacement from positions of profit and power of the traditional
Anglo-Norman ruling class. Once the government withdrew
or modified four proposed measures which seemed to
threaten the merchants of the towns and the landed gentry
and professional lawyers of the Pale, resistance to the
church bills abated.

In a session of October 1537 Parliament passed an act de-
nying papal authority in Ireland and prescribing for officeholders an oath acknowledging the royal supremacy. Another act called for the dissolution of thirteen named
monasteries. None of this originated with the Irish Parliament, but neither was it heroically resisted there. To English martyrs like John Fisher and Thomas More, the struggle between king and pope did have doctrinal (and heretical)
implications, but they were humanists and cosmopolites
whose vantage point, close to the seat of royal power, afforded them a clearer view of unfolding events. Ireland produced no such instant opponents, men in high place so pro-
foundly troubled by their monarch's proceedings that they
defected from his cause at the cost of their lives. The character of Irish resistance to religious change was to be much
more gradual and oblique.

The overthrow of "native rule" and the substitution of
royal for papal authority in the Irish Church were attempted almost simultaneously and constituted merely the
secular and ecclesiastical aspects of a single expansionary

force. The episcopal bench was simply a power center which the Crown endeavored to control, as part of the larger effort. Although many of Henry's thirteen post-1534 episcopal appointments were of Celtic and Anglo-Norman Irish, the most controversial was that of George Browne, an English protege of Thomas Cromwell, to the archdiocese of Dublin, in 1536. Together with Bishop Edward Staples of Meath, Browne constituted the pro-reform and antipapal party within the Henrician Irish hierarchy. The archbishop of Armagh, George Cromer, was also an Englishman, but he had served his see since 1521 and had no instinct to share in Henry's quarrel with Rome. He simply withdrew from public life after 1534, hoping to offend no one. Instead, his inconspicuousness aroused the suspicion of all, and the papacy suspended him from his functions in 1539, though he probably remained a loyal Roman Catholic until his death in 1543.

The papacy responded increasingly to what it regarded as royal usurpation of its critical role in the choice and oversight of the church's hierarchy. As in the case of Archbishop Cromer it could, and did, suspend those whose loyalty was doubtful. It could appoint to sees which were vacant or even rivals to sees where there was a royal appointee. The nature of the diocese and the extent to which it was controlled by English authorities in Dublin frequently determined the outcome of these disputes. A diocese like Dublin itself was hardly worth bothering over, for any papally appointed archbishop could not hope to claim his see or its revenues. Thus Archbishop George Browne, though an ardent reformer, faced no papal rival. But the provinces provided greener fields, and there were more than forty papal appointees to Irish bishoprics between 1534 and 1553. Some became resident in their sees. Others held little more than an empty title. It was the embryonic beginning of an administrative system of two separate churches, which in time would give rise to two separate and antithetical religions.

No one could know how long Henry VIII's dispute with

Rome would last, or whether it would be ended by his successors. As it happened, the dispute grew into a profound
and enduring division which was only briefly interrupted,
from 1553 to 1558, by the monarchy of the Catholic Queen
Mary, Henry's daughter by his pious first wife, Catharine of
Aragon. As supreme head of his Church, Henry VIII steered
a theologically conservative course. In Ireland, as in England, the major impact of his innovations was institutional
and administrative, rather than liturgical or doctrinal.

The most palpable and obvious alteration of Irish religion was the attempt to dissolve the monasteries. We have
seen what a long and important role monastic foundations
had played in Irish society since at least the sixth century.
In 1534 there were more than four hundred monastic
houses and probably between four and five thousand mo-
nastics. The friaries, in particular, had become the chief religious centers in many parts of the country and were by no
means remote from the daily life of the people. At the same
time the monasteries in Ireland, as in most of western Europe, were generally in decline. The monastic ideal, after
many revivals, was at a low ebb. A great deal of wealth, ac-
cumulated over centuries, in many cases supported a deri-
sory number of religious in the performance of functions
which were not always regarded as necessary or useful by
lay society.

The monastic system was ripe for reform, and even those
who believed in the monasteries and desired their survival
had to admit that some prudent reorganization and consolidation was essential. Thus the bill of 1537 which proposed
the dissolution of thirteen named houses did not evoke a
storm of indignation in the Irish Parliament. What was unforeseen, and probably unforeseeable, was that Henry VIII
would find the logic of dissolution so infinitely appealing. If
a little dissolution was good, then more was better, a proposition made all the more persuasive when the wealth of
the dissolved houses was acquired by the Crown instead of
by the remaining monasteries. At some point Henry determined to eliminate the monasteries altogether, and by 1540

he had almost entirely accomplished his purpose in England and Wales. In Ireland the commissioners for carrying out the dissolutions began in the Pale (where their efforts were most effectual) and worked their way outward, extending into Gaelic areas only after 1541. By the king's death in 1547 something more than half of the monasteries had been dissolved and slightly less than half of the communities of mendicants.[4] Northwest Ulster, northern Connacht, and southwest Munster remained virtually untouched.

The vigor of the dissolution may have been attuned to the political situation in each area. In the Pale, for instance, dissolution was carried out energetically in the late 1530s by the deputy, Lord Leonard Grey, partly to illustrate the power and determination of the Crown, and partly because local Anglo-Norman families were willing to support the work in return for a share of the spoils. Thus the prominent Barnewall family was enriched with a favorable lease on the former property of the Convent of Grace Dieu in northern County Dublin, and acquired lands of the former Carmelite friary of Knocktopher in county Kilkenny.[5] A period of greater restraint followed the fall from grace, and subsequent execution in 1540, of Thomas Cromwell, the chief architect of the dissolution in both islands. Sir Anthony St. Leger replaced Grey as lord deputy, and St. Leger proved more willing to conciliate local interests and restrain the commissioners in their dissolving activity.

Just as there was no Irish counterpart to the English martyrs Thomas More and John Fisher, so also was there no Irish counterpart to the pilgrimage of grace, the great popular rising of 1536 against the dissolution of the monasteries in the north of England. Even the infamous campaign against religious images carried out at about fifty shrines within the Pale during the winter of 1538–39 provoked little protest, partly because the commissioners may have been more restrained and less iconoclastic than later chroniclers reported. King Henry was a heretic, but not a Protestant. His concern was not to protestantize Ireland, but to bring its Church within his control and integrate it

into his more ambitious conception of Irish government.)
Henry and his successors faced an uphill fight, but not because the Irish were congenitally Roman Catholic and adverse to all forms of Protestantism. The larger obstacle was
that the Church was becoming identified with the expansive and intrusive foreign power of England. It was the Anglo-Normans rather than the Celtic Irish who first reacted
against this intrusion, perhaps because it was they who had
dominated the hierarchy of the old Church and they who
suffered most from displacement. It was they who also
shared in the spoils of the dissolved monasteries; but perhaps what they gained was not commensurate with what
they lost, for in the Pale Lord Deputy Grey and his English
followers acquired for themselves as large a share of monastic wealth as did the Anglo-Norman palesmen who far
outnumbered them.[6]

With the Geraldines' resistance crumbling and the Church
yielding slowly (at least superficially) to royal authority,
Henry VIII contrived to have an Irish Parliament enact on
June 18, 1541, "that the king's highness, his heirs and successors, kings of England, be always kings of this land of
Ireland."[7] Technically, the Irish Parliament did not create
this new power. That would have demeaned the monarchy
by suggesting that its authority was derived from its subjects rather than God above. Parliament merely "recognized" the new relationship, but it thereby ended the more
modest twelfth-century "lordship" and gave legal expression to an assertive royal policy which was increasingly evident in the field. The Tudors were now kings of Ireland,
but this was as much a declaration of intent as a statement
of accomplishment. English authority had been reasserted
in Dublin and the Pale, but the hinterland was as ungov-
erned as ever.

In a legalistic sense, the act of 1541 was a consequence of
Henry's break with Rome. It was too easy to argue that the
"lordship" which the English monarchy had enjoyed since
King John derived such legitimacy as it had from papal
sanction, and that what the papacy had granted the papacy

could rescind. But if Henry's policy was expansionary, it had the small redeeming quality of being universalist. The Parliament which recognized Henry to be king included, for the first time, Gaelic lords and representatives of Gaelic areas. He aspired to be king of all Ireland, not just Anglo-Norman Ireland. Particularly through the policies of Lord Deputy St. Leger (1540–1546), Henry sought to incorporate Gaelic chiefs into a broader Irish state on an equal footing with the Anglo-Norman lords. St. Leger was impowered to make royal grants and create peerages for Gaelic chiefs who were willing to surrender to the king on particular terms. This was known as the policy of "surrender and regrant," and in accordance with it numerous Irish were brought into a direct feudal relationship with the English crown.

Surrender and regrant broadened the base of support for the Tudor monarchy by attaching to it important Gaelic lords who had previously been autonomous. At the same time, however, it tended to undermine the support which the Gaelic lords enjoyed among their own people. Surrender and regrant was, in effect, a form of bribery by which great lords were encouraged to repudiate, or minimize, some of their traditional and communal responsibilities in return for English recognition of their pretensions.

The surrender of Con O'Neill is a case in point. The lord of the most formidable Ulster tribe, O'Neill made his submission to Lord Deputy St. Leger in December 1541. Although he desired the ancient Norman title of earl of Ulster, Henry VIII kept that title for the crown and fobbed him off with the earldom of Tyrone. In accordance with English custom the title was made heritable, and Con designated his son Matthew to succeed him. This was a violation of tradition. Many of Con's followers regarded his wealth and power as privileges conferred upon him by his people rather than as his absolute, devisable possessions. Con's overlooked son, Shane, had an obvious interest in supporting any obstruction to his brother Matthew's succession. Thus the Anglicization of Con O'Neill into the earl of Tyrone attached the great chief to the government, but divided his people into quarreling factions, a phenomenon repeated many times over in other parts of Ireland.

Through surrender and regrant Henry VIII was endeavoring to bring the Gaelic Irish into an expanded Irish polity, but at another level he was infiltrating born Englishmen into positions of power and influence. This was true of the episcopal bench and also of the Irish council, where English appointees stirred the jealousies not only of the Gaelic Irish, but also the Anglo-Normans, who were the traditional holders of such office under the medieval lordship. The costs of administering Ireland remained great, something on the order of £5000 per annum, so that direct rule, whatever its benefits, continued to be a drain upon the English treasury. But at Henry's death, in 1547, the island was by no means disaffected. The pattern of the Middle Ages had been shattered, but no clear alternative had been put in its place. The Church, minus some monastic foundations, carried on much as before the Henrician innovations. When the first Jesuits came to Ireland in 1542 they reported the country to be barbarous, and when they attempted to gain the support of Con O'Neill they found he had just made his submission to St. Leger and would not even see them. The Tudor conquest had begun, but it was not at all clear how, or where, it would finish.

The reigns of Henry's first two successors, Edward VI (1547–1553) and Mary (1553–1558), were too brief and contradictory to leave a distinctive imprint upon Ireland. Government vacillated according to the outlook and policy of the particular lord deputy or lord justice. Sir William Brabazon (1547–1550), Sir James Croft (1551–1552) and Sir Thomas Cusack (1552–1553) carried out a generally harsh program of military repression. Sir Anthony St. Leger, back in power from 1553 to 1556 preferred negotiation and persuasion. Neither approach was stunningly successful, and each produced in time the demand for its contrary.

Although but a child of nine at his accession, Edward VI was a doctrinaire Protestant, bred up in the new theology by the relatives of his deceased mother, Jane Seymour.

From an administrative point of view two approaches were possible in Ireland. Either the new faith could be soft-pedaled in an effort not to exacerbate already strained relations; or the new religion could be vigorously promoted as an essential element of the political reform of the kingdom. The first way had the merit of postponing indefinitely an embarrassing moment, but it left a religious vacuum which Rome could hardly fail to exploit. Serious proselytizing, on the other hand, would require immense dedication and major resources: money for education, a Protestant, Gaelic-speaking clergy, and a level of control over the society as a whole which the government did not yet have. Inasmuch as the Reformation had no recognizable Irish roots, it would either have to be promoted among the Irish by means of education and persuasion, or it would have to be imposed upon them by an array of administrative and judicial machinery. Even in England, where anticlericalism and reform theology had many adherents from an early point, the innovations had to be sedulously and vigorously imposed on many parts of the country; and the old faith lingered on despite the best efforts of Church and Crown.

Ireland was even more retrograde: less willing to change, less convinced of the necessity. When John Bale, the only ardent reformer appointed to the Irish episcopate under Edward VI, reached Ireland in 1553 he despaired of the hierarchy in both Church and State. Protestantism had made great strides in England with the adoption of a much-reformed prayer book in 1552. Bale tried to bring his backsliding diocese of Ossory (in County Kilkenny) up to date by introducing the new prayer book. It proved a disastrous course. Clergy and laity alike revolted. When the sickly young Protestant king died in 1553, his devoutly Catholic half-sister Mary came to the throne and stopped in its tracks the progress of Protestantism in England and Ireland. John Bale's flock was publicly overjoyed when it heard that the new queen had proclaimed the old faith:

They rung all the bells . . . they flung up their caps to the battlement of the great temple [St. Canice's cathedral in Kilkenny],

with smiling and laughs most dissolutely . . . they brought forth
their copes, candlesticks, holy water stock, cross and censers,
they mustered forth in general procession most gorgeously, all
the town over, with *Sancta Maria, ora pro nobis* and the rest of
the Latin litany.[8]

Bale left Ireland an embittered man, convinced of the island's hopelessness, certain that its inhabitants were mired
in ignorance and superstition. On the other hand George
Dowdall, the conservative Henrician appointed archbishop
of Armagh in 1543, left Ireland in 1551, apparently in despair at what he saw as the successful efforts of Lord Deputy Croft to prohibit the celebration of mass and enforce
the use of the earlier (1549) Edwardian prayer book. Both
could not have been right in their pessimism, but each saw
an element of a complex picture. Mary's reign seemed to
vindicate Bale's dolorous forecast, and Dowdall returned to
be her archbishop of Armagh. Most of the reform-inclined
bishops had taken wives, and Mary now ejected these fallen
shepherds from the hierarchy. The lord deputies, first St.
Leger and then from 1556, Thomas Viscount FitzWalter,
were ordered to restore the church to its pre-Edwardian
condition, and in 1557 an Irish Parliament gave statutory
expression to the reconciliation with Rome. The lands of
the dissolved religious orders were *not* restored to the
Church, however, so that the blow dealt monasticism by
Henry VIII was very little mitigated by his well-intentioned
daughter. Where monastic communities survived it was because they had not yet been dissolved (as many had not)
rather than because the Catholic queen revived them.

The citizens of Kilkenny might throw their caps in the air
with joy, but Mary was not an unmixed blessing for Ireland. She had no intention of retreating from her father's
ambitious designs, and through her second lord deputy,
Thomas FitzWalter, later earl of Sussex, she began a new,
and portentous, phase of the Tudor conquest. This was the
so-called "plantation" of counties Leix and Offaly, two
Leinster counties on the southern edge of the Pale. The sub-
missions obtained under surrender and regrant were not
proving sufficient to reduce the island to well-ordered tranquillity. Ungovernable regions remained, and a standing

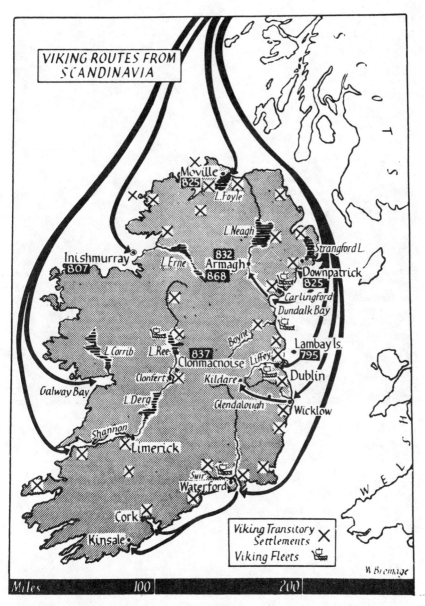

13. *Map showing Viking invasion routes.*

The Romans, like modern military planners, attacked with concentrated forces across the shortest possible distance. Not so the Vikings. A truly naval people, they roamed the seas. No shore was safe from their depredations. Their impact upon Ireland was diffuse, peripheral, and widespread.

Map by W. H. Bromage, from Edwards, *An Atlas of Irish History*, p. 44.

14. The Rock of Cashel, County Tipperary, earliest surviving portions from the eleventh century.

This easily fortified location was from a very early point the seat of the kings of Munster, and later became the site of one of Ireland's four archbishoprics. The earliest portions visible (the round tower) date from about the eleventh century.

from De Paor and De Paor, *Early Christian Ireland,* #63.

15. Cormac's Chapel, Rock of Cashel, south facade. Built by Cormac Mac Carthaigh, king of Munster, in 1127–1134.

The chapel, built of large, well-dressed, rectilinear, stone, has the simplicity and solidity of an igloo, combined with the lovingly applied detail of a wedding cake. It is an unusual and striking example of pre-Norman Irish architecture. Clearly it incorporates Romanesque continental influences, and in that sense is not purely "insular." But it suggests a "native" style which all but disappeared under the weight of later Norman influence.

from De Paor and De Paor, *Early Christian Ireland,* #70.

89

16. Nuns' Church at Clonmacnoise, County Offaly, c. 1166.

It is hard, perhaps, to compare mere doorways of a ruinated chapel with the whole surviving facade of Cormac's Chapel, but the broader portals, and the elaboration (and even liberation from the mass of the walls) of the columns and arches, which begin to take the form of discrete architectural elements, illustrate the Norman influence on Irish architecture in the late twelfth century.

from De Paor and De Paor, *Early Christian Ireland*, #76.

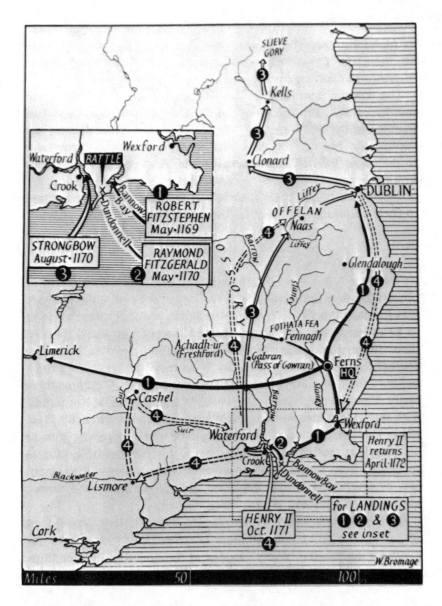

17. Map showing the Norman invasion routes.

The map illustrates the extent to which early Norman activities were concentrated in the Southeast. Although Norman warriors were soon to advance on the north and the west, the southeast was the region in which their influence was most enduring.

Map by W. H. Bromage, from Edwards, *An Atlas of Irish History*, p. 46.

18. Map showing Norman towns and major castles.

The Normans left architectural footprints wherever they went, for they were among the Middle Ages' most talented and prolific builders, and their favored medium was durable stone. Their walled towns, castles, and churches, in various stages of ruin, remain prominent parts of the Irish landscape. Many of their techniques and styles were adopted by their Gaelic neighbors, so that Norman architectural remains can also be found in areas of solid Irishry.

Map by W. H. Bromage, from Edwards, *An Atlas of Irish History*, p. 50.

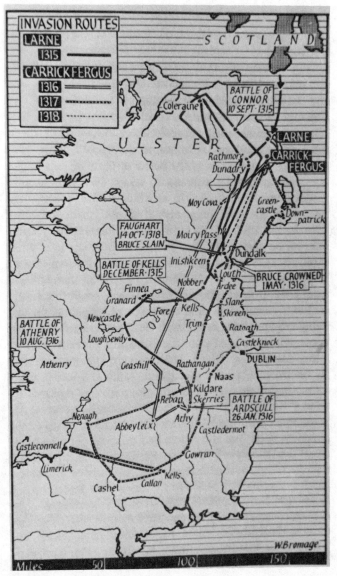

Within the map:

INVASION ROUTES
LARNE
1315 ——
CARRICKFERGUS
1316 ====
1317 ········
1318 - - - -

SCOTLAND

BATTLE OF CONNOR 10 SEPT·1315

Coleraine

ULSTER

LARNE
CARRICK-FERGUS

Rathmore
Dunadry

Moy Cova
Green-castle
Down-patrick

FAUGHART 14 OCT·1318 BRUCE SLAIN

Moiry Pass
Dundalk

BATTLE OF KELLS DECEMBER·1315

Inishkeen
Louth
Ardee
BRUCE CROWNED 1 MAY·1316

Nobber

Finnea
Granard
Fore
Kells
Slane
Skreen

BATTLE OF ATHENRY 10 AUG·1316

Newcastle
Trim
Ratoath
Castleknock

Lough Sewdy
DUBLIN

Athenry
Geashill
Rathangan
Naas

Kildare
Reban
Skerries
BATTLE OF ARDSCULL 26 JAN·1316

Nenagh
Athy

Abbeyleix
Castledermot

Castleconnell
Gowran

Limerick
Kells
Cashel
Callan

W.B.romage

Miles 50 100 150

19. *Map of the Bruce invasion, 1315–1318.*
    The track of the Bruce campaign is a complicated one, but it suggests the way in which an excursion from Scotland provoked a widespread revolt against English authority in Ireland, and underscored the vulnerability of the Crown's "lordship of Ireland."

Map by W. H. Bromage, from Edwards, *An Atlas of Irish History,* p. 53.

bz aptanf·loca demcp̃ ꝗ̃ fuifcp̃ ꝓ
iua ·hoftib; inuia reddenf · natu
ralem difficultarem induftria
plurimum ⁊ arte muniunt·

rat autem Bernici' uul
tare gridif ⁊coꝛpoꝛe p̃plo.
vir bellicoꝰ ⁊audaꝛ ꞇ gente fua·
fr crebro continuocp̃ belli cla
moꝛe uoce rautifona · Timeri a̅
cunctif ꝗ̃n dilugi malenf · Nobi
lium oppreffoꝛ · humiliũ erectoꝛ·
Infeftuf fuif · fuoꝰ alienuf · ꝗ̃aꝛ'
omnium contrariꝰm · ⁊ iꝑe c̅r̅
onm · Rotbericuf aut̅ miffif ad
ꞅꞇephaniden nuntiuf · donanf
cp̃ u̅ modicif e̅a p̃miffif ꝗ̃n pꝛo
miffif · ut a patria ꞇ ꝗ̃uf nullũ
s uendicare potuerat · cũ pace ⁊
amoꝛe difcedec · uaruif fuafit uer
bif·nec ipfrafit · Nuntci u̅o ad ꝗ̃
chardiden querfi ut in exteras

20. *A rendering of Dermot MacMurrough, from a twelfth-century manuscript of the* Expugnatio Hibernica *of Giraldus Cambrensis.*

Dermot was, of course, unknown to the twelfth-century illuminator of Gerald of Wales' account of the conquest of Ireland. But because Dermot had "invited" Henry II and his Norman vassals to intervene in Ireland on his behalf, he played a central role in the Norman version, or justification, of how they had come to Ireland. Hence, an attempt to portray him.

Slide from the National Library of Ireland.

21. *The chief of the MacSweeneys at his feast, a woodcut from an edition of John Derricke's* The Image of Ireland with a Discoverie of Woodkerne, *first published in 1581.*

The Image of Ireland *is one of the classics of Irish ethnography, and compares with John White's watercolors of the American Indians encountered at the Roanoke Island colony just a few years later (1584–85). Note the tonsured clerics, the minstrel with Irish harp, and the animal skin being used as a cooking cauldron, on the lower left.*

Slide from the National Library of Ireland, Dublin.

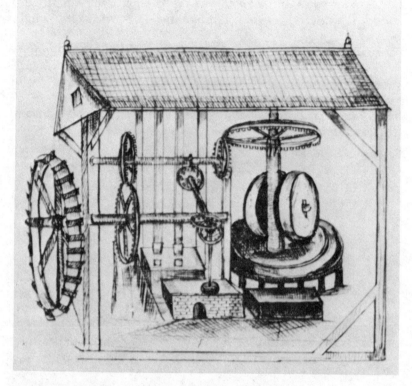

22. Sketch of a water mill for grinding corn, from a manuscript by Thomas Dingley (or Dineley) entitled "Obervations in a voyage through the Kingdom of Ireland," written about 1680.

Dingley's sketch of a water mill reminds us of the industrial Ireland which had long existed, albeit on a small, rural, and usually primitive scale. Waterpower was abundant, and was used in many locations for milling. In the late eighteenth and nineteenth centuries it was adapted to the needs of the textile industries: linen and cotton.

Slide from the National Library of Ireland.

army of between one and two thousand men was an expensive necessity. From at least the time of Gerald of Wales in the 13th century British observers had periodically concluded that the difficulty with governing Ireland was the Irish. This theme, varying between a lament and a concrete suggestion, was revived in the 1540s and eventually gave rise to Mary's "plantation." Basically, the scheme involved clearing an area of its unruly population, and substituting a population of planters from whom greater loyalty could be expected. It was an ambitious, in some ways ingenious, attempt at social engineering.

Leix and Offaly, the country of the O'Connors, O'Mores, and O'Dempseys, had long been a refuge for the enemies and marauders of Palesmen. No local jury could be trusted to find the inhabitants in rebellion and declare their lands escheated to the crown. Therefore the Irish Parliament was got to enact "that Leix should become Queen's County and Offaly King's County, that the whole territory should be confiscated, and that the English system of local organization and law enforcement should be establishment."[9] The details of the plan called for the native population to be confined to one third of the two counties, and for the other two-thirds to be planted with Englishmen born in England or Ireland. "Englishmen born in Ireland" might, or might not, include Anglo-Normans, according to administrative whim.

The plantation made very slow headway. The O'Mores, O'Connors, and O'Dempseys wreaked havoc with the new settlers. But when an idea's time has come, no amount of disastrous experience seems capable of discrediting it. For a hundred years English statesmen were convinced that the only major shortcoming of "plantation" as a means of dealing with Irish disorder was that it had not been sufficiently implemented. Future governors showed more interest in improving or extending the scheme for plantation than in considering its inherent limitations.

When Elizabeth I came to the English throne in 1558 she

made a clean sweep of the major offices of both Church and State, but in Ireland she was content to rely upon Mary's last lord deputy, the earl of Sussex. Caution was needed, for one of Henry VIII's greatest accomplishments, the submission of the Ulster O'Neills, was threatening to come unstuck. Con O'Neill's son, Shane, was attempting to supplant his preferred brother, Matthew, as heir to the earldom of Tyrone. Elizabeth's great and understandable fear was that an angry Shane would seek support for his cause in nearby Scotland, and that the Scots would be encouraged to fish in those troubled waters by *their* anglophobic allies, the French. Recognizing that Shane had the effective support of the O'Neills, the government induced him to come to London in late 1561 for serious negotiations. It was sufficiently moved by his power and arguments to leave open the whole question of the succession to the earldom of Tyrone. Shane was acknowledged as the *de facto* lord of northern Ulster, but the extension of English authority through "surrender and regrant" began to look much more doubtful than it had in the hopeful days of Henry VIII.

Shane O'Neill's pretentions to the overlordship of much of Ulster was resisted by his neighbors, the O'Donnells, Maguires, MacMahons, O'Reillys, and others, who turned to Queen Elizabeth for support against him. Once again the crown tried to negotiate with Shane, but by March 1566 Elizabeth was ordering her new lord deputy, Sir Henry Sidney, "to consider how this 'cankred, dangerous rebel' might be 'utterly extirped.' "[10] In May 1567 Shane was defeated in battle by the O'Donnells, and to escape their vengeance he surrendered himself to some of the Scots who had recently settled in Antrim. Why he expected their mercy remains a mystery. In any event, they killed him. The English eventually secured his head and displayed it from the point of a pike on the wall of Dublin Castle, a ferocious but customary means of advertising the fate of those deemed rebels. Although Lord Deputy Sidney's vigorous campaigns against Shane impressed the inhabitants of Ulster with the Crown's growing power, Shane's death brought the subordination and assimilation of the northern province little closer.

In the south, government authority was still circumscribed by the continuing struggles among the Anglo-Norman lords, now often referred to as "the old English" to differentiate them from "the new English" (mainly Protestant) immigrants of the Elizabethan period and after. The Fitzgeralds and Butlers remained at each others' throats even though neither could any longer aspire to the lord deputyship. Sidney realized that the Crown's authority would be minimal until government in the provinces (as in Dublin) was out of the hands of local magnates and firmly in the grasp of royal functionaries. But English policy, however logical, destabilized the existing order of things, such as it was, without having anything better to put in its place.

When, for instance, the government acted in 1567 against the refractory earl of Desmond and sent him to prison in London, the result was the revolt of Munster two years later. Not only the Fitzgeralds and their followers, but even their enemies, the Butlers, had interpreted the removal of Desmond and a sequence of attendant events as proof of predatory English designs upon the land and wealth of the province. This was a perversion of Henry VIII's objective of better and more thorough government, but it was not entirely the result of unvarnished greed. To "govern," one must be able to reward the governors. As more and more governors were drawn from England these "new English" became conspicuous beneficiaries of royal generosity. Furthermore, the least burdensome kind of reward on the English Exchequer was a grant of Irish land, and since the medieval punishment for rebellion usually included confiscation of the rebel's lands, much of the wealth with which New English governors were rewarded was wealth taken away from Old English and Irish landholders. The "governed" might well wonder who was benefiting more from more government, they or the new class of governors.

Visible justification for this suspicion was the fact that in the late 1560s Munster was awash with English fortune hunters. The chief ports of the province lay within easy reach of the Atlantic sea-lanes which West Country Englishmen were plowing with growing boldness. The Old English towns of Cork and Waterford, with their established commerce and shipping, made congenial bases from which to explore the opportunities to acquire land in the fertile countryside.

The most notorious of these quests was that of Sir Peter Carew, a Devonshireman who adroitly engaged in what one historian called "genealogical buccanneering." On the strength of alleged descent from Robert Fitzstephen, the twelfth-century Norman invader, Carew claimed lands in Meath and Carlow, and more fantastically, hundreds of thousands of acres in Kerry, Cork, and Waterford. Less troubling than this exercise of gall was the fact that in 1568 Carew secured the backing of the Irish Council for the first part of this claim, and seemed on the verge of getting its support for the second part as well.

Elsewhere in Munster Richard Grenville, the storied sea-dog, and Warham St. Leger (son of Sir Anthony, the former lord deputy) secured lands for development on Cork harbor, and a group including Humphrey Gilbert, the future explorer, planned a new town on the west Cork coast from which to exploit the adjacent fishing grounds.[11] The native lords of Munster were justified in thinking that they had more to fear from the new governors, and their compatriots, than from each other.

Religion in the 1560s was not yet a widespread ground for contention, but it was on the verge of becoming so. The English interlopers and fortune seekers were almost exclusively communicants in the new faith. Outside the Pale the Irish were still little threatened in the maintenance and practice of the old religion. An Irish Court of High Commission was established in 1564 to enforce reform of the Church, but progress was pathetically slow and limited to the few sees where active reforming bishops had been appointed. Nevertheless, when a rebellion broke out in Munster in 1569, its leader, James Fitzmaurice Fitzgerald, a cousin of the earl of Desmond, claimed to be acting in defense of "the Catholic faith by God unto his church given and by the see of Rome hitherto prescribed to all Christian men."[12] His followers' concerns were more secular, but the revolt foreshadowed the fateful conjunction of religious and secular discontents in the future, especially after Elizabeth I's formal excommunication by papal bull in 1570.

Fitzmaurice's rebellion was quashed by the lord deputy, Sir Henry Sidney, with about 1,000 troops. Humphrey Gilbert carried out the final pacification of Munster with a ruthlessness which contemporaries regarded as novel in Irish warfare. It is at least possible that the developing religious antipathy was partially responsible. Fitzmaurice escaped to France in 1575 and busied himself plotting the much more serious insurrection to be launched in 1579. By then, the post-Tridentine alignments were much more pronounced. The Council of Trent had ended in 1563 leaving the papacy at an apogee of worldly strength, and fortified with a mandate to lead a crusade against the heresies of the north. Elizabeth was excommunicated in 1570, and her growing support for the rebellion in the Netherlands against Philip II of Spain gave "his most Catholic Majesty" extra incentive to oppose English designs wherever possible. Irish resistance to English rule ceased to seem merely parochial, the traditional obstinacy of a remote and wayward people. Instead it began to appear, in English eyes, as part and parcel of a diabolical conspiracy to restore the dominion of an Anti-Christ Rome over England. English soldiers and governors in Ireland were increasingly likely to see lingering Roman Catholicism as the root cause of the intransigence and barbarity of the Irish.

Changes in attitude or outlook often defy precise description. Henry VII and Henry VIII had wished to bring Ireland to some decent order, not to crush and overwhelm it. They had no desire to extirpate its culture or aristocracy, but only to assimilate both to the English monarchy. By degrees that objective changed under Elizabeth until English policy was openly hostile toward Irish, and especially Gaelic, society. Assimilation was replaced as an objective by "reformation," a remodeling which went far beyond religion to include law, language, custom, and even social habits. Those had been decried by the fourteenth-century statutes of Kilkenny and even by the twelfth-century chronicler, Gerald of Wales, but never had they been denounced with such vehemence as in the closing decades of the sixteenth century. A conviction that the very fabric of Irish life was worthless, or at least inferior, underlay the numerous schemes to supplant it with something else.

"Plantation" was the institutional expression of this inchoate disdain for Irish society and culture. It had begun under Queen Mary but was to accelerate dramatically in the reign of Elizabeth. Although the major theater of Elizabethan plantation was to be Munster, it took some time to provoke the prerequisite rebellion of its great magnate, the earl of Desmond. Elizabethan plantation activity had its beginnings in eastern Ulster. Despite the claims of the O'Neills, the Crown held itself to be the rightful heir of the long extinct Norman earldom of Ulster. Con O'Neill had been given the earldom of Tyrone instead. In the early 1570s Elizabeth began, on the urging of her trusted councilor, William Cecil, to make grants to English adventurers of whatever they could conquer and plant in the two Ulster counties of Antrim and Down. It was hoped that these colonies would establish enclaves of English authority in the wild north and also provide a barrier to the growing and vexatious migration of Scots across the North Channel.

Sir Thomas Smith, a scholar and courtier, received a grant in 1571 to the south shore of Belfast Lough reaching down into the Ards peninsula of County Down. A year later the earl of Essex (Walter Devereux, father of the famous rebel Earl of Essex) received a grant to most of Antrim. Acting as an entrepreneur on its own account the Crown offered to pay the costs of 600 of the 1,200 soldiers employed in the adventure in return for a share of the lands taken. Both schemes were extensively promoted in England with the kind of printed propaganda which a decade later would lure colonists and investors to Virginia. Despite the optimistic imaginings of the publicists, both Ulster colonies collapsed. Apart from its initial wager on their success the Crown was reluctant to help bail them out of the serious and unforeseen difficulties they encountered. The areas they claimed were far from being empty frontiers. In the Ards, for instance, Smith's colonists encountered not only the Gaelicized Norman family named Savage, but also Brian MacPhelim O'Neill of Clandeboye, a man who had loyally supported the Crown against Shane O'Neill and his successor, Turlough Luineach O'Neill, and who did not take kindly to being treated as a rebel. It was impossible—or at least unrewarding—to treat Ireland like the wilderness of North America. It was not new-found-land, but very old land with layer upon layer of previous relations, however discordant, with English authority.

It is difficult to generalize about savagery, partly because it is not uniformly reported in all places and times. Still, there seems to have been a marked increase in the level of militarily unnecessary killing in the middle Elizabethan period. Humphrey Gilbert's pacification of Munster in 1569, Essex' slaughter of 200 followers of Brian MacPhelim O'Neill at Belfast in 1574, and of 500 Scots on Rathlin Island (off the north coast of Down) in 1575 all point toward a growing ferocity in the Anglo-Irish relationship and a broadening of the population it afflicted. Needless to say, the Irish responded in kind and there is no satisfactory way of assigning primary responsibility to one side or the other.

It may have been partly *because* the private ventures at plantation in Ulster proved so unsuccessful that Munster became the principal theater of Elizabethan colonizing activity and took so different a form. Perhaps it was merely that the O'Neills were more remote from English encroachment in their stronghold of County Tyrone. The south was kept in ferment, on the one hand, by English fortune hunters, and on the other, by James Fitzmaurice Fitzgerald, the papal crusader, who in 1579 returned to Ireland from the continent. This time he came with the blessings of Pope Gregory XIII and an army of 700 men which landed at Smerwick, on the Dingle peninsula of County Kerry. Once again, for Fitzmaurice personally, it was a religious campaign, but for many of those who joined him it was merely a convenient opportunity to strike out against English authority. Fitzmaurice was killed in a skirmish just a month after the Smerwick landing, but the cause was taken up by his cousin, Sir John of Desmond, brother to the earl. The fate of Munster hinged to a large degree on the decision of the earl himself. His stake was huge, and for months he sat prudently and cautiously on the sidelines. Finally the newly appointed governor of Munster, Sir Nicholas Malby, proclaimed Desmond a traitor and precipitated him into rebellion.

Sympathetic risings flared in Connacht, Ulster, and Leinster where James Eustace, Viscount Baltinglass, raised the papal standard. Edmund Spenser, the poet, was in Ireland in 1580 as secretary to Lord Grey of Wilton, the new lord deputy. He later recollected "there was no part free from the contagion, but all conspired in one to cast off their subjection to the Crown of England."[13] Lord Grey repressed the rebellion and capped his triumph with the increasingly familiar massacre. A ragtag expedition of 600 Spaniards and Italians landed at Fitzmaurice's old fort at Smerwick in September 1581. Holed up in unfamiliar country, after the rebellion they had come to aid was largely repressed, the papal force was soon besieged by Lord Grey and his ally, the earl of Ormonde. When Desmond made no move to relieve them, the Italians and Spaniards surrendered to Grey, who had them executed to a man.

Desmond and his associates were attainted in 1586. Their vast holdings passed, in theory, to the Crown, which chose to make them the heart of a great new Irish plantation. An elaborate scheme was drawn up in London, according to which half a million acres of productive, confiscated land (thoughtfully surveyed in 1584, two years in advance of the rebels' attainder) would be distributed to English planters in rounded parcels not to exceed 12,000 acres. The hope was to establish on the former Desmond lands an English "gentry" of landlords, with an imported English "yeomanry" below it as hard-working, sturdy tenants. Complicating this hope was the fact that the confiscated lands were not a compact unit, but were scattered across the Munster counties of Waterford, Cork, Limerick, Kerry, and Tipperary. Many lay in remote areas which were less attractive to new settlers than the old ports from which speedy exit was easier should troubles with the native population recur.

By 1588 the Munster plantation had attracted some 3,000 English immigrants, and the number (including men, women, and children) may have been as high as 12,000 ten years later. It was certainly the largest migration of Englishmen to occur in the Elizabethan period, and it was not until the 1630s and 40s that migration to North America surpassed in numbers the migration to Ireland. In this sense Ireland was England's first colony and the Irish plantations were the forerunners of the later ventures along the Atlantic littoral of North America. On the other hand, the new plantations in Ireland could not, try though they might, wipe clean the medieval slate and treat Ireland as a newly discovered and conquered land.

Despite its grand aspirations, the Munster plantation resembled its predecessors in falling far short of expectations. The new population was too small and too dispersed to secure the large province either for itself or the Dublin government. The attempt to limit the seignories (the largest blocks of land to be held by any one landlord) to 12,000 acres was soon foiled by enterprising fortune hunters, Sir Walter Raleigh among them. There was no shortage of well-born Englishmen (often younger sons) eager to become rich on fertile Munster acreage, but there were few yeoman farmers ready to give up the comforts and security of England, such as it was, for small-to-middle size holdings in a reputedly strange and dangerous land.

Lacking sturdy English tenants (or finding that such tenants demanded disagreeably low rents as a condition for coming), the large landlords made leases, often on attractive terms, to the very Irish whom the plantation had been intended to displace. In addition, the whole plantation had to be scaled down because of numerous claims that land which had initially been confiscated (as belonging to Desmond and his followers) was, in fact, the freehold property of men who had not been found to be in rebellion, and who could not be shown to be tenants of those who were.

Only in a destructive sense could the Munster plantation be called a success. The power of the Desmond Fitzgeralds as lords of Munster was permanently broken. In 1565 Sir Henry Sidney's instructions as lord deputy had called for establishment of regional government in the south along the lines of the Tudors' highly effective councils of the North (in England) and Wales. These had been important devices for extending the power and influence of the crown to remote, and traditionally anarchic, parts of Britain. The first lord president of Munster, Sir John Perrot, had been appointed in 1571, but it took the plantation to give the presidency any substance and elements of local support.

Connacht too was given its own provincial government and lord president (in effect, a local governor with his own local council) in the middle of Elizabeth's reign. After some vigorous soldiering in the early 1580s by Sir Nicholas Malby, lord president since 1576, a formal settlement or "composition" was worked out between the government and the local aristocracy in 1585. Like the Henrician policy of surrender and regrant, the composition of Connacht secured, or confirmed, the lands and privileges of the native lords, some of whom were Old English, and others Gaelic. Those who were confirmed in their estates had to enter indentures to "pay a yearly rent to the crown of ten shillings a quarter for usable land, to appear at hostings with an agreed number of men, and to abolish Irish jurisdictions and the system of land and stock allocation that was part of them."[14] Connacht was thus brought under more effective English rule without either the overthrow of its chief men, or the confiscation and plantation of their lands.

By the last decade of the sixteenth century Leinster, Munster, and Connacht all bore the imprint of "direct rule," though in various forms. Ulster alone remained virtually undented. The surrender of Shane O'Neill to Henry VIII and the creation for Shane of the earldom of Tyrone had not circumscribed the independent power of the O'Neills, or the northern lords in general. The ephemeral plantations in Down and Antrim had done little more than increase the turbulence of an already divided province. Ulster became the great challenge to the last decade of Elizabethan government in Ireland.

It was a decade marked by major European war, and particularly by bitter, widespread conflict between England and Spain. Perhaps it was vital that Ulster be reduced so as to deny any haven to a future Spanish Armada. In any event, the English were determined to end Ulster's splendid isolation, and a promising, if brutal, beginning was Lord Deputy Fitzwilliam's arrest, trial, and execution of Hugh Roe MacMahon, the recently acknowledged lord of County Monaghan in southern Ulster. The lands of Monaghan were then divided in 1591–92 among the surviving MacMahons to constitute a sort of "native" plantation.

The rest of Ulster was less easily reduced. Ulstermen were not favorably impressed by the experience of their neighbors in Connacht. They were aware of the growing list of grievances which the Connachtmen had against Sir Richard Bingham, the lord president there since 1584. There were abundant tales of English cruelty and duplicity, and their effect was less to intimidate than to provoke profound suspicion of English designs.

The political key to Ulster was Hugh O'Neill, second baron of Dungannon from 1562, and in effect, the English-backed claimant to the lordship of all Ulster. Lord Deputy Sidney had brought O'Neill to England to be educated and Anglicized, and on his return to Ireland he proved, for a time, an exceedingly useful ally. For this he was rewarded with a patent for the earldom of Tyrone, but the title was still claimed by Hugh's rival, Turlough Luineach O'Neill. When Turlough died in September 1595, Hugh finally achieved recognition among his countrymen as The O'Neill; but two years before that, in 1593, some of the chief lords of Ulster had begun to confederate against the government. Maguire of Fermanagh was the first to enter openly into rebellion. Hugh Roe O'Donnell, escaping from imprisonment in Dublin Castle, was soon inaugurated as The O'Donnell, in which capacity he joined the fray. As in Munster where the earl of Desmond for long held aloof, Hugh O'Neill waited and watched, carefully calculating the odds and the stakes. For a while he played the part of an intermediary between the government and the rebel earls, but the English soon came to doubt his good faith.

O'Neill must have concluded that his powerful position in Ulster depended more upon the esteem of his countrymen than upon English titles and favor, for in 1595 he attacked a large English force attempting to bring supplies to government soldiers in Monaghan. O'Neill was speedily proclaimed a traitor, and all the pieces had now fallen into place for an Ulster rebellion strongly centered in Tyrconnell and Tyrone, the heartland of the O'Donnells and the O'Neills. Hugh affiliated himself to an appeal to Philip II for Spanish troops, and the Ulster lords were later to offer the Spanish king the crown of Ireland in return for his aid. Preoccupied with the struggle against his authority in the Netherlands, Philip was noncommittal, but in English eyes Ulster had become a theater in the acrimonious war with Spain.

The Tudors never faced a more formidable Irish challenge. Ulster was remote, well-supplied with its own produce, and well organized. At the battle of the Yellow Ford, near Armagh, in August 1598, an English army of more than 4,000 men was defeated, its commander, Sir Henry Bagenal, killed, and more than half its men killed, wounded, or lost. Never before had Irish insurgents been able to resist an English force of that magnitude. The great victory at the Yellow Ford enhanced the prestige of the Ulster lords throughout the island. English authority was in a state of collapse and O'Neill appealed for adherents in the other three provinces, wrapping the cause of Irish independence in the cloak of Roman Catholicism.

The response was enthusiastic and widespread. The English settlements in Munster, and even parts of Leinster, were overrun. Along with Dublin, the old towns of Cork, Waterford, Limerick, and Youghall became places of refuge for the new settlers. A few "loyal" lords—the earl of Thomond in Connacht and the earl of Ormonde in Munster—refused to join the rebellion, but they had become virtual strangers in their own land. The arrival in April 1599 of a new lord lieutenant, Robert Devereux, earl of Essex, revealed the novel importance being assigned to Ireland. Essex was the son of Walter Devereux, one of the early Elizabethan planters of eastern Ulster. But more than that, he was a great, even a scandalous favorite of the aging queen, though many years her junior. Essex had grand ambitions for military glory, and Elizabeth gave him the golden opportunity he coveted, but not, perhaps, the wherewithall to exploit it.

Essex came to Ireland with an army of 16,000 men, boasting that he would triumph over O'Neill on the battlefield. Instead, the twenty-one weeks of his presence left matters in the same ruinous state as had prevailed before his coming. Rather than challenge O'Neill frontally, Essex directed his forces to the less rigorous work of pacifying Leinster and Munster. When the disgruntled Elizabeth ordered him northward where the real threat lay, Essex allowed himself to be drawn into a parley, rather than a battle, with O'Neill. All that he achieved was a cessation of hostilities that favored O'Neill far more than it favored the forces of the Crown. Essex returned to England with a reputation tarnished beyond recovery and clouded with suspicions that he had hoped to conspire with O'Neill against the queen. It was only under Essex's successor as lord deputy that the tide began to turn.

A capable and meticulous professional soldier, Charles Blount, Lord Mountjoy, reached Ireland in February 1600 and began a painstaking advance on Ireland with fire and sword. To undermine an enemy he could not always find or bring to battle, he destroyed Ulster's fields, burned its inhabitants' houses, and slaughtered the livestock. Combatants and noncombatants suffered alike. Munster was reduced to order by a new lord president, Sir George Carew. Slowly the Ulster rebellion was forced on the defensive, and its survival became dependent upon help from abroad. As always, this proved a slender reed upon which to lean. Continental powers tended to evaluate requests for aid from Ireland in terms of their own self-interest. Pope Clement VIII hesitated to support the Ulster rebels wholeheartedly for fear he would jeopardize the Catholics of Leinster and Munster, whose recusancy the English were generally still tolerating. Philip III of Spain was already engaged in peace negotiations with the English and was circumspect, at best, about a new Spanish committment to Ulster. Finally, he grudgingly dispatched an expedition of some 4,500 men under Juan del Aguila, and it came ashore at Kinsale in County Cork in September 1601.

The Spanish expedition was too little, too late, and it landed in a part of the island where it could too easily be isolated from the still unsubdued rebels in the north. Mountjoy had 7,000 men at his disposal and used them to seal off the Spanish in Kinsale. Despite English efforts to keep them at arm's length in the north, first O'Donnell and then Tyrone slipped south in an effort to break up Mountjoy's siege and unite their own forces with the Spanish. By December, the English besiegers were themselves besieged by the 5,500 men of O'Donnell and Tyrone. When a battle broke out between the English and Irish forces on December 24, Mountjoy prevailed. The Spaniards took no part in the battle, but with all hope of relief lost they surrendered to Mountjoy on January 2, 1602. Though the battle had been fought in Munster, it signified the overthrow of Gaelic Ulster. O'Donnell took ship for Spain, and died a few months later. Tyrone returned to Ulster, but entered negotiations with Mountjoy which led to surrender on fairly generous terms a year later.

Ulster had been ravaged by nine years of warfare, but its settlement was, initially, less harsh than that imposed on Munster after the Desmond rebellion. Tyrone maintained his title, and Rory O'Donnell, brother of Hugh, was created earl of Tyrconnell in 1603. Plans for the establishment of a lord presidency in Ulster were abandoned. Nevertheless, Ulster had lost its immunity from English expansion. The indigenous Gaelic leadership had been emasculated, politically speaking, just as the Old English leadership of Munster had been overthrown a few decades earlier. The Tudor conquest was complete (though Elizabeth did not live quite long enough to see Tyrone's surrender) in the sense that the traditional and historic organs of Irish resistance had been dismantled. This is not to say that Ireland had been reduced to tranquillity. The seventeenth century would see renewed rebellions, one of them (in 1641) arguably the most terrible in Irish history. But the rebellions of the future would require the help of new men, new ideas, and new institutions.

The most basic objective of Tudor policy had been achieved. Functionaries of the Crown now held the reins of power. Local lords no longer had to be respected like petty kings. Yet the Tudor victory had a hollow ring to it. So much force had been needed, so many more sticks than carrots, that the fusionist ideal of a bicultural society harmoniously owning allegiance to a single English monarch had been left as much a smoking ruin as the countryside itself. Henry VIII, like the Angevins before him, had wanted to be *everyone's* king, but by the end of Elizabeth's reign there were good grounds for regarding the monarchy as shamefully partisan. Did the monarchy care only for the New English, the Protestant immigrants of recent decades? How could it command the allegiance of the Old English and the Irish whose varied cultures but common religion the English monarchy (and increasingly, the English people) professed to disdain? And if the Crown was adverse to the majority of the population—including not just its poorest and meanest members, but also its traditional privileged classes—how could it maintain and extend effective government? These were the awkward important questions which attended military success.

4

THE MAKING OF THE PROTESTANT ASCENDANCY: THE SEVENTEENTH CENTURY

CENTURIES ARE artificial things, and dynasties—such as the Tudors or the Stuarts—are no more than the genealogical counterpart of centuries, measuring time by clusters of successive lives rather than hundreds of successive years. The death of Elizabeth I, the last Tudor, on March 24, 1603, had little specific impact on Ireland. Her successor, the first Stuart, was James VI of Scotland, son of her cousin, Mary Queen of Scotland and her second husband, Henry Stuart, Lord Darnley. He took the title of James I in England, thus uniting the crowns of Scotland and England for the first time in their long and stormy history.

Despite his years of rule in the northern kingdom, James came to the English throne as something of a cipher, in particular as concerned his religious proclivities. The son of an ardent Roman Catholic mother, a martyr for the faith in the eyes of some, James had nevertheless been reared by strict Calvinist tutors at the insistence of the Scottish aristocracy. Which of these antithetical paths would he follow? Which accorded with his innermost beliefs? England had become, by 1603, a self-consciously Protestant nation, but in Ireland there was a growing gulf between the officially Protestant Church of Ireland and the still largely unreformed mass of the population (not to mention a very large part of the former clergy). Where would the new king bring his weight and influence to bear?

By Elizabeth's death religious disillusionment and distress were commonplace in Ireland. Old English families had begun to send their children to the continent to obtain the orthodox religious upbringing no longer available at home. A papal hierarchy of Irish bishops and archbishops had been created, but was almost entirely nonresident, and living abroad. The English government's attitude toward Catholicism was vacillating and uncertain. Recusancy (refusal of the rites of the reformed church) in Ireland was far too widespread to be treated with the same severity that was employed in England. When necessary, Catholicism was ignored, or tacitly acknowledged. Propagation of the gospel according to the new faith made slow, or little, progress. The reformers' crowning achievement was the founding in the 1590s of Trinity College. It was intended as the first unit of an eventual University of Dublin but became, in effect, the first—and for two hundred and fifty years the only—university in Ireland.

Protestant theologians believed that mankind needed learning in its struggle toward the light. The old conduits of ecclesiastical authority leading from Rome were judged corrupt and unreliable. The laity, or some substantial part of it, had to be equipped to seek out divine truth for themselves. Trinity College was meant to provide a beacon in the search and thus to contribute to the protestantization of Ireland. But by the 1590s polarization of the population had proceeded to a point at which lines were clearly drawn. Trinity was immediately suspect of heresy in the eyes of most of the Irish and Old English. Its students tended to come from the ranks of the already converted who were mainly of English birth or recent English origin. Few Catholic souls were won, and the college became the seminary of a colonial Protestant minority. This was not an unimportant function, but it contributed to the hardening division of the population, rather than to its fusion into one insular, reformed church.

Like Trinity College, the Church of Ireland became increasingly an institution of the English-born newcomers. It flourished where they were numerous, withered where they were few. This was ironic because the Church of Ireland was an ancient and deeply Irish body reared on the spirit and the flesh of the early Irish saints. Churches dedicated to St. Patrick, St. Brendan, and St. Brigid became uncongenial, even abhorrent, places to their collateral descendants. The Irish and New English alike were drawn to those sacred places on which the Church of Ireland frowned, especially the suppressed monasteries and friaries. In such places retrograde clergy, out of sympathy with the innovations brought about by the state church, could administer the traditional rites to a like-minded laity.

Why did the ideas and institutions of the Reformation encounter such profound resistance in Ireland? Seen from the vantage point of the nineteenth and twentieth centuries in which Irish Catholicism became an immensely powerful force, the failure of the Reformation in sixteenth- and seventeenth-century Ireland may seem inevitable. But we should beware of assuming that the past was merely an earlier version of the present with all the same attitudes and polarities that eventually came to exist.

It is helpful to remember that there was stout resistance to "innovation" in many parts of Britain. What distinguished Ireland was not so much the force of the resistance as its relative remoteness from effective ecclesiastical authority. In most of Ireland the Crown had little or no effective control until at least 1604. If there was a general Irish reaction to the attempted innovations in religion it was little more than apathy for at least several decades. As the extension of English rule proceeded under the banner of Protestantism that apathy turned slowly to fear and detestation. Rome, quite naturally, chose to exploit the resulting turmoil. From its point of view it was doing no more than attempting to sustain the faith and the faithful. That it ultimately succeeded so overwhelmingly cannot have been the result alone of the heroic exertions of several hundred missionary priests. The kingdom of Bohemia was saved from Protestantism (in the 1620s) only with the help of the armies of the Holy Roman Empire and the unhindered efforts of the Society of Jesus. No support of that magnitude was available in Ireland, and we must conclude that the remarkable survival and resurgence of Catholicism was as much *because* of the efforts to suppress it, as in spite of them.

James I was not unmindful of the potential for religious conflict within and between his kingdoms. A much maligned king, with an undoubtedly irritating manner and more than his share of shortcomings, James made a conscious and energetic effort to thread his way between the perilous religious extremes of his time. He was personally content for his subjects to enjoy "liberty of conscience," which amounted to freedom to follow the old faith if they objected to the new. But the political repercussions of this liberality soon proved unacceptable on both sides of the Irish Sea. James' English subjects emerged from two decades of war with Spain convinced that only a Protestant God and their own Protestant virtues had saved them from a Romish fate worse than death. Most were disinclined to make generous concessions to those they had only recently regarded as mortal enemies, and they viewed the intransigent Catholics of England and Ireland as potential fifth columnists and traitors. James was forced to take a much more militantly Protestant position than he thought either right or useful, particularly as regarded Ireland.

When his episcopal Protestantism was enunciated in 1605 it gave rise in England to the celebrated Gunpowder Plot in which a group of disillusioned Catholics vainly attempted to blow up king, lords, and commons in one spectacular puff. The number of English Catholics was minuscule (some 35,000 in 1603 out of a population of perhaps five million), so that the political consequences of repressing them were negligible. But as an enquiry of 1604 in Ireland made clear, the Protestant Church of Ireland was functioning effectively in only a very small total area and embracing only a small segment of the population. The rest of the country was either without formal religion, or making do in the old faith, with or without assistance from Roman clergy.

James did not wish to risk confrontation with the Catholic majority, an act which could be contemplated only because the majority was yet unorganized, dispirited, and without leadership. But the Crown was in some ways the prisoner of its own Protestant servants. The leading Protestant bishops and the majority of the Irish Council (of which those bishops were members) saw no hope for the conversion of the Irish either to the new faith or to English manners and customs so long as Roman Catholicism was tolerated. To support the men on whom he depended for the administration of Ireland, and to convince his Protestant English subjects that he was not himself a secret Catholic, James issued a proclamation in October 1605 demanding conformity to the Protestant faith in Ireland, and ordering the Catholic clergy to leave the realm by December.

Despite this bold stance there was little chance that such an order could be enforced. The only places where both Protestant services and law-enforcing machinery were available were in the Pale and the old towns, so that the principal sufferers from the new severity were the Old English. This absurdity moved the English Privy Council in April 1607 to order the government of Ireland to relent in its prosecution of Catholics. The old religion and its clergy remained officially illegal in Ireland while both were ubiquitous in practice. Once more, as so often under Elizabeth, the effort to go hammer and tongs against Catholicism collapsed, as it were, under its own political weight. Ardent reformers despaired of ever supplanting Roman rites and authority among the Irish and became all the more convinced that the only hope was the importation and plantation of an already Protestant population such as that wax-

ing in England and Scotland. Events in Ulster between
1607 and 1609 gave them the golden opportunity they
hoped for.

The rebellion of Hugh O'Neill had ended in 1604 on negotiated terms that spared the north the massive confiscations which followed the Desmond rebellion in Munster.
Nevertheless, the government had triumphed, and Sir Arthur Chichester, the new lord deputy from 1605, and Sir
John Davies, his attorney general, sought to translate military superiority into meaningful political control. All the
trappings of English local government were installed: sher-
iffs for the individual counties, justices of the peace, and
coroners of the crown. Not far in the back of Chichester's
mind was inauguration of a provincial lord presidency like
that which had been established previously in Munster and
Connacht. These institutions challenged the traditional authority of O'Neill in the nine counties of the north. Scottish
migration into Antrim and Down, which had begun in Elizabeth's reign despite the queen's wishes, was now officially
encouraged by the Scottish James. Chichester himself
helped to plant part of the area with colonists brought from
England, and the first Protestant bishop for the area,
George Montgomery, was inserted into the Ulster see of Ra-
phoe, Derry, and Clogher in 1605.

Little by little O'Neill was circumscribed and the north
penetrated by English influence. Recognizing the hopelessness of his position, O'Neill decided to join Rory O'Donnell,
Cuconnaught Maguire, and a large group of kinsmen, in
sudden flight to the continent. On September 4, 1607, they
took ship from Lough Swilly, leaving behind abundant and
unanswerable suspicions as to what aborted plots necessi-
tated their hasty departure. In song and romance the
"flight of the earls" has become a poignant exodus of what
remained heroic and quintessentially Gaelic in Ireland.
There is at least an element of truth in such a view. The
Ulster earls had been the last hope of effective resistance to
swelling English power. With their departure, the subjection of the island to English law, custom, government, and

religion, was almost a foregone conclusion. On the other hand, the nine years' war had already crushed their power, so that their flight was more an admission of that reality than the cause of future weakness.

In their absence the earls were judged outlaws in the court of King's Bench, and plans were set afoot to confiscate their lands. This relatively modest scheme was transformed by the short-lived revolt of Sir Cahir O'Doherty in April 1608. O'Doherty had helped the government in its case against the refugee earls, but having served this purpose was unceremoniously dropped from favor. His embittered revolt was supported by some of the O'Hanlons and O'Cahans, giving the government a pretext to despair of *ever* imposing order on the native population of Ulster. O'Doherty was killed in July, and assizes held the same summer found most of the land in Armagh, Cavan, Coleraine, Donegal, Fermanagh, and Tyrone to be in the king's disposal, by virtue of the misconduct of its former holders. It was a draconian verdict based on "the general principle, that the treason of the few justified the expropriation of all."[1]

The government had formerly professed a sympathy for small freeholders in their struggle to remain independent of the great Gaelic lords. Now it tarred them with the same brush in order to achieve—or justify—a massive restructuring of Ulster. The outlines of the new plantation were hammered out in London in late 1608. Down, Antrim, and Monaghan were not involved, the first two being already areas of Scottish and English plantation, and the third having been assigned to the native MacMahons in 1591–92. In the six counties to be newly planted the basic principle was segregation. English and Scottish settlers were to be placed on lands completely cleared of their native inhabitants. Natives could reside only on "land granted to favoured Irishmen, to the church, and to military officers who had served during the late war."[2]

Coleraine threatened to be the most difficult county to plant, and in 1609 the City of London was induced to take it on as a corporate venture. The plantation in the other five counties was complicated and subject to numerous vagaries, but in general resulted in the establishment of about 100 "undertakers," slightly more than half of them Scots, on about a quarter of the total acreage. Some fifty "servitors," Irish who had fought on the English side in the late wars, received about one fifth of the lands distributed, and about 300 "native Irish" former landowners in the province were compensated with another quarter of the total. The substantial amount that was left, a little more than a fourth of the whole, was distributed to the Church (particularly the northern bishoprics), Trinity College (large grants in Armagh, Fermanagh, and especially Donegal), Lord Deputy Chichester (who got the peninsula of Inishowen between Lough Foyle and Lough Swilly), and some Old English proprietors who were restored to their lands in County Cavan.

The key to the plantation's success or failure was the diligence of the undertakers in settling their lands with English and Scottish tenants, and in providing the capital improvements (fortified houses, bridges, roads, barns) necessary for a secure and flourishing colony. The undertakers received cheap land, but were saddled with numerous requirements to improve and develop it. The greedy and the hard-pressed were disposed to evade the conditions of plantation and maximize their rents by taking native Irish as tenants. English and Scots tenants tended to demand lower rents as the price for venturing into a strange and unsettled island. Even in Coleraine the City of London and its component companies succumbed to the more profitable Irish tenants, and the government was eventually forced to acknowledge the inevitable and replace the prohibitions against Irish tenants with fines for taking them.

The Ulster plantation "failed" in the sense that it fell far short of its framers' dreams, but no event in the seventeenth century had more enduring consequences for the future of Ireland. Ulster proved the one province of Ireland where immigration in the early-modern period was substantial, and the one province where the Celtic and old English population did not maintain a clear majority. The Scottish migration to Ulster was largely responsible, and some of the reasons for it remain obscure. Expansive forces were at work within Scottish society, and instead of resisting their outlet in Ireland, as Elizabeth I had done, the Scottish James I encouraged it. As well as dominating Down and Antrim Scottish settlers played an important part in planting the six escheated counties.

The huge scale of the confiscations and of the subsequent immigration caused the Ulster plantation to be the most disruptive act of English government since the beginning of direct rule. It was the underlying cause of the most profound rebellion in Irish history, that which began in October 1641 and was not altogether extinguished until the vengeful campaign of Oliver Cromwell in 1649–50.

The architects of the plantation hardly foresaw the explosion it would help to cause. On the contrary, because it was the most extensive and rationalized plantation in Ireland, it seemed the most promising. Ancient problems like the poverty of the Church had been solved at a stroke, at least in the north. The inherent difficulties of administering a barbarous society were avoided by replacing it with one that was more familiar and more governable. But where were the displaced, disregarded natives to go? What was to become of them and their keen resentment of the newcomers and the government which protected them?

The thirty years between the plantation of Ulster and the rebellion of 1641 saw the spread of English influence in the south as well as the north. Instead of massive immigration of middle-size and even small farmers, Munster experienced the growth of an English plantocracy. Large areas came to be dominated by a few wealthy and enterprising men, their relations, friends, and clients. The richest and most famous of them was Richard Boyle, the first earl of Cork.

Parliament was another area where new English influence mushroomed. As testimony to the completion of the conquest of Ireland the Irish Parliament of 1613 was the first to draw representation from all thirty-two Irish counties. To give political representation to the newly established Protestant landlords (and also to create more reliably pro-English sentiment in Parliament) the Crown created some forty new parliamentary boroughs in locations (mainly in Ulster) likely to be dominated by New English proprietors. This insured a majority of Protestants (132 to 100) in the Irish Parliament of 1613, but left a substantial Catholic minority, most of whose members were from Leinster and Munster.[3]

The problem of governing Ireland in the reigns of James I (1603–1625) and Charles I (1625–1649) was basically one of manipulating the Catholic and Protestant factions, and of preventing them either from paralyzing government by their opposition to each other, or paralyzing it by allying against the Crown. The Protestants had become a force with which to reckon, but not yet a force through which to rule. In other words, they posed something of the same difficulty for English government which the old English had posed in the fifteenth and early sixteenth centuries. The Stuart kings, following in the footsteps of Elizabeth, had come to rely upon, first, English governors and officials, and second, New English planters and their clients. But *unlike* Elizabeth, James I and Charles I both desired an accommodation with their Catholic subjects in Ireland, partly as a balance to their increasingly assertive Protestant subjects in England.

To exploit this ambiguity in English policy the Catholic members of the Irish Parliament in 1626 put forward a set of demands which, from 1628, were known as "the Graces." These fifty-one demands of an assorted character were urged on Charles I more or less as the price of Catholic cooperation. Their major thrust was to remove from Catholics disabilities which put them at a disadvantage in their struggle to preserve and acquire landed wealth. Charles I accepted the Graces in return for the promise of an annual subsidy of £40,000 from the Irish Parliament for a period of three years. The Graces, however, were made conditional upon their enactment by the Irish Parliament, and the politics of the 1630s revolved largely around whether the Graces would actually be enacted, and if so, in what exact form.

The question was no longer whether the Crown had power in Ireland, but rather who would benefit from the power it had unquestionably obtained. In the 1620s, for instance, a good deal of the Crown's new rights of patronage in Ireland had gone to benefit the English royal favorite, George Villiers, duke of Buckingham. At Buckingham's bidding—and to the very great profit to him, his friends, and relations—Irish knighthoods, baronetcies, and peerages proliferated extravagantly. New men and families were fastened upon the wealth and dignity of Ireland without any palpable benefit to the Crown. Even the Protestant Church of Ireland failed to get much of the wealth which was intended to shore it up for the struggle against Rome. Protestant planters like the earl of Cork contrived to transfer much valuable ecclesiastical property to themselves, so that the Church, like the Crown, became an institution with rich friends, but comparatively slender means of its own.

In 1633 Charles I appointed as lord deputy a man who self-consciously set out to change all of this. Thomas Wentworth, a Yorkshireman who had most recently been the king's lord president of the Council for the North, came to Ireland with an articulated sense of Ireland's potential as an asset to the Crown, but also of the chronic problems which had long rendered the kingdom a liability. Wentworth perceived the Crown as an embattled institution. His objective was to strengthen it and to do this he launched a campaign against the particularist factions, both Catholic and Protestant. He sought to increase royal revenues, decrease the expenses of Irish administration, and raise an army which could be employed by the Crown in either foreign or domestic entanglements.

Much of Wentworth's program required a resumption for Church and Crown of property to which they were entitled, but which had slipped into the hands of entrepreneurial laymen. Wentworth did not stick to playing off Old English against New, or Catholic against Protestant. His blunt method was to take on all comers, defying the two landed interests simultaneously and threatening each with royal wrath. No previous lord deputy had exercised such legatine powers, and they depended upon Charles I's almost unlimited confidence in, and reliance upon, his talented servant. Wentworth was not above feathering his own nest with Irish lands, but unlike Buckingham in the 1620s, he did not build up and enrich a class of clients.

Ostensibly, Wentworth gave Ireland the kind of order the Crown desired it to have, and provoked shrill protests and lamentations from among the privileged, whether Catholic or Protestant. In fact, he contributed to the growth of a new kind of instability. The opponents to Charles I in England regarded Wentworth's work in Ireland as a singular threat and were obsessed with the possibility that a predominantly Catholic Ireland might one day support an English king in a civil war with his English Protestant subjects. Wentworth's victims in Ireland were more than happy to aid his opponents in England, and when an English Parliament was convened in November 1640, its first act was to impeach Wentworth, who had some months earlier been relieved of the lord lieutenancy of Ireland, but raised to the peerage as the earl of Strafford.

For eleven years Charles I had been endeavoring to rule his dominions without calling a parliament in England, and when the mounting expense of his attempt to impose a version of English religion on the Scots finally forced him to relent, Strafford and Ireland were foci of the pent-up opposition. The impeachment of Strafford failed, for it required formal proof that he had committed treason, no easy thing to demonstrate in a man who had faithfully followed every order of his sovereign. But he was, instead, made the object of an act of attainder, a legislative assertion of guilt which was passed by the House of Commons, narrowly passed by the House of Lords, and unhappily acquiesced in by a fearful Charles I. Strafford was beheaded in May 1641, and his death signaled the inability of the king to protect his servants from the wrath of Parliament. Strafford was no Catholic and no particular protector of Catholics in Ireland. Yet in a way he never intended, he represented a bulwark against the antipopery of an increasingly vocal segment of the English population. With Strafford gone and the king trembling before his own Parliament, Catholics in Ireland—even those who had hated the Lord Lieutenant—were justified in feeling that another English storm was about to burst over them, that the equilibrium which had existed since 1604 was about to end, and that the grudging, tacit, toleration of their religion was about to be replaced by rigorous persecution.

The rebellion that broke out on October 23, 1641, was, at least in part, a response to these new circumstances in England. It had two initial components: a plot to capture Dublin, which failed; and a widespread rising in Ulster, which was overwhelmingly successful. The new Protestant settlers were driven off the land and streamed into castles, ports, and fortified towns, seeking refuge wherever it could be found. Many were killed outright, or died of starvation and exposure in the course of flight. Thousands of Catholics were killed in Protestant reprisals. The statistics of the cruelty have been endlessly debated, but without any conclusive estimate of their true dimension. Despite prodigious exaggeration and falsification of the events, it was clearly a dark and bloody time. Many of the refugees took ship for England where, as beggars in the western ports or London, they made a piteous impression and further inflamed English reaction to the Irish rising.

The rebellion seemed to vindicate English Protestant fears of a giant Catholic conspiracy in which their own King Charles played a part. It hardly helped matters that some of the rebels claimed to have a warrant for their action signed by the king, and it is beyond doubting that Charles had been fishing for support in the troubled waters of Irish Catholic discontent. That he actually intended to sponsor the rebellion that occurred is most unlikely. But English Protestants were not merely paranoid in fearing for their religion. Roman Catholics had clearly strengthened their position in Ireland since Elizabeth's death. Numerous Catholic clergy, and even a few prelates roamed the island, ministering to the faithful, sometimes quite openly. The Catholic population of England, though minuscule, was probably increasing. And worst of all, Charles I had taken a French Catholic queen, put certain Catholics in high office, and shown himself strongly opposed to the sterner forms of Protestantism spreading among his subjects.

The reaction of English Protestants to "the bloody rebellion" or "the massacre," as it was often called, was predominantly one of stark horror, mingled with suspicion of the king. Charles sought to exculpate himself, but without alienating his Catholic subjects in Ireland, for he hoped still to have their political and military support. Many of these Catholic subjects, especially the Old English in Leinster, professed utter innocence of the rebellion and begged for arms to help resist it. These were not forthcoming because the Protestant lords justices in Dublin (who constituted the government in the absence of a newly appointed lord deputy) interpreted the rebellion as universal rather than local. They believed, and reported, that the Catholic population of Ireland was rising *en masse*. They trusted no Catholic, and whether or not their assumption was correct, it proved self-fulfilling.

In early 1642 the rebellion spread slowly throughout the island until only pockets of Protestant resistance remained. To some extent, the rebellion spread, because of the evident English failure to send an army of reconquest. Parliament feared that if an army was raised, the king would take command of it and turn it against Parliament. The king would not take a militantly anti-Irish stance for fear it would preclude an eventual, negotiated settlement. The result was paralysis. The Scots sent troops to Ulster, but only the merest trickle of men and munitions reached the besieged Protestants elsewhere. England's preoccupation with its own internal conflicts and a developing civil war virtually sealed the two islands off from one another for eight long years.

In this vacuum a movement for insular independence developed. An impressive array of Catholic peers and large landholders from both Gaelic and Old English backgrounds assembled in the summer of 1642 and took the name of the Confederates of Kilkenny from their meeting place. They quickly established an executive and a legislature which claimed to govern Ireland in nominal obedience to Charles I as a king on the verge of a civil war with his subjects in England. They sedulously distinguished between the king, whom they wished to support, and his intrusively Protestant larger kingdom, which they wished to resist. Their plan was simply to offer their much-needed loyalty and support in return for recognition of a relatively independent and openly Catholic state in Ireland.

The king was placed in an impossible bind. If he conceded what the Confederates of Kilkenny desired he would alienate his supporters in England, few of whom were Catholic. If he refused, Ireland's help was lost to him. Charles did what monarchs usually do in such a situation: equivocate. His failure to make concessions of substance subjected the Confederates of Kilkenny to internal division, for the Gaelic Confederates were reluctant suitors to what they saw as a basically English monarch, and they much preferred to look for some Catholic protector on the continent. In this view they were strongly supported from 1643 onward by two successive papal legates attached to the Confederates. Neither Pietro Scarampi nor Giovanni Battista Rinuccini could see the use or necessity of a continuing connection between a Catholic Ireland and a Protestant monarchy in England.

In 1648 controversy over loyalty to Charles I finally split the Confederates irreparably. The Old English entered a truce with the king's lord lieutenant, James Butler, marquis of Ormonde, and Rinuccini departed the island angrily, hurling excommunicatory thunderbolts at those who dared to follow the path of compromise. As it turned out, the Ormonde Truce did little to improve Charles I's fortunes. In December of the same year he was placed on trial by the victorious Parliament, and in January 1649 he was publicly beheaded as a traitor to his own people. The Ormonde Truce was important, however, because it had the effect of absolving Catholic Ireland of blanket responsibility for the heinous events of 1641. But this absolution, or more properly, reduction of responsibility, had been achieved only so far as the king and the royalists were concerned.

The real tragedy was that it counted for nothing in the eyes of the English party that had triumphed. Or rather, it was another mark against the Catholic Irish that they had been willing to consort with the defeated and convicted king. Once the royalist forces in England had been throughly defeated in the so-called second civil war (1648) and Charles I dispatched to his maker, the victorious Parliament was free to deal with an Ireland that had languished in disorder and rebellion for eight years. In the late summer of 1649 the Parliament's lord general, Oliver Cromwell, led a 30,000-man army of repression to Ireland. After eight years the alleged atrocities of 1641 were republicized in order to justify a vendetta against the Irish people.

That crimes against Protestants—some of them horrendous—had been committed in 1641 and after is not at issue. What concerns us is the use that was made of these incidents to transform the character of the eventual reconquest and settlement. Within six months of the rebellion's outbreak in 1641 an assumption of universal Catholic culpability had been codified in legislation which promised to repay with confiscated rebel land loans made to Parliament. In theory the loans were to finance repression of the rebellion, but in fact the funds raised were frittered away uselessly. Nevertheless, Parliament had thereby committed itself to the confiscation of vast amounts of Irish land, and this was widely understood to portend a harsh and expropriatory settlement. When the Cromwellian conquest finally came about in 1649–50 the atrocity propaganda of the

1640s was republished and rehearsed in an effort to justify a settlement which, from every other point of view, was cruel and unusual.

The reconquest began with the expedition of Oliver Cromwell to Ireland in the late summer of 1649. Striking out from his base in Dublin Cromwell conducted his well-drilled and experienced army of 30,000 English soldiers through a series of triumphant sieges and engagements. What distinguished the campaign from those fought by the same forces in England was the commonplace slaughter of women, children, noncombatants, and unarmed captives. This was not entirely the result of the English soldiers' zeal. Cromwell's army was as well-ordered as any in seventeenth-century Europe (indeed, it was one of the best), but the lord general believed that he was an instrument of divine retribution for the atrocities committed against Protestants in 1641, and he accordingly gave orders to deny mercy to Catholics on a number of occasions.

When Cromwell left Ireland in early 1650 the Catholic armies were broken, and a huge Protestant garrison remained behind to mop up lingering resistance and impose the forthcoming settlement. The thrust of that settlement was to transfer from Catholic to Protestant ownership an additional forty percent of the landed wealth of Ireland. It also sought to concentrate what survived of Catholic land-ownership throughout the island in the most remote and westerly parts, particularly Connacht. The new proprietors were meant to be those who had lent money to Parliament in the 1640s under the scheme of "adventure" for Irish lands, and the soldiers who had accompanied Cromwell to Ireland and who were to be paid for their services from the land they had helped to reconquer.

The Cromwellian settlement was probably the most ambitious and radical attempted anywhere in seventeenth-century Europe. Very nearly a whole nation was expropriated by its conquerors, not just a small band of identifiable rebels. To make possible such sweeping transfers of land, the century's most ambitious land survey and mapping was carried out by the polymathic physician, Sir William Petty. An inventor, experimenter, and indefatigable theoretician, Petty was one of many well-placed Cromwellians to accumulate a fortune in confiscated Irish land. The maps and surveys he prepared enabled the Cromwellian authorities to begin the immensely complicated transfer of land from the various categories of Irish deemed to be rebels, to the various categories of English deemed to have a valid claim to it.

So manifold and contradictory were the thousands of claims and counterclaims that they had only begun to be sorted out when Oliver Cromwell died in September 1658. Little additional progress was made with the settlement before the tumultuous era of revolution ended with the restoration of the Stuart monarchy in 1660. Ireland had been Cromwellian for less than a decade. Like Scotland after 1651, Ireland had been subject to a basically military government; but Scotland had seen nothing like the profound social and economic restructuring which was attempted in Ireland. The island had been governed as a garrison state in the 1650s. The English government (the Commonwealth from 1649–1653, the Protectorate from 1654–1660) resented the huge, continuing military expenses and tried to reduce the size of the army, but there was no real prospect of a settled, self-supporting civilian state. The Cromwellian garrison included many Protestant sectaries, especially Baptists, but little effort was made to proselytize among the Irish. They were widely regarded as irredeemable, and thus the two societies glared at each other across the barricades of a veritable occupation.

This picture of "fanatic" Protestants pitted against "unyielding" Catholics is not complete. Oliver sent his younger son, Henry, to Ireland in 1655, and the Protector's son—who eventually became lord deputy—was slowly drawn into a circle of conservative clergymen, army officers, and reemerging Jacobean planters. Like some of their counterparts in England these establishmentarians feared the anarchistic tendencies they observed in the lower ranks of the

army and among the more feverish religious sects. Henry
Cromwell shared their distaste for radicalism and was
drawn to the wealthy Protestant families which had established themselves before 1641. This was a crucial development, for many Protestant survivors had nominally served
Charles I during the chaotic 1640s and were in danger of
being relegated to a status only slightly less inferior than
that of the Catholics. Thus Oliver's son provided a kind of
bridge over which the early settlers could reach a safe and
respected place in Cromwellian Ireland. When Charles II,
the refugee son of the martyred Charles I, began his bid to
return to the throne of his ancestors in 1659, he found a
congenial reception in Ireland from many of the Protestant
planters Henry Cromwell had favored. Men like Sir Charles
Coote and Sir Roger Boyle had made their peace with the
Cromwellians and even made successful careers with them,
but they had not been involved in the trial and execution of
Charles I or in the radical innovations of his successor.

The fact that Charles II regained his throne with the help
of pre-Cromwellian Irish Protestants made it almost impossible for the restored king to undo completely the Cromwellian Settlement. The Catholic position in 1660 was quite
simply that it was time for the monarchy to reward its
friends and punish its enemies, and they had no doubt that,
despite a few lapses, they had been far more constant in
their loyalty to the Stuarts than had the Protestants of
either Ireland or England. The Catholics hoped for a return
to the *status quo ante bellum,* a reversal that could only be
produced by another round of wholesale convictions and
confiscations, this time, of Protestants. Charles II could see
the justice of this, but he was too hesitant and cautious to
bring it about. It was an admonitory example that his
father had gone to the block in 1649, at least in part, for
angering his Protestant subjects by befriending a Catholic
minority with which he sympathized.

Charles II took a cautious, politic tack in which he sought
obliquely to restore "innocent papists" to their former
lands, but eventually betrayed most of them when a storm

of Protestant indignation blew up in response. Thus the protestantization of Irish society reached a new height at the Restoration. The new Irish House of Commons, in contrast with its predecessors of 1640 and 1634 was now exclusively, rather than predominantly, Protestant. A handful of noble Catholic families regained their lands, but they were a distinct anomaly. "Society" was now Protestant, and Dublin became a Protestant capital. There was some expansion of the Protestant middle and lower classes as well, though it seems unlikely that more than a fraction (perhaps a third) of the Cromwellian soldiers and civilian administrators made Ireland their home after the Restoration. After 1660 there was some influx of Protestant merchants and artisans, particularly to Dublin, and of course, after the revocation of the Edict of Nantes in France (1685) there was an immigration of Huguenots, many of them skilled in textile manufacture.

The 1660s brought about, instead of the hoped-for reversal of the Cromwellian land settlement, its virtual legitimization, with only minor revisions. The result was *two* Irelands: an official Protestant one, and a disenfranchised, expropriated, and sometimes refugee, Catholic one. The Catholics were by no means bottled up in the West as the Cromwellians had intended, but remained in almost every part of Ireland as an under-class of servants and lesser tenants. Thousands emigrated, continuing a tradition already well-established by the late sixteenth century. The earliest exiles had been drawn principally to Spain, and to military service in the Spanish armies in the Netherlands, but by the latter half of the seventeenth century Irish refugees were spread across the face of Catholic Europe. Many were in Austria, and especially France, where an Irish brigade served the monarchy from the time of Louis XIV to the French Revolution. The culture of aristocratic Catholic families became cosmopolitan and flourished both inside and outside the island homeland.

For the peasantry there was little escape, except for the dismal American ventures into which they were sometimes

coerced. English colonial entrepreneurs carried off boat-
loads of them in the 1630s to help people the pestilential
Caribbean colonies of St. Kitts and Barbados, and thousands of Irish were drafted for the settlement of Jamaica
after its capture from the Spanish in 1656. Irish names are
also to be found on the lists of those carried to Virginia in
the middle years of the century, but nowhere in the Caribbean or central Atlantic colonies did the Irish emerge as a
prospering and self-conscious ethnic group. On the contrary they were widely regarded as a troublesome and unreliable admixture, and numerous colonies passed laws
aimed at preventing or limiting their immigration.

One of the anomalies of Ireland in the reign of Charles II
is that parts of it prospered despite the preceding decades
of turmoil and devastation. An economic revival was under
way even before the death of Oliver Cromwell, and it was
probably the result of new capital investment in Irish land
by Protestant landlords more confident than before that the
island was finally theirs. Exports to England, especially of
livestock, boomed and gave rise to protectionist English
measures on behalf of English-bred cattle. The Protestant
planters had no sooner begun to thrive in Ireland than they
awakened the jealousies of their English counterparts.

Late seventeenth-century Ireland was by no means a *tab-
ula rasa* on which the Protestant plantocracy could write a
whole new script. There were persistent fears of risings and
plots from both the left and the right of the religious middle (the Church of Ireland). Rumors of Catholic conspira-
cies were legion, especially in periods of tension with
France, which, after 1648 replaced Spain as the prime
threat to Protestant northern Europe. Little less threatening were the plots of the "fanatics," a name liberally applied to dissident Cromwellians, Baptists, Presbyterians,
and other Protestant sectaries. Much more than in England,
the "middle way" of the established church was a tightrope
which only a tiny minority of the population could (or
wished to) walk. But the greatest threat to Protestant Ireland was that the Cromwellian and Restoration land settle-

ments would come unstuck, and that the Catholic sympathies of Charles II and James II would eventually lead to
profound revisions in the ownership of property.

"Ireland is the capital out of which all debts are paid,"
the earl of Clarendon remarked, but by 1660 there was not
enough capital in Ireland to repay all that was owed. Justice for Catholics, or even simple satisfaction of those who
deserved well of Charles I and Charles II meant confiscation of land held by Protestants. The land question was the
Pandora's box of the age, and from his controversial accession to the throne in 1685 James II threatened to open it.
The first Stuart monarch to succeed as an avowed Catholic,
James took as his second wife an Italian Catholic princess,
Mary of Modena. Since his heirs, the children of his deceased first wife, the Protestant Anne Hyde, were both females, there was a good chance that he could yet produce
a male Catholic heir to supersede the claims of his daughters. James was thus the bright hope of Catholic Ireland,
and he justified this hope by moving steadily to reverse the
Protestant hegemony there. His principal agent was an
English Catholic, Richard Talbot, whom he raised to the
Irish earldom of Tyrconnell in 1685 and made lord deputy
of Ireland in 1687. James did not attempt to dismantle the
Church of Ireland, but treated it with neglect while encouraging the revival of the Catholic church and clergy.

The crisis of James' reign occurred in England rather
than Ireland and was precipitated in June 1688 by the birth
of a son to Queen Mary. The royal birth made a self-perpet-
uating Catholic monarchy seem the unavoidable destiny of
Protestant England. Recoiling from this grim prospect a
group of influential aristocrats invited William of Orange,
leader of the Dutch republic, to intervene in English affairs.
William's mother was a Stuart, but his best excuse for involvement was his marriage to Mary, the elder of James II's
daughters by his first marriage. At William's arrival with a
powerful army, support for James II evaporated. James II
fled the country, fearing the fate of his father, Charles I, and

the throne was more or less awarded to William and Mary, in view of its alleged "vacancy."

In Ireland the issue was less cut and dried. James II meant life and hope to thousands of Catholics who were unwilling to abandon his cause without a struggle. What had been an almost bloodless (and so-called glorious) revolution in England took the form of a bloody civil war in Ireland. Some Protestants again fled the country, while others took refuge in the walled towns. By early 1689 Tyrconnell had established his authority in Dublin and most of the south, but was hoping for military and economic support from Louis XIV of France, patron of the exiled James. Protestants prayed for an invasion of Ireland and restoration of Protestants hegemony by the new English king.

The struggle between Protestants and Catholics in Ireland could not long remain isolated from the struggles of the great powers. Neither Louis XIV nor William III cared particularly for Ireland, except insofar as it figured in the larger European conflict between them. Even James II lacked any feeling other than a hope that Ireland might prove a useful lever for recovering his lost crown in England. The civil war between Protestants and Catholics once more laid Ireland open to exploitation as an arena in the international conflict between an ascending France and her allied opponents.

Urged on, and financed, by his French patron, James II landed in southern Ireland in March 1689. After a triumphal progress to Dublin he summoned an Irish parliament which met in May. Just as Protestants had managed to assemble an exclusively Protestant House of Commons in 1661, Catholics now contrived to turn the tables. Of 230 representatives in the new Parliament, only six were Protestants. No representatives were returned from the Protestant areas of Ulster, and lord deputy Tyrconnell suspended the charters of certain southern boroughs where the election of Protestants was likely. There were few Gaelic Irish in the House of Commons, for most of the members were

Old English, a reminder of the enduring vitality and prominence of this former ruling class. In the lords there were five Protestant lay peers, as well as four bishops of the Church of Ireland, and this tiny party constituted the entire opposition.

This so-called Patriot Parliament set about addressing the grievances of decades, but was restrained by a cautious James II, ever mindful of Protestant opinion in England. A declaratory act asserted that the Parliament of England could not legislate for Ireland—an ancient refrain which would have future reverberations—but James II blocked a bill which would have ended the subordination of Ireland to the Crown by repealing Poynings' law. The king also tried to stop the act repealing the Cromwellian and Restoration land settlements, but here was the crux of his supporters' hopes. Unless the land settlements were annulled, the state of the expropriated Catholic landholders would remain forlorn. James acquiesced, and the resulting legislation provided a statutory basis for returning to the land ownership pattern of 1641. Years of adjudication would be necessary to satisfy all the claims thus created, and the Jacobite era in Ireland was not to last that long. Having dealt with the major grievances of its members, insofar as it could, the Parliament voted James II a subsidy of £20,000 per month for a period of thirteen months. In July it was "prorogued," or adjourned.

While the Parliament was still in session the Jacobite forces were trying to capture the fortified Protestant city of Londonderry in northwest Ulster. A siege was begun in April 1689, and by mid-summer the 20,000 inhabitants of the town were on the verge of starvation. A Williamite naval force arrived at Lough Foyle (the arm of the sea on which Londonderry lies) in mid-June, but made no effort to overcome the boom by which the besiegers had blocked off access to the town from the water. Finally, in late July, the expedition assaulted and broke the boom and brought relief to the desperate town. The Jacobites raised their siege on July 31, and were dealt another defeat the same day by Protestant forces at Enniskillen in southern Ulster.

The Jacobite cause seemed in decline, but William III could not afford to let it linger. In August William sent a newly raised army to Ireland under the elderly duke of Schomburg, a Huguenot general who had entered Dutch service after the revocation of the Edict of Nantes in 1685. Schomburg landed at Belfast and quickly took the Jacobite stronghold in the old Norman castle at Carrickfergus. He accomplished little in the remainder of the year and his troops were soon decimated by sickness and disease. William regretfully decided to go himself to Ireland in 1690 and thereby miss out on the much more interesting campaigning on the continent. It was, he wrote to one of his allies "a terrible mortification."[4]

Both sides built up their forces in anticipation of the approaching confrontation. William landed in Belfast Lough in mid-June with 15,000 troops in 300 ships. Seven thousand French troops had reached the Jacobites at Cork in mid-June, but had to be replaced by 7,000 Irish troops to be sent to the continent. William moved south from Belfast and met the Jacobites, moving north, at the river Boyne, about 40 miles north of Dublin. Some 36,000 Dutch, Huguenots, Germans, Danes, English, and Ulster Protestants, under William, faced some 25,000 Irish and French, under James. Battle was joined on July 1, and the result was a triumph for William. James fled south and on July 4 took ship for France. William's forces occupied Dublin, embarrassing the Protestants who had collaborated with the Jacobites rather than flee to England or join William's forces.

William's victory at the Boyne had turned the tide, but not yet ended the war. In the west the Irish rallied along the Shannon under the leadership of Patrick Sarsfield, the scion of an Old English family who had made a name as a brilliant cavalry officer. William marched to Limerick, the chief strong point along the Shannon, and laid siege to the town in early August. Sarsfield successfully assaulted his artillery and ammunition train with the result that William ran out of ammunition in late August. Unwilling to linger unproductively in Ireland, William returned to England and turned over command of the army in Ireland to Baron von Ginkel, a Dutch general.

In 1691 Ginkel brought the war to conclusion. In late June he breached the defensive line of the Shannon with an attack upon Athlone. Even more decisive was a pitched battle fought several weeks later at Aughrim, sixteen miles southwest. St. Ruth, the French general commanding the Jacobite force, was killed, and the rout of his army turned into a slaughter. Galway town surrendered to Ginkel in return for assurances that the merchants could keep their lands in Connacht. Limerick remained the last citadel of Jacobite resistance, and Ginkel invested the town in late August. The French sought to keep the Jacobite cause alive simply to pin down English forces in Ireland and prevent them from engaging on the continent, but the Irish defenders of Limerick saw little point in useless heroics. In late September Sarsfield entered into negotiations.

Two sets of articles, one military and one civil, were agreed upon and signed on October 3, 1691. Together they constituted the so-called Treaty of Limerick. The military articles permitted the Jacobite forces in the town to depart to France. The civil articles provided, first, for freedom of worship for Catholics, such as was "consistent with the laws of Ireland or as they did enjoy in the reign of King Charles II." The second of the civil articles offered pardon and property rights to the defenders of Limerick (and any remaining Irish garrisons) who stayed in Ireland and took an oath of allegiance to William III. It also guaranteed that they could "carry on their professions or trades as freely as they had done in Charles II's reign."[5] In return for these provisions, Limerick was handed over to Ginkel. Most of the Jacobite army—some 12,000 men—took ship for France.

The war in Ireland was over and yet another land settlement lay ahead. The Protestant hegemony was reestablished on a firm footing—one sees in retrospect—to last for the better part of two centuries. What feeble protection the Treaty of Limerick offered Catholics against Protestant economic and political preponderance the next few decades would clearly show.

The year 1691 marked another stage in the expansion of the English position in Ireland. Whereas the seventeenth century began with the completion of the Tudor military conquest and the overthrow of the Gaelic province of Ulster, the century ended with a successful defense of the new Protestant order. The Williamite triumph in England and Ireland meant that there would be no further Catholic monarchs from whom to hope for sympathy and support. There would be no repetition of James II's attempt to turn the clock back, to recognize the Catholic Church, and to restore to Catholic families the lands they had lost in the decades of turmoil and confiscation. In retrospect, 1691 secured the Protestant ascendancy. To the Protestant Irish of the time, the rebellion of 1688 was merely a repetition of the rebellion of 1641, which in turn was a repetition of 1595. To them the Irish threat could never be discounted, because the history of the past century showed too clearly the enduring volatility and treachery of Catholic Irish society. Hence, there could be no generosity for the vanquished, no relaxation of the victorious grip.

In a sense, 1691 was the birthdate of the Protestant ascendancy. A long gestation preceded it, and there would be growth and change after it, but the basic form of the ascendancy had been determined. There would be little further immigration from England or Scotland. More important, the era of massive property confiscation was over, because the bulk of the property which had belonged to Irish Catholics had now been transferred to English and Scottish Protestants. The Williamite confiscations that followed the Treaty of Limerick virtually completed this process of wealth transfer, and by 1703 Catholic families were left with only 14 percent of the island's land.

The eighteenth century is sometimes called the period of "the Protestant nation." This term makes little sense unless

one understands that the Catholic majority had been reduced to a second, inferior, and less visible nation. The
wealth of its aristocracy largely expropriated, its clergy fugitive, its army serving a French king abroad, and many of
its natural leaders in exile, Catholic Ireland became the
vast, submerged portion of an iceberg. It provided the "ascendancy" with its tenants and artisans, and eventually
some of its merchants and professionals. The commonplace
comparison between black Africans in the Americas and the
Irish in Ireland overlooks the important difference that the
Irish suffered subordination in their own land. It was an essential aspect of their tragedy, and the key to their eventual
salvation.

5

IRELAND AS A PROTESTANT "NATION": THE EIGHTEENTH CENTURY

EIGHTEENTH-CENTURY Ireland was like a rich and varied stew over which a thin, elegant crust of pastry had been laid. This crust was the "ascendancy," a social fabric made up of Protestant landlords, officeholders, and churchmen. Collectively, they ruled the island—insofar as the subordination of Irish government to the monarchy allowed—and enjoyed the lion's share of its wealth. The ascendancy built the handsome houses and squares of Georgian Dublin, and in doing so turned a former military and administrative strongpoint into a center for society.

In the countryside the ascendancy threw up scores of ambitious—sometimes magnificent—residences. Castles were no longer thought necessary, on the whole, for organized resistance had been finally ended with the Williamite triumph. Great estates were often surrounded with miles of imposing wall, but these were less a military obstacle than architectural proclamations of wealth and ownership. The names of the houses themselves were proclamations of newfound wealth and status. Some incorporated the names of the founder's wife, as with Bessbrook, Castle Constance, and Annesgrove. Others institutionalized a family surname, as with French Park, Mount Plummer, or Drewscourt, or simply employed fancy, as with Harmony Hall, Mount Venus, Mount Music, or Castle Comfort.[1]

The ascendancy was a thin upper crust, but it was, itself, a composite of Protestants of varying wealth, religious outlook, and length of settlement in Ireland. Only the common antipathy to Roman Catholics gave the ascendancy coherence.

In the "stew" below the crust there was also variety. Despite the exodus of "wild geese" to Catholic Europe, many old Catholic families retained land in Ireland. By 1699 nearly 1,200 claims by Catholics for the restoration of their estates under the Treaty of Limerick had been heard by the Irish Privy Council, and most were granted. But with only fourteen percent of the land in Catholic possession, the old Catholic gentry was reduced to negligible minority status. Most of the Catholic population owned no land, but leased it, on varying terms, from those who did. They worshiped—when they worshiped—in a proscribed faith, and many of them, especially in the west and the south, spoke a language regarded as barbarous by the ascendancy. Far the greatest part of the population of Ireland consisted of these "peasants" or "country people" who would in due course coalesce into a "nation" and assert their primacy in the island. But in the eighteenth century they were politically inconsequential and the entire period is often described as the era of "the Protestant nation," for Catholic Ireland existed only in a subterranean, even clandestine fashion.

The Catholic majority was powerless to prevent the development of Ireland into an officially and ruthlessly anti-Catholic state in the decades after the Treaty of Limerick. The Irish Parliament had become a Protestant preserve, and in the opening decade of the eighteenth century it passed a series of acts, the most famous in 1704 and 1709, designed to penalize or discourage the practice of Roman Catholicism, especially among the propertied. These so-called penal laws were a repudiation of the first of the civil articles of the Treaty of Limerick, but they were an accurate reflection of the lingering fears of Protestant colonists that Catholic Ireland remained a potential "fifth column" and a grave threat to the new landholding class.

The penal laws were meant to induce Catholics to conform to the Protestant Church of Ireland, and they succeeded to some degree. Many leading Catholic families converted in the course of the eighteenth century, so that by 1778 Catholic proprietors were receiving only 1.5 percent of the total annual rent income of the island.[2] The penal laws saddled the bulk of the population with civil, social, and economic disabilities which were offensive even when, as was often the case, they were not rigorously enforced.

The act of 1704, for instance, provided that Catholics could purchase no interest in land, except a lease for not more than thirty-one years. A Catholic was forbidden to acquire land either by inheritance or marriage, and if he was among the few who already owned land, he could not bequeath it by will. Instead, at his death the land was divided in equal portions among his sons, unless, that is, the eldest conformed to the Church of Ireland, in which case the eldest inherited all. If the eldest son conformed within his father's lifetime, he could claim the estate before his father died, leaving the father a mere life-tenant on his own property. Other laws aimed at obstructing Catholic education, or prevented Catholics from holding public office by imposing sacramental tests. The cumulative effect of the penal laws was to keep Catholics in a position of inferiority rather than extirpate the Catholic faith, which was, in any event, too fragmented, amorphous, and deinstitutionalized to be readily suppressed.

By the middle of the seventeenth century Protestantism in Ireland—whether in the Church of Ireland or the nonconforming sects—had lost such missionary and evangelical zeal as it briefly enjoyed. From the time of the Cromwellian conquest, if not earlier, Catholic Ireland had been largely dismissed as beyond hope of conversion and salvation. The Church of Ireland was more and more an establishment church, committed to defense of the faith of an embattled minority, rather than propagation of that faith among those who had not seen the light. The bulk of the population clung forlornly to the one church that would have them, a church almost without fabric or walls, its clergy few and fugitive, as well as often inadequately educated. Despite the heroic spirits who gave their lives to it, Catholicism in eighteenth-century Ireland was a hulk, a frail and feeble thing which partly owed its survival to the clumsy efforts of the Protestant nation to destroy it. Excluded from landed wealth, from political life, from the "official" Church, the Irish erected a counterculture, not so much rebellious as evasive, of which Catholicism slowly became an essential part.

Eighteenth-century Ireland was thus crystallized into two distinct, and in some ways antipodal, cultures. It was an ordered, hierarchical society where well-heeled Protestants could enjoy immense authority, considerable importance, and the rarefied pleasures of aristocratic life. It also offered a certain amount of opportunity to less well-heeled Protestants to make modest fortunes in industry, commerce, or land. As a system of distributing the wealth of the island it could last only so long as the much more numerous underclass lacked the means or the determination to overthrow it, and only so long as the overclass retained sublime confidence in the justice of its privileged position. No one at the time could have predicted whether that would be months, or centuries, but in the event Protestant hegemony endured for less than two hundred years after the Treaty of Limerick, and showed signs of severe strain before even the first century had ended.

The stories of the two nations—one Protestant and one Catholic—must be told separately, even though they coexisted in the same land and impinged upon each other in numerous ways. The story of the Protestant nation has mainly to do with the emergence of the very conception, and then the struggle for independence from England. As the Irish Catholic majority subsided into relative passivity after the Jacobite rebellion of 1688–1691, English arms began to appear less vital to the security of Protestant rule, and the negative consequences of the English connection began to be noticed and lamented.

In fact, episodes of resentment preceded 1688. Exports of Irish wool to any country but England had long been forbidden, but further exclusionary mercantilist principles were applied to Ireland by the so-called Cattle Acts of 1663 and 1667. Acts of the English Parliament, these statutes first restricted and then prohibited exports of Irish cattle, sheep, swine, beef, pork and bacon to an England which was becoming a booming market for these commodities, particularly young, grass-fed cattle. English cattle raisers wanted protection against an Irish agriculture which was enjoying a dramatic recovery, and the cattle acts sharply reduced the exports of those animals. Whether or not Irish agriculture was seriously injured by such legislation has remained a subject of controversy. With the live animal market curtailed, Irish producers shifted to the export of butter and salted provisions, for which there was great demand from transatlantic shipping, so that exports as a whole did not decline in response to mercantilist legislation, but increased. On the other hand, the fact that English Protestants, sitting in the English Parliament, had appeared to put their own economic interests above those of their coreligionists now planted in Ireland contributed to an evolving perception of English oppression of Protestants in Ireland, as well as Catholics.

The late seventeenth and early eighteenth centuries saw the growth of the idea that Ireland as a whole, colonists and colonized alike, suffered under the heavy thumb of English power. The view was given written expression in 1698 by an Irish MP, William Molyneux, who published a pamphlet entitled *The Case of Ireland's being bound by act of Parliament in England stated*. In a vain attempt to block commercial legislation aimed at the Irish woolen industry, Molyneux argued that the English Parliament had no right to legislate for (or against) Ireland, which was an entirely separate and distinct kingdom of the realm.

Molyneux was followed in the reign of George I by the

most brilliant and caustic of all the Protestant critics of English power in Ireland, Jonathan Swift. A churchman and scion of Protestant Ireland, Swift vaulted St. George's channel to flourish in the heady air of Queen Anne's court. Embarked on a brilliant career, Swift overreached himself, as did the Tory party with which he was so intimately associated. Aspiring to an English bishopric, he had to be contented with the deanery of St. Patrick's Cathedral in Dublin, to which he was appointed in 1713. Queen Anne's death in 1714 sealed his fate, for the whiggish George I had no instinct to reward one of the most savage and effective of Tory propagandists. His ambitions defeated, his wordly career a shambles, his personal life unhappy, Swift came in the 1720s to dwell upon the grievances of Ireland. His response to the English restraints upon Irish woolen manufactures (anonymously published in 1720) was *A proposal for the universal use of Irish manufacture; . . . utterly rejecting and renouncing everything wearable that comes from England.*

Swift's contribution is not easily grasped. In an age without billboards or spot commercials, the craftsman of words, the consummate shaper of literate or audible argument was a force in society capable of focusing dispersed resentments into powerful persuasion. In 1724 Swift excoriated English government in a series of published letters signed under the pseudonym M. B. Drapier. Swift's anger, like that of many Protestant Irish, had been aroused by the grant in 1720 of a patent (in effect, a royal license) to an English merchant, William Wood, to mint and circulate copper coins of small denomination in Ireland. No government mint had been established in Ireland, and since 1660 the right to mint coin had been given or sold by the Crown at its pleasure. Wood had bribed a mistress of George I to procure the profitable patent, and the people of Ireland were footing the bill by having to accept debased coinage. "Wood's Half-Pence" became a cause célèbre in the campaign to free Ireland from the consequences of corruption at court. In the Drapier Letters Swift enlarged the issue to one of "Liberty." In the famous fourth letter he held up to ridicule the notion that

Ireland was in any way subordinated to the kingdom of England. "I have looked all over the English and Irish statutes" Swift wrote

without finding any Law that makes Ireland depend upon England; any more than England doth upon Ireland. We have, indeed, obliged ourselves to have the same King with them; and consequently they are obliged to have the same King with us. . . . Let whoever think otherwise, I, M. B. Drapier, desire to be excepted. For I declare, next under God, I depend only on the King my Sovereign, and on the Laws of my own Country; And, I am so far from depending upon the People of England, that if they should ever rebel against my Sovereign, (which God forbid) I would be ready at the first command from his Majesty, to take Arms against them.

The Drapier expressed Swift's more bold and sanguine side. By the end of the 1720s his feelings took the embittered and acidulous form of *A Modest Proposal for Preventing the Children of Ireland from being a burden to their parents or country.* The English had interfered with Ireland's export of wool, cattle, and other agricultural products. Swift coolly proposed that Ireland exploit an as-yet-unrecognized resource, the abundance of small children from wretchedly impoverished families. By the mere practice of cannibalism, these could become a prized source of food.

I have been assured by a very knowing American of my acquaintance in London, that a young healthy child well nursed is at a year old a most delicious nourishing and wholesome food, whether stewed, roasted, baked or boiled; and I make no doubt that it will equally serve in a fricasie or a ragout.

For the purpose of argument Swift lumped Protestant and Catholic Irish together as victims of English oppression, thereby implying that the underclass would somehow suffer less if the Protestant establishment in Ireland were given more autonomy. This was a debatable proposition, but it strengthened the picture of colonial tyranny Swift was endeavoring to create. In the short run Swift served the Protestant nation and its claims to greater independ-

ence; but in the long run Swift contributed to the notion of
Ireland as an island entitled to govern its own affairs, apart
from whether they were Catholic or Protestant affairs. His
themes were independence and responsibility, sobriety and
patriotism. Ironically defending his proposal to eat children, Swift wrote in *A Modest Proposal:*

let no man talk to me of other expedients: of taxing our absentees
at five shillings a pound; of using neither clothes nor household
furniture, except what is of our own growth and manufacture; of
utterly rejecting the materials and instruments that promote foreign luxury; of curing the expensiveness of pride, vanity, idleness,
and gaming in our women; of introducing a vein of parsimony,
prudence, and temperance; of learning to love our country,
wherein we differ even from Laplanders, and the inhabitants of
Topinamboo; of quitting our animosities, and factions, nor act
any longer like the Jews, who were murdering one another at the
very moment their City was taken.

These obvious prescriptions were intended for a Protestant
Ireland, but they have become part of the unwritten consti-
tution of virtually every Irish nationalist movement since
Swift wrote them down.

Molyneux and Swift were early publicists of the Protestant nation and its claims to independence, but there was
nothing like unanimous support for this position. A wealthy
landlord might spend much, or even all, of his time in England enjoying London's cosmopolitan pleasures. He would
have English relatives and, quite possibly, an English education. Furthermore, he could well have English estates or
investments to look after, even if the greater part of his
wealth was located in Ireland. Such a man might take a
seat in the Irish House of Lords (if a peer), or the House of
Commons, but not necessarily with any burning desire to
attack or undermine the English connection. If he ever experienced any irritation, or resentment, at the subordinated
authority of the Irish Parliament, the perquisites and emo-
luments distributed to supporters of the Crown by its
agents, the so-called undertakers, could help to soothe his

feelings. Why should a person of this description tip so pleasant and agreeable an apple cart in order to proclaim the questionable benefits of an independent Ireland?

The colonial situation in eighteenth-century Ireland was quite similar to that in English North America, with the important exception that Ireland was geographically much closer to the mother country. Furthermore, it possessed its own Parliament even though it was subordinated both by the fifteenth-century Poynings' Act, and by the enlargement of that statute in 1719 in the so-called Declaratory Act of the sixth year of George I. This latter act asserted an English right to legislate for Ireland and exercise a right of final judicature. It reasserted the right of the English Privy Council to suppress or alter Irish bills, and it confirmed the effect of the perpetual mutiny act of 1707 which placed the Irish army beyond the control of the Irish Parliament.[3]

By American standards, most of Protestant Ireland was Tory, and the movement toward independence halting and feeble. Many of Ireland's most disaffected Protestants crossed the sea to America, and when they finally threw themselves into the struggle against English colonial domination, it was in America, rather than in Ireland. The area from which Protestant emigration was most pronounced was the north, that section of the country which had been most densely settled by Scots-Presbyterians in the seventeenth century. In Ulster there were tens of thousands of hard-pressed small farmers, artisans, and tradesmen. By the late seventeenth century there was little remaining chance to find cheap land or abundant economic opportunity, and the marginal fortunes of small farmers rose or fell with the vagaries of the Irish weather.

Substantial emigration from Ireland to North America began in the reign of George I (1714–1725) and was directed at first to New England. In the second half of the 1720s it gathered force and moved southwest to focus on the Pennsylvania colony, and from the 1730s on, South Carolina. The migration reached a climax on the eve of the American Revolution. Religious, as well as economic, in-

centives played their part, for the prevailing Presbyterian-
ism of the Scots-Irish was as repellent to the Church of Ireland as similar forms of Puritanism were to the Church of
England. Immigrants expected greater freedom for their
faith in the New World, and along with settlers coming di-
rectly from Scotland, succeeded in implanting important
aspects of Scottish culture, society, and religion in the upland and mountainous regions of the middle-American colonies. As a result of this process, Protestant Ireland lost an
important part of its yeomanry, and America gained some
of its most independent and durable frontiersmen.

When the Revolutionary War broke out in America, opinion in Ireland was naturally divided. Ulster Presbyterians
tended to favor the American rebels, sympathizing with
their struggles against an English monarchy which they,
too, found oppressive. Church of Ireland establishmentarians rushed to condemn the Americans. Leaders of the Irish
Catholic community used the moment of crisis to promote
the first important measure to mitigate the penal laws. Less
significant acts had been passed by the Irish Parliament in
1771 and 1774 with the British government generally urging on the Protestant plantocracy a liberality which it
feared and resisted. The need for Catholic loyalty during
the American rebellion helped obtain the Irish Parliament's
acceptance of an act of 1778, which repealed important
parts of the infamous popery act of 1704. Henceforth Catholics were allowed to take long leases on land, and to in-
herit or bequeath it without special impediments. It was
the beginning of the painfully slow process by which all
disabilities were to be removed from Irish Catholics over
the following half-century.

The impact of the American War on Protestant Ireland
was quite different. When France joined the struggle in
1779, England was hard-pressed to maintain its 12,000
man garrison in Ireland. British troops which served both
as an internal police force and as a defense against invasion
from France had to be drawn out of the island, and a power
vacuum was thus threatened. To deal with it, an Irish Prot-

estant militia called the Volunteers was raised, and for the first time since William of Orange, Ireland was without both the benefits and burdens of an English military presence. The Irish House of Commons responded to the novelty in an almost giddy manner and began to badger England with its economic grievances and demands for free trade, unhampered by English mercantile legislation.

A hard-pressed English government made concessions which in peacetime would have been unthinkable. An act of 1781 amended Poynings' Law, repealed the Declaratory Act of 1719, and rescinded the right of the British Parliament to legislate for Ireland or act as a final court of judicature for Irish cases. This spate of legislative action was the so-called Constitution of 1782, and though it was facilitated by external forces, its architects were two indefatigable MPs, Henry Flood (1732–1791) and Henry Grattan (1746–1820). The wealthy son of a chief justice of the court of King's Bench, Flood entered the Irish Commons in 1759, and in the 60's and early 70's became the vocal leader of a small party of dissidents known as the "Patriots." In 1775, however, Flood accepted the post of vice-treasurer, possibly from self-interest, but also out of conviction that the cause of independence could be better served, at least temporarily, by cooperation with the government. To the Patriots, Flood's action appeared a betrayal (though he was discharged from his office in 1781), and he was succeeded as leader of the group by his younger colleague, Grattan. Thus the achievements of 1782 were overseen and directed by Grattan, who received most of the credit for them from posterity, as well as the more tangible reward of £50,000 from a grateful Irish Parliament.

The Constitution of 1782 brought the Protestant nation to its apogee. The formal independence of the Irish Parliament and the Irish judicial system had been achieved, but a Crown-appointed executive remained in the person of the lord lieutenant. In England, "cabinet government" was evolving in the direction of dependence upon parliament. That is to say, if a government (or cabinet) lacked support in Parliament, it was increasingly likely to be discharged from office by the Crown. In the Ireland of 1782, by contrast, the lord lieutenant was in no way dependent upon the Irish Parliament, and a critical disjuncture was thereby created. Furthermore, the Protestant nation rested upon a pathetically tiny Protestant electorate which was itself divided along religious and social lines. Schemes for electoral reform were flourishing in England in the 1780s, and it was only a matter of time before pressure developed for rationalization of the antiquated franchise in Ireland. Any expansion of the electorate would inevitably erode the clubby monopoly of political power held by the Protestant landlords, but middle-class Protestants, many of whom had served as Volunteers, wanted the vote and the greater degree of representation which only thoroughgoing electoral reform could bring about.

The century had seen the growth, as well, of a middle-class Catholic community, many of its members merchants, and this body also hoped to benefit from an expansion of the electorate and eventual relief from the penal laws. The Protestant landlords in the Irish Parliament moved cautiously, lest, by widening the base of support for their new-found independence, they lose control of it. An act of late 1782 which removed the impediments to the purchase of land by Catholics took care to exclude the land of parliamentary boroughs. Otherwise, it was feared, Catholics might come to control elections by purchase of lands in boroughs, even though they could not yet vote, or sit in parliament.[4] From 1782 to 1800 the Protestant nation walked a tightrope, unable either to leap forward to a widened polity, or backward to naked dependence upon England as its guarantor. The balancing act might have lasted somewhat longer if Ireland, along with the rest of Europe, had not been buffeted by the repercussions of the French Revolution.

From 1789 the example of France inspired would-be reformers to become radicals, and cautious conservatives to become obdurate reactionaries. It was, by and large, Protestants of the middle sort who were most inflamed. Pious

Catholics were appalled by reports of the outrages committed against Church and clergy in revolutionary France, and emigré priests fanned their fears of the atheistic gospel with which France was threatening to corrupt all of Europe. Anticlericalism was almost unknown in Catholic Ireland, for there were too few priests, and far from being privileged and indolent, they tended to share the sufferings of their harassed flock. But to some middle-class Protestants, cheated of a real place in the constitution of 1782, the French Revolution illuminated the injustice of Europe's ancien régime. The wealthy and powerful were, in this view, everywhere conspiring to maintain and aggrandize themselves at the cost of all whose misfortune it was to exist beneath them. In Anglo-Irish terms these villains were the corrupt British monarchy, in the person of King George III, and the sycophantish flatterers whom the Crown appeared endlessly to enrich at the expense of humbler subjects.

Much of this sentiment was concentrated in the north, long a hotbed of unprivileged Protestants, particularly Presbyterians who had historic religious grievances against the Church of Ireland as well. Catholics, too, were gradually influenced by the revolution in France, for it made the point that men could endeavor to model the world to their ideal, rather than suffer forever the indignities and barbarities to which they were born. Thus it emboldened Catholics to push further for the removal of the penal laws which had burdened them for over a century. The Crown sought to placate these Catholics, but was limited by what the Protestant landlords who dominated the Irish Parliament would tolerate in the way of "relief." A bill of 1792 removed all disabilities on marriages between Catholics and Protestants, admitted Catholics to the practice of law, and removed the remaining restrictions on Catholic education, but failed to give Catholics a vote.

The British government of William Pitt the Younger saw the concessions of 1792 as insufficient to secure the loyalty of Ireland's Catholics, and it virtually imposed upon the Irish Parliament the momentous act of 1793. This statute

gave Catholics the right to vote both in local elections and
for members of Parliament. It gave them the right to bear
arms, and removed the remaining restrictions on their
holding of land. Finally, it opened to them all but the highest civil and military posts. After the act of 1793, a Catholic
could still not be lord lieutenant, lord deputy, chancellor of
the exchequer, commander-in-chief of the forces, or a pro-
vost or fellow of Trinity College, but a whole world of state
employments was at least nominally open to him. The right
to vote had been obtained, but it was circumscribed both
by the enduring prohibition upon Catholics sitting in Parliament, and by a system of property qualifications and
borough (town) governments which effectively shielded the
ascendancy from the Catholic voter.[5]

As the war with France, rather than the revolution itself,
became the preoccupation of English statesmen, firmness
and repression replaced conciliation and appeasement, as
policies for dealing with Irish discontent. There was the
usual fear in times of grave crisis that reformers might in-
terpret generous concessions from government as signs of
weakness and self-doubt. Lines hardened on both sides, and
the mid-1790s gave rise to an improbable and remarkable
amalgamation of Protestant and Catholic dissidents into
the Society of United Irishmen. Founded in Belfast in 1791
with the help of a Protestant radical named Theobald
Wolfe Tone, the society aimed at achievement of complete
religious equality and thorough reform of the Irish Parliament. The Society aspired to overthrow the legacy of sectarian hatred which it blamed on the ancien régime in the
British Isles. Little in the history of Ireland since the mid-
sixteenth century prepares us for this extraordinary collaboration in which the antipodes made common cause
against what they dramatically perceived to be a common
foe.[6]

The emergence of the United Irishmen by no means signified the healing of the massive rifts in Irish society, for
these bridges between the warring sides were rarefied exceptions to a general rule of continuing, and in some ways

worsening, conflict. At the same time that the Society of United Irishmen was being formed in Belfast, bloody vendettas were being carried out between Catholic and Protestant tenants and small farmers in other parts of Ulster, particularly County Armagh. Sectarian terrorist societies such as the Protestant "Peep o'day boys" and the Catholic "Defenders" were established to wreak havoc upon one another and their respective members. The spirit of enlightened rationalism flickered fitfully in the gloom of an Ireland that was still largely primitive, divided, and bitterly sectarian.

An Irish Parliament that had objected only feebly to Pitt's Catholic relief bill of 1793 proved adamantly opposed to its logical sequel, a bill of 1795 which would have admitted Catholics to seats in Parliament. The resurgence of Protestant conservatism dashed the hopes of a mildly reformist viceroy, William Wentworth Fitzwilliam, second earl Fitzwilliam, who was recalled to England in the aftermath of the bill's failure. Henceforth it was unrealistic to believe that Catholics would soon be admitted to full participation in the political life of a separate Ireland. The initiative among the reformers passed to the men of violence, who held up the dream of a French-supported revolution in Ireland. By January 1796 Wolfe Tone was in Paris lobbying for the French military aid which he was sure would precipitate a gigantic rebellion against English authority in Ireland. His assiduous efforts obtained a sizable naval expedition later that year, and it sailed for Ireland with some 30,000 men under the command of Admiral Hoche.

Intricate military plans are always subject to mishap and misfortune, and Tone's ardently desired flotilla broke up in an Atlantic fog. Half of the fleet, with Tone, reached Bantry Bay in County Kerry, but the other half, with its commander, missed the rendezvous. General Grouchy would not order a landing with only half his forces assembled, and the fleet withdrew, fearing otherwise to be intercepted by superior British forces. Tone wrote in his diary for December 21 that his ship was near enough the strand "to toss a biscuit ashore" and lamented "there cannot be imagined a situation more provokingly tantalizing than mine at this moment—within view, almost within reach, of my native land, and uncertain whether I shall ever set my foot on it."[7]

The English soon realized what an unpleasant diversion had been prevented by the providential Atlantic fog, and they began a campaign of repression, particularly in Ulster, intending to break the strength of the United Irishmen and insure that no subsequent French expedition would find fertile soil for a native rising. The French, for their part, had many more immediate concerns than Ireland, which was in their view, at best, a side show worth a wager, but not a major commitment. The United Irishmen feared that their cause faced extinction, and their last desperate hope was that a spontaneous uprising in Ireland, however ill-starred, would seduce the French into a major intervention on their behalf. But no well-coordinated campaign proved possible, and instead, local insurrections went off like small Chinese firecrackers in the late spring and summer of 1798. The participants ranged from privileged, high-minded, and well-educated idealists on the one hand to rude and unlettered Protestant-hating peasants on the other. The noble nonsectarian spirit, always most notable in and around Belfast and Dublin, gave way to the historic sectarian passions, especially in counties Wexford and Wicklow, where the rising was predominantly one of Catholics against Protestants.

Whatever else it was, or might have been, 1798 became a bloodbath and, as usual, civilians paid the heaviest price. The British army, with some justification, treated the occasion as a reverberation of 1641 and 1688. An attempt to overthrow the British government in time of bitter war with France was grounds enough for a charge of treason, but the anti-Protestant aspect of the peasant rebellions tarred the entire enterprise with the brush of seventeenth-century religious fanaticism. The army put down the rebellions with undiscriminating savagery, adding another layer to the rich legacy of crimes against the island committed by English conquerors. The final sad postscript to the year's revolutionary hopes was the late summer landing in County Mayo of a tiny French expedition, which achieved some remarkable early successes before being defeated and forced to surrender by a confident English army ten times its size.

It is often observed that England experienced no French Revolution, but nowhere did it come closer than in its turbulent and divided kingdom of Ireland. The year 1798 shook the fabric of Protestant Ireland. The years since 1782 had contributed to the illusion that Ireland could be governed by the Irish—Protestant Irish, albeit—with some considerable independence of England. But in 1798 once again the full panoply of English military power, some 40,000 soldiers, had been needed to deal with insular dissidents. How viable was a state so palpably dependent upon the "foreign" power of Britain to preserve it from the ravages of its own unruly population?

Such, at least, was the thought which stirred the English prime minister, William Pitt (the younger), to explore the possibility of a union of the Irish and English parliaments. A similar procedure had been followed in 1707 when the separate state of Scotland, its monarchy united with that of England since 1603, had been merged with England in an act of union. The application of such a merger, with certain differences to Ireland would, Pitt thought, broaden the responsibility for preserving order there, but also deprive Protestant Ireland of the cherished measures of independence which had been won since 1782.

The merger had to be approved in the Irish Parliament, and Pitt's Irish Secretary (the member of the British cabinet with chief responsibility for Ireland), Robert Stewart, Viscount Castlereagh, set about obtaining a majority in support of the measure. He did this, in part, by use of the venerable eighteenth-century methods of bribery and intimidation, which could be highly effective in dealing with a small body of privileged men. By the spring of 1800 the

Irish Parliament had been persuaded to vote for its own extinction, and the century-long notion of an independent
Protestant Ireland was brought to an abrupt end.

The details of the Act of Union will be discussed in chapter 6, but here we consider it merely as an end point. The
Protestant hegemony remained firmly established, but
without its own legislative apparatus. The destinies of Ireland had been transferred to a Parliament at Westminster
that was five-sixths composed of Englishmen, Welshmen,
and Scots (550 out of a body of 650). This assembly might
continue to aid and abet the Protestant interest in Ireland,
but it had no inevitable self-interest in doing so, and was
therefore inherently less reliable. The Act of Union was attended from the first by William Pitt's desire to provide
Irish Catholics with the right to sit in the new Parliament.
This well-known concession secured extraparliamentary
support for the act in prominent Catholic circles. Protestants were not supposed to feel threatened by such a development on the grounds that any Catholic representatives
from Ireland would never amount to more than a pitiful
minority in the union Parliament. In practice, many Protestants had for so long found shelter behind the barricades
of statutory discrimination against Catholics that they
were afraid to see these disabilities removed.

Catholics themselves were not necessarily agreed on the
usefulness of political rights, some sensing that the only
immediate beneficiaries would be the small group of
wealthy merchants, landowners, and professionals who
could hope for a seat in the new union Parliament. But Pitt
had virtually promised that Catholic "emancipation" would
attend the Act of Union, and this assurance foundered upon
the immovable rock of King George III's bigotry. The monarch saw correctly that the extension of full political rights
to Catholics in Ireland would make necessary a comparable
toleration of English Catholics, and antipopery was still too
active a fountainhead of English national identity to be jet-
tisoned without perilous turmoil. Antipopery riots had paralyzed London as recently as 1783, and George III refused

to risk new upheavals for the sake of Ireland. Thus the Act of Union passed without a companion act of emancipation, and it was only belatedly, in 1829, that Daniel O'Connell was able to achieve this element of the original design. Like the disregard and violation of the civil articles of the Treaty of Limerick in the years after 1691, the long delay between "union" and "emancipation" was easily interpreted as further evidence of England's boundless malice and perfidy wherever Ireland's Catholics were concerned.

We have traced the rise and fall of the Protestant nation, but we need to describe the fabric of the larger society which had come into being since the completion of the English conquest in the late seventeenth century. This is not easily done, for it requires statistical evidence from what was, until the census of 1841, a largely unstatistical age.[8] But even with rudimentary records concerning population there is no doubting a dramatic increase of numbers. From something over two million in 1690 the Irish population grew to three million by 1730, to four million by 1780, to six million by 1810, and to over eight million by 1841.[9]

What caused this unprecedented population increase? The simplest and most important historical questions are always the most difficult to answer, and there are many hypotheses, but no unshakable consensus as to the reasons for what occurred. Simple explanations have the merit of intelligibility, and so the potato has often been put forward as a major cause. Introduced from Peru in the late sixteenth century by Sir Walter Raleigh (who acquired a great estate at Youghall in County Cork) the potato made undoubtedly steady inroads on Irish (and generally, European) agriculture. Its nutritional (caloric) yield per acre exceeded that of any other known crop, and its cultivation therefore dramatically decreased the amount of land necessary to sustain a single individual, or family, at a subsistence level. It does not necessarily follow, however, that the potato was the *cause* of the population increase of the late eighteenth, and early nineteenth, centuries. In France, for instance, the peasantry was so doubtful of the potato's benefits that its cultivation had to be energetically advocated by the monarchy. In early eighteenth-century Ireland the potato merely took its place beside traditional grains as one component of a mixed agricultural economy. At some point between the middle and end of that century, the potato gained its ascendency and became the principal staple of the Irish peasant's diet. Late eighteenth-century visitors to Ireland commented favorably on the vigorous appearance and health of a people nourished by abundant quantities of milk and potatoes.

It is at least possible that this transition to a potato-dominated diet was actively encouraged by a landowning class which perceived that potato culture meant cheap labor. With potato crops, fewer acres were needed to provide for the subsistence of tenant labor. More of a landlord's land could be worked for his exclusive benefit. Whether or not the potato was responsible, landlords' total rents quadrupled between 1760 and 1815.[10] The proliferation of potato culture may have promoted population growth by encouraging marriage at younger ages. A tiny plot of land planted with potatoes would support a young family, but the survival of all depended perilously on the annual success of this single crop. Younger ages at marriage in turn produce longer and more prolific periods of fertility, and children may have been eagerly sought as a form of eventual social security for parents who could expect no institutional care in their old age. The relationships between these forces are complex and uncertain, but it is clear that from approximately 1740 onward Ireland experienced exceptional population growth along with a boom in the economic value of agricultural production, and the broadening cultivation of the potato.

The political aspirations of the Protestant nation did not arise in an eighteenth-century vacuum. On the contrary, they were powerfully fueled by an expanding colonial economy. It was not a backwater which the Protestants wished to take over politically, however benighted conditions might be among the native Irish. The island's economic growth is most readily seen in the expansion of imports and exports (in a period of negligible inflation). Imports rose from about £800,000 in 1700 to over £5 million in 1800. Exports grew from approximately the same 1700 level of £800,000 to nearly £4 million in 1800, and leapt to over £7 million by 1816, as a result of the British need for Irish products during the Napoleonic Wars.[11] A large part of this impressive expansion was the contribution of linen, exports of which had soared from 500,000 yards in 1698 to over 40 million yards in the 1790s. By 1800 linen exports accounted for nearly half of Ireland's total exports. Like wool, linen was a cottage industry and was worked by peasants and small farmers all over Ireland as a cash complement to their agriculture. In the closing years of the seventeenth century a conscious British decision to discourage the Irish woolen industry (codified in an act of 1699) and to encourage Irish linen manufacture (by making it a duty-free import to England from 1696) coincided with the arrival in northern Ireland of French Huguenots skilled in the production of fine linen cloths. By 1770 the northeastern Ulster counties of Down and Antrim were each selling some £400,000 worth of linen a year, followed by Armagh (£280,000), Coleraine (£260,000) and Tyrone (£100,000). The only counties outside of Ulster to sell as much as £100,000 worth of linen a year were Dublin and Louth, both in eastern Leinster.

The extraordinary expansion of the linen industry was thus highly localized in the northeast, and it has been argued that its benefits were equally confined to the landlords of that area. Linen has repeatedly been faulted for failing to lay the base for real industrial expansion in Ireland, in contrast to cotton, which transformed England's Midlands, and particularly Lancashire, into a land of steam-powered textile mills in the pattern of the new "factory system." Linen manufacture continued to expand in the nineteenth century (when it became even more localized in the Belfast area), but the world market for linen never really recovered from the impact of cotton as a rival textile, and the profits of cotton manufacture did not extend to Ireland.[12] Linen is an excellent example of an enterprise which flourished in the industrial era, made fortunes for a handful of entrepreneurs, enhanced the affluence of the Protestant magnates, and supplemented the livelihood of many small farmers, but did not, ultimately, provide a base for enduring prosperity or capital accumulation.

Much the same could be said of the other chief commercial enterprises of eighteenth-century Ireland. Most of them were associated with provisioning, the preparation and sale of preserved food, principally butter and barreled beef. In this area it was the south, rather than the north, which was preeminent. The Munster ports of Cork and Kinsale lay along the track of the growing North Atlantic commerce. French as well as English ships found it easy and economical to provision themselves in southern Ireland, or to load provisions as cargo for export to the American colonies. Irish provisions were generally regarded as cheaper, rather than as superior, in quality. From the 1780s onward, grain too became a significant Irish export, and exports of grain to England played a role in England's replacement of the American colonies as the chief market for Irish foodstuffs.

Despite the large volume of bog, mountain, and other unproductive land, Ireland is well-suited to food production and is today a major supplier of the British and European table. But as we have seen, population was rising rapidly, along with exports. Without increases in productivity resulting from more efficient agriculture and manufacture these parallel tendencies had to lead eventually to a lower standard of living for the mass of the population. The potato was, in a sense, the major innovation in Irish agriculture, and for a time—perhaps as long as a century—the potato helped to forestall what might almost be seen as an inevitable crisis. The English need for Irish produce during the Napoleonic Wars further masked this underlying crisis by creating the appearance of impressive economic growth.

The sustained failure of the potato crops from 1845 onward merely unhinged what had long been developing into a dangerously precarious structure.

Eighteenth-century Ireland was, in many respects, a flourishing place. Landlords prospered, their incomes increasing and making possible such luxuries as the Georgian country houses which, in various states of grandeur or disrepair still embellish the countryside. Castletown, the magnificent house in County Kildare built by William Connolly (1662–1729), entrepreneur and Speaker of the Irish House of Commons, is the most celebrated example, but there are dozens of others. Not all of the wealth went for extravagant houses and a self-indulgent life inside, and around, them. Some of the revenues were plowed back into "capital improvements" that produced lateral benefits for others. The earl of Grandison, for instance, about 1752, settled a colony of weavers from Ulster on his estate at Dromona, County Waterford, and built two well-designed villages for them: Villierstown and Mount Stuart.[13] Thomas Vesey laid out a small model town for his tenants at Abbeyleix, as did the earl of Aldborough for weavers at Stratford-on-Slaney in County Wicklow.[14] But, for the most part, the disposable wealth of the rich enhanced their own worldly lives without contributing more than marginally to the productive capacity of the country at large, or the quality of life of the mass of its inhabitants. The people in "the big houses" provided employment for architects, masons, glaziers, silversmiths, dancing masters, and the like (many of whom came from England or the Continent), but the work of those employees did not, in turn, raise the island's ability to sustain its growing population.

Perhaps the most flagrant form of economic self-indulgence was not the living of a sybaritic life at Castletown, or some other palatial country seat, but absenteeism in Dublin (where society increasingly resorted, built town houses, and capered), or more commonly, England and abroad. Habitual absence from one's property dramatized one's irrelevance to the country economy. If life in a semi-feudal so-

ciety went on *without* the landlord as well—or as badly—as
it went on *with* him, what necessary role did he play in the
system? Why was a tenant obliged to pay rent to him
through time everlasting? The most primitive means of
claiming land is by occupying it. Wherever right to possession is in serious question, long or frequent absence may
serve to undermine this claim. The landlord's claim was
usually strengthened by his visibility and by his concern
for the affairs and lives of his tenants and all who were dependent upon him. Habitually absent, he could come to
seem a remittance man, a rentier, the purely passive recipient of altogether unearned (and possibly undeserved?)
rents and profits.

Remittances of rent to absentees amounted to about
£100,000 in 1698, out of a total landed rent-roll of about
£1.3 million. By the 1720s the rent roll had increased to
something over £1.6 million, but remittances to absentees
may have jumped to £300,000, or between a fifth and sixth
of all landed income.[15] One authority argues that although
the total remittances to absentees doubled between 1720
and 1780, their proportion of total rental income declined,
because rental income tripled in the same period.[16] But in
any event, the absentee was merely the most visible symbol
of Irish economic disorder, and not its underlying cause.

The eighteenth century saw not only the zenith of Protestant privilege and affluence in Ireland, but the beginnings
of its decline. By the end of the century Protestants had lost
their near monopoly of wealth. The constraints of the penal
laws upon Catholic ownership and inheritance of land had
inspired many to enter trade. In the coastal towns of the
south and west, particularly, Catholic families began to establish themselves in the provisioning trade, dry goods,
moneylending, and other urban arts. The Roches of Limerick were preeminent, and some Catholic merchant families
had offshoots extending to the ports of France, Spain, and
even South America. When Edward Byrne, a wealthy merchant, died in 1792 he left an estate of £400,000.[17] That was
a spectacular rise for a member of a family which, accord-

ing to a survey of 1664, occupied sixty-three houses in County Dublin, only three of which had more than one hearth.[18] Another parvenu of the same stamp was John Keogh, a late eighteenth-century Dublin tradesman who became one of the leading lights of the Catholic Committee.

The apex of the social pyramid in Catholic Ireland was slowly changing. The fugitive bishops and the handful of harried Catholic nobles were now being joined by a stream of Catholic entrepreneurs, businessmen, and professionals. Catholic *noveau riche* were naturally eager to acquire the security and social cachet which only land could confer and as noted above, an act of 1778 repealed those sections of the Popery Act of 1704 which obstructed Catholic landholding and inheritance. At least some of the sentiment favoring this repeal came from Protestant landlords who saw it as a means of driving up the price and value of their holdings.

Despite the bloodbath of 1798 and the subsequent Act of Union, the eighteenth century closed on a Catholic Ireland which was no longer prostrate and defeated. Particular Catholics were beginning to acquire wealth, land, and self-esteem, all prerequisites to the reemergence of a strong leadership. Furthermore, their religion was no longer the object of universal English contempt, as it had been a century before. The wild anticlericalism and atheism of the French Revolution had given English statesmen a grudging appreciation for the conservative virtues of the Catholic Irish clergy who were nothing if not enemies of revolution. In 1795 there was established with government support the Royal College of St. Patrick at Maynooth (just west of Dublin), an official seminary for the education of Catholic clergy in Ireland.

Economic and religious disabilities were slowly being removed. The growth of democratic ideas was making increasingly difficult the defense of the most arbitrary forms of privilege, widespread though they were. But therein lay the contradiction, for Ireland was, in toto, a monstrous case of arbitrary privilege. It was owned, exploited, and controlled by an exogenous minority. The Act of Union in 1800 transferred the political focus of that control to the West-minster Parliament in England, but there was very little reason to believe that it would be exercised in a novel spirit of generosity or compassion for the subject population. Thus Ireland entered the nineteenth century as something of an anomaly: an island whose arrangements, whose society was in growing contradiction with the changing ideas of what was fair and just. What remained to be seen was whether, or how, this contradiction would be resolved, and with what explosive consequences.

6

CATHOLIC IRELAND
RESURGENT: THE
NINETEENTH CENTURY

T HIS CHAPTER, and the one which follows, summarize the
history of Ireland from the Act of Union in 1800 to, more
or less, the present day. There is a natural tendency for
the story to become more detailed as it approaches the
present. Yesterday's events strike us as more momentous
than those which occurred a millennium ago. And there is
so much more that we can find out about yesterday, because the records are abundant, and include modern won-
ders such as photographs, movies, and sound recordings.
Volumes have been written about this dramatic, colorful,
and in some ways tragic two centuries, and it would require at least several hundred pages to construct a narra-
tive that did justice to the principal developments, events,
and personages.

The aim of these two chapters is more modest. It is not
to tell the full story, but rather to show how the recent and
distant pasts connect, and how patterns and forces long established in Ireland expressed themselves in the nineteenth
and twentieth centuries. Thus a conscious effort has been
made to concentrate on what seem the most significant
tendencies, and to minimize detail that in this context de-
tracts from the central purpose. Readers who seek a fuller
account will find suggestions in the bibliography.

event better expresses the joint, or seam, between an earlier Ireland and the Ireland of our day than the Act of Union. In one sense it was the high-water mark of the conquest of Ireland which had been begun in the twelfth century and completed in the seventeenth. As Wales had been "united" with England in 1536 (more than two hundred years after its conquest by Edward I), and Scotland had been "united" with England and Wales in 1707, so Ireland was finally constitutionally absorbed into the United Kingdom in 1800. (The event had been foreshadowed during the Protectorate of Oliver Cromwell, 1654–1658, when the union of England, Scotland, and Ireland was promulgated by the paper constitution called the Instrument of Government. It was reversed at the Restoration of Charles II in 1660.) In another sense, however, it institutionalized—one might say "constitutionalized"—the single element of the Anglo-Irish relationship that would preoccupy the following two centuries: political domination.

The Act of Union assumed that Ireland, like Scotland and Wales, was basically assimilable to England, despite the manifestly greater difficulties of ruling it. It set the political framework in which, and against which, modern Ireland emerged. We have already seen how the *social* framework evolved in the sixteenth and seventeenth centuries to produce a Protestant Anglo-Scottish ascendancy. The Act of Union ended the political autonomy this ascendancy had achieved in 1782 and transferred political power over Ireland to a Union Parliament at Westminster. The 100 elected Irish MP's, regardless of who they were, and what were their politics, could never account for more than a sixth of the total legislature. The great bulk of Irish matters would thus be disposed of by an assembly in which Irish representation was merely symbolic.

The Union abolished the Irish Parliament and substituted for it Irish representation at Westminster. Exactly 100 Irish-elected MP's were to sit in a House of Commons of 658 members, while 28 Irish peers and 4 bishops (from the Protestant Church of Ireland) were given places in a

newly expanded House of Lords. The Church of England
and the Church of Ireland were united. Free trade was enacted between the two countries, with certain qualifications. The financial systems of the two countries were left
distinct, but for a period of twenty years it was stipulated
that Ireland should contribute two-seventeenths of the total
expenditure of the United Kingdom. This was not an unrea-
sonable proportion, given the respective size and strength
of the two economies, but it failed to anticipate that the
first fifteen of the next twenty years would see England
locked in a desperate and expensive war with Napoleonic
France. As a result the Union eventually imposed upon Ireland an unrealistic share of this extraordinary financial
burden.

On the whole implementation of the Union went smoothly,
although a disconcerting note was struck by Robert Emmet, a Protestant patriot who lead an abortive insurrection
of United Irishmen in Dublin in 1803. The rising was easily
quashed, and historians have generally dismissed it as a
scuffle with little support or hope of success. But faced with
condemnation to death as a traitor, Emmet left his mark
with a stirring oration in the dock. Versions of the speech
differ, but basically, Emmet denied that in seeking French
support for his insurrection, he had intended to "put our
country under the dominion of a power which has been the
enemy of freedom in every part of the globe. Connection
with France was, indeed, intended, but only as far as mu-
tual interest would sanction or require. Were they to assume any authority inconsistent with the purest independence, it would be the signal for their destruction."[1] Emmet
knew the futility of such an argument in court. He concluded with a disquisition upon his imminent death:

My race is run—the grave opens to receive me, and I sink into its
bosom. I have but one request to ask at my departure from this
world, it is the charity of its silence. Let no man write my epitaph; for as no man who knows my motives dare now vindicate
them, let not prejudice or ignorance asperse them. Let them rest
in obscurity and peace, my memory be left in oblivion, and my

tomb remain uninscribed, until other times and other men can do justice to my character. When my country takes her place among the nations of the earth, *then*, and not till then, let my epitaph be written.[2]

These brave words have a ring of melodrama about them to the modern ear, but they have had immense appeal for generations of Irish patriots who have found enduring inspiration in Emmet's example and rhetoric. Like Emmet, they have usually had to assume the failure of their venture, and their own demise. And yet, an inner bitterness has driven them on, offering no consolation but the hope of posthumous triumph. Every insurrection, rising, conspiracy, and rebellion would be defeated until an eventual, unpredictable success. That single victory would transform every previous effort, however squalid or ludicrous, into a noble chapter of the long struggle for national freedom. Emmet's rising was one of many which would be redeemed by that retrospective grace.

The Union had been one element of William Pitt's bifocal policy for dealing with an Ireland that seemed perpetually on the brink of revolution. The other element was Catholic emancipation: the removal of the remaining, principally political, disabilities on the Catholic citizens of the new "United Kingdom." English antipopery reached a zenith in the early eighteenth century. By 1800 it was an anachronism, a tradition which had outlived its usefulness and ceased to correspond to objective reality. To the sophisticated Pitt, it was much more important to respond to the grievances of British and Irish Catholics than leave them unattended, like so much gunpowder, to be ignited at will by an incendiary France.

There were those, however, with King George III among them, who saw Catholic emancipation as distasteful, dangerous, and unnecessary. In 1807 when Arthur Wellesley, the future duke of Wellington, was chief secretary for Ireland he wrote caustically to London: "We have no strength here but our army. Ireland, in a view to military operations, must be considered as an enemy's country."[3] As long as it could be dominated by military force, there was no compelling need to make disagreeable concessions to its Catholic inhabitants, and this ungenerous view was even easier to defend after France had been thoroughly defeated in the campaigns of 1812–1815. Thus the Catholic emancipation, intended by Pitt to accompany the Act of Union, proved impossible to achieve for many years thereafter, a fact interpreted as betrayal by those Irish Catholics who had been persuaded to support the Act of Union.

When Catholic emancipation was finally obtained, or rather, when the removal of historic disabilities was finally completed, it was the result of an unprecedented campaign and mass movement. The demand did not disappear in the first two decades after the Union, but Catholic leaders pursued it though a casual process of negotiation with the British government. The government sought control, or at least influence, over the appointment of Catholic bishops and parish priests, and also state provision for the payment of the Catholic clergy.[4] These were familiar arrangements between Church and State in other Catholic countries. Why not in Ireland? Catholic opinion was divided on the matter. Was it a prudent, even advantageous alteration of the Church, or a craven surrender of all that was most sacred? The balance was tipped in the 1820s by Daniel O'Connell, a prospering Catholic lawyer from County Kerry.

O'Connell had gone through a radical stage in his youth, but the trauma of Robert Emmet's 1803 rising sent him scurrying back to join the forces of law and order. A successful barrister by 1798, O'Connell became involved with the Catholic Committee and was soon known for his vigorous opposition to any concessions of influence over the Catholic Church to the British government. In this he was opposed by most of the Catholic aristocracy and the great Protestant reformer, Henry Grattan, who saw compromise as the path of reason. The slowness of the British government to reward the advocates of compromise gradually strengthened O'Connell's hand, as more Catholics came to despair of emancipation in any acceptable form from a

British government not coerced into offering it. Almost single-handedly, O'Connell transformed the quest of a privileged few into a struggle of the Catholic masses. The polite dialogue between the Catholic aristocracy and the ecclesiastical hierarchy on the one hand, and the British government on the other, was slowly replaced by the clamorous demands of six million Catholics.

To appreciate O'Connell's campaign, it is necessary to understand something of the Irish political system. The Act of Union moved Irish representation from a Dublin Parliament to Westminster, and it reduced the number of elected members of the House of Commons from some 300 to exactly 100. This reduced the number of elections, or rather, places in which and for which elections were held, but it did not basically alter the size or nature of the electorate. The electoral system which had grown up in Ireland was similar to that in England, with members of Parliament elected from the counties, on a uniform county franchise, and other members elected from special parliamentary towns or boroughs on a franchise that varied from town to town. Borough elections were routinely controlled by wealthy local members of the aristocracy, or by prominent town merchants, but in county elections there was at least the possibility of a real contest and a popular choice. The Catholic Relief Act of 1793 extended to Catholics in the counties, but not the boroughs, the same voting rights as had traditionally been enjoyed by Protestants. This was the "forty-shilling freehold" franchise, and it meant that adult males who owned property worth forty shillings a year in rent were eligible to cast a vote. This was a very small amount of property (a man would have needed about fifty times that amount of annual income, or about £100, to live as a modest gentleman in early nineteenth-century Ireland). By 1829 there were approximately 100,000 voters, of whom some 80,000 were Catholic 40-shilling freeholders added to the electoral roles by the act of 1793. Since they could not vote for Catholics to represent them, and since there was no secret ballot with which they could protect themselves from the threats of their generally Protestant landlords, the new Catholic electors of 1793 had virtually no impact upon the nature of Irish representation, either before or after the Act of Union. It was this anachronistic situation Daniel O'Connell sought to change.

Sidestepping the conservative hierarchy of the Catholic Church, which was inclined to view the English government as a bulwark against French atheism and radicalism, O'Connell in 1823 founded his own organization, the Catholic Association. Its objective was to use constitutional means to remove the remaining disabilities on Irish Catholics, the most important of which was the prohibition against sitting in Parliament. In 1824 associate membership was opened to anyone who contributed a penny a month in dues, a rate which brought membership within the reach of hundreds of thousands of people. An elaborate volunteer organization was set up to promote payment of this "Catholic rent" in every corner of the country. The movement grew like wildfire in Leinster and Munster, with smaller receipts in Connaught, and distinctly lean pickings in Ulster.[5] The response among the Irish population to O'Connell's campaign was staggering and unprecedented. O'Connell was rapidly accepted as a man of destiny, the long-awaited deliverer of Irish Catholics from the tyranny of British Protestantism. When the government of Lord Liverpool (itself split on the desirability of Catholic emancipation) introduced legislation in 1825 to outlaw the Catholic Association, O'Connell avoided dissolution by refounding his movement as the *New* Catholic Association.

From 1826 the association began to use its wealth and influence in behalf of pro-emancipation candidates for Parliament. Organizing the previously submissive forty-shilling Catholic freeholders, early successes were achieved in Waterford, Louth, Monaghan, and Westmeath.[6] Those contests proved the prelude to one of the most dramatic elections in modern Irish history. When, in June 1828 the popular and, in fact, pro-Catholic MP William Vesey-Fitzgerald was forced to stand for reelection in County Clare, because of his appointment to a cabinet post, O'Connell was prevailed upon to oppose him. It was a contest between "the emancipator," as O'Connell had come to be called, and a hapless supporter of the duke of Wellington's government, which opposed emancipation. O'Connell won handily and defied the government to deny him his rightfully acquired seat in the House of Commons.

Fearing rebellion, the government relented and introduced an act of emancipation which the king grudgingly signed in early 1829. The act permitted Catholics to hold all offices of state except that of regent, lord chancellor of Ireland or England, or lord lieutenant of Ireland. It included a number of minor restrictions on the practice of Catholicism, but these were ignored in practice from the outset. More significantly, O'Connell agreed to dissolve the Catholic Association and tacitly accepted a bill disenfranching the forty-shilling freeholders by raising the county property qualification fivefold to £10. The ingenious effect of this amendment was to reduce the Irish electorate from over 100,000 voters (in a population of nearly eight million) to around 16,000. The immediate price of the admission of Catholics to political life was thus the denial of the vote to tens of thousands of small-farmer Protestants and Catholics who had previously enjoyed it. A religious gate had opened, but an economic one had closed.

O'Connell's victory, in one sense, produced a betrayal of the very rank and file which had made it possible. Revolutions are not made without sacrifice, and the elimination of the 40-shilling freeholder was seen by some as a necessary, justifiable, and temporary concession in the long struggle against British domination. In any case the campaign reinforced sectarian division in Ireland. The United Irishmen of the eighteenth century had sought to join Catholic and Protestant Irish together in the struggle against Britain. Though it was not his specific wish, O'Connell set Protestant and Catholic against one another, adding highly combustible fuel to the fires of the Orange Order and the "Brunswick Clubs," as some of the Protestant groups opposed to emancipation had called themselves. After O'Connell, Irish nationalist movements were emphatically Catholic. Emancipation's most immediate benefit was to enhance the upward mobility of a small Catholic middle class. But the campaign by which emancipation was achieved, the mass movement with a charismatic leader skilfully manipulating and shaping the bitterness of centuries, was an influential precedent and a harbinger of things to come.

The Act of Union and the campaign for Emancipation established much of the *political* framework of modern Ireland. The cluster of events called "The Famine" played an equally momentous role in determining the *social* framework. No event of modern Irish history is so diffuse or impenetrable. Had the famine not occurred, we should probably remember the 1830s and 1840s as a period of gradual reform, a period of marked "modernization" within an island which retained harsh extremes of privilege and deprivation. In the administration of justice, for instance, important reforms were made between 1835 and 1840 while O'Connell was restively allied with the Whig government of Lord Melbourne and Thomas Drummond was undersecretary for Ireland.[7] Catholics were appointed to responsible positions in the legal system and a sincere effort was made to encourage the rendering of impartial justice.[8] In matters of public health the government was far more willing to take a strong role in Ireland than in England, where a long tradition of handling such matters though local authorities intervened. On the eve of the famine there were over 600 state-aided public dispensaries spread about Ireland, and there had been significant recent progress in government provision of fever hospitals and asylums for the deranged.[8]

The most striking area of state provision of public services was elementary education. Sectarian rivalry was intense in the first three decades of the century as the Catholic Church emerged from the shackles of the penal laws and launched an educational counteroffensive. Protestant societies—one with the inspired name of the "Society for the

Discountenancing of Vice"—fought back, hoping to maintain the hegemony for Protestant doctrine which the penal laws had previously assured. Efforts at nondenominational education, the most celebrated of which was the Kildare Place Society founded in 1811, tended to fall victim to the acute suspicions of one side or the other. In 1831 a Whig government announced plans for a National Board of Education which was to administer a centralized system of nondenominational elementary education. A large section of the Church of Ireland turned its back on the National Board and the increasingly evangelical Presbyterians of Ulster bargained for concessions as a result of which "by the mid-century, the Presbyterians were receiving State aid for what was, de facto, virtually a self-contained system of denominational [i.e., Presbyterian] schools."[9]

The Catholics too withdrew gradually from cooperation with the National Board, yet by 1849 there were more than 4,300 elementary schools with nearly half a million pupils operating under the scheme. The education provided included no Irish history, language, or literature. The prescribed texts were "uncontroversial and inexpensive, but dull and unimaginative. Large chunks of platitudes on polite behaviour . . . represented a turgid amalgam of social ethics and political docility. In this way it was hoped to inculcate a loyalty to the State and to the status quo."[10] Despite this insensitivity to Irish culture and tradition the years preceding the famine were not ones of neglect or stagnation, but saw English statesmen struggling to adapt English solutions and English institutions to Irish conditions. On the other hand they were not years which saw an attempt to shake or revise the deeply imbedded privileges which were the legacy of the Tudor–Stuart conquest and the foundation of the Protestant position.

The social and economic structure of Ireland was static, but demographic change was subjecting it to unprecedented forces. After centuries of only gradual growth, between 1780 and 1821 the population of Ireland may have been increasing at a rate as high as 17 percent in each decade. From 1821 to 1831 it slowed slightly (to 15 percent per decade), and from 1831 to 1841, more dramatically (to 5.25 percent). Nevertheless between 1821 and 1841 the population grew from 6.1 million to over 8 million. The 1841 census showed that "about seventy per cent of the rural population was either landless or dependent on inadequate holdings of less than five acres."[11] In the wealthier, less densely populated eastern counties this percentage of countrymen with tiny land holdings was much lower, while in a poor and "congested" (i.e., crowded) western county like Mayo, it was nearly 85 percent.

As noted in the previous chapter, cultivation of the potato had been increased dramatically to help feed this burgeoning population. The potato was an efficient subsistence crop and much of the "new" population, in the west and south of the island, was sustained by the potatoes grown on parcels of land so small that the occupants would have starved had they relied on any other crop. Some of this added population was channeled out of Ireland by emigration, a marked phenomenon long before the famine. In the period 1780 to 1845 approximately 1.75 million people left the island. The exodus to North America alone averaged over 30,000 a year between 1815 and 1845, but an equally substantial outflow was directed to Great Britain, where thousands of Irish joined the unskilled and semiskilled laborers of London and the new industrial regions of Clyde and Merseyside.

Our picture of Ireland on the eve of the famine is one of a society in delicate equilibrium. The greater part of the island's landed wealth was beyond the reach of the greater part of its population. The sedulous efforts at "reform" could not, and did not, touch this basic structural fact. On the margin of the society (beyond the generally comfortable world of the great estates) a rapidly growing population was either fleeing the island in hope of greater opportunity elsewhere, or being sustained within Ireland by the fickle grace of the monoculture Potato. In retrospect one can see that the exposure to disaster was abundant, and the wonder is not that a famine occurred, but rather that it did not occur before 1846. The potato was a slender reed upon which to lean, and the potato crop failed, partially or totally, fourteen times between 1816 and 1842.[12] But no government of the time had the means or the disposition to correct so profound a fault in a whole island's economy, much less the full realization that it existed.

The Great Famine had its immediate origins on the eastern seaboard of the United States and Canada, where potato crops were ravaged by blight in 1842. In August 1845 the disease made its first European appearance in the south of England, and by September it had crossed to Waterford and Wexford from which it spread to about half of the island.[13] By the time it reached Ireland nearly one-sixth of the season's potato crop had already been dug, and thus escaped damage. It was not until 1846 that the blight made a serious impact. The crop of that year was almost a total loss. Some nine to ten million tons of potatoes were destroyed, the anticipated production of approximately 1.5 million acres of land. By comparison, approximately 2.5 million acres had been planted in 1841. The blight abated in 1847, but the trauma of the previous season had lead to complete demoralization and consumption for food of the "seed" potatoes which were necessary to plant a new crop. Only 284,000 acres were planted in potatoes, and they yielded only 2 million tons. The year 1848 saw the number of acres sown nearly triple to 743,000, but a cold, wet growing season produced a yield per acre almost half that of the previous year (30 barrels compared to 57), so that real recovery began only in 1849.[14] There was a small decrease in the acreage sown with potatoes that year, but the yield was over 4 million tons, a 12 percent improvement over 1848.

The blight was narrow, in that its impact was upon potatoes alone, but protracted, in that it took nearly five years for the potato culture to return to its former vigor. In the meantime, Ireland had suffered a human disaster of terrible and unprecedented proportions. The blight struck precisely the poorest members of the population, quite simply, destroying the food upon which they depended. The substantial harvests of cereals and livestock, though unaffected by the potato blight, were generally in the possession of the affluent. Though some of it was charitably given away, most of it went to market in England and elsewhere, in the usual way. The Conservative government of Sir Robert Peel began an ambitious system of public "food depots," which forestalled much suffering in 1846. But Peel and his party were forced from office later that year and the Whig government of Lord John Russell which succeeded was dominated by the doctrine of *laissez-faire*.

Since the poor had not the money to buy alternative food, and it was thought immoral for the government to give away food or money, a system of public works was established in which the poor were meant to earn the money with which to buy the needed food. The costs of this assistance were to fall entirely on the parish taxes, or "rates," which in most cases meant the landlords, and in badly affected regions of the county the landlords were already suffering from the inability of their tenants to pay their customary rents. Between September and December 1846 the numbers dependent upon this form of assistance jumped from 30,000 to half a million. The system of relief collapsed under this pressure and was replaced in 1847 by a combination of soup kitchens and workhouses. The measures adopted were pathetically inadequate to the scale of the unfolding disaster, and much of the bitterness the famine engendered resulted from the callous disregard for Irish life and suffering which those measures betrayed.

The blight of the potato triggered a famine, a chronic scarcity of food as well as the money necessary to buy it. The result was not so much outright starvation as chronic and widespread malnutrition. In its wake marched virulent disease: typhus, relapsing fever, dysentery, and scurvy. It is probable that between 1845 and 1851 a million people died who would not otherwise have done so. Another million left the country for destinations in Britain and abroad (see Chapter 8). There is no way to evaluate scientifically the suffering of either those who stayed, or those who left. Each group faced dreadful trials, and in each a fortunate few found for themselves or their offspring a better life. The whole shape of Ireland was drastically altered by the event, and if the Protestant ascendancy remained, for the time being, solidly in control of the land, its members none the less lost part of the legitimacy of their title. The small— mainly Catholic—landholders were all but purged from the island. In 1841 there were more than 310,000 holdings of from one to five acres but by 1851 there were only 88,000, and by 1910, only 62,000.[15] By contrast, holdings of over fifteen acres increased modestly, and holdings over thirty acres increased dramatically.

The famine not only produced suffering, death, and emigration; it also effected a profound consolidation of landholdings. The monoculture potato patch became the exception rather than the rule. Larger farms tended to concentrate on cereals, especially oats, and also meadow for grazing cattle. Tillage reached its maximum extent in 1851 and thereafter gave way to increased emphasis on grazing. The value of livestock on Irish farms actually increased by 38 percent from 1841 to 1852 as the country turned on the awful hinge of the famine toward a more productive, and efficient, agriculture. A drastically reduced population "not only maintained, but actually increased the area under cultivation."[16] Consolidation produced the abiding institution of modern Irish agriculture—the small family farm. It was probably already established in the eastern counties, but the famine introduced it to the more conservative west.

With the almost obsessive concern to conserve the family farm as a viable unit of production came the abrupt rise of the average age of marriage as children were denied marriage portions of farm land. Between 1845 and 1914 the average age of marriage rose from 25 to 33 for males and from 21 to 28 for females. New family units could *not* be frivolously formed as they had been in the pre-famine days of the prolific potato. The desires of individual family members had now to be ruthlessly subordinated to the need to maintain the unit of production.[17] The typical small family farm was a Catholic farm, except in Ulster, where it was typically Protestant. The small family farmer, even if he was a tenant rather than a freeholder, posed a slightly different problem for the Protestant ascendancy, from that posed by the hordes of pre-famine cottiers. He was a man with a stake in the land, rather than a cowed dependent, and multiplied thousands of times over, he provided the beginning of a Catholic rural middle class which aspired to ownership and landed wealth.

The famine for a time eclipsed the growth of nationalist sentiment. Until his death on May 15, 1847, Daniel O'Connell remained the most celebrated exponent of the movement for constitutional separation of Ireland from England. The great "emancipator" of the 1820s had turned his attention in the 1830s to the cause of Repeal, the undoing of the Act of Union and the return to Ireland of the powers of government which had been transferred to Westminster in 1800. But how was such a cause to be furthered in the political framework which had emerged? Except for public disorder and rebellion, the only channel of influence lay in the Irish Parliamentary representation at Westminster. As a member of the Union Parliament O'Connell became a politician, struggling to build up a loyal following of Irish MP's whose votes on English domestic issues could be traded to whichever English political party (Whig or Tory) offered the most to Ireland, as O'Connell perceived it. From 1835 to 1841 O'Connell and his followers were allied to the Whigs, but although a number of reforms were achieved, there was no dramatic concession to nationalist objectives. As a protest against the inadequacy of Whig policy toward Ireland, O'Connell founded in 1840 the Loyal National Repeal Association, largely on the model of his immensely successful Catholic Association of earlier days.

The Repeal campaign failed to fire the popular imagination, and the Repealers won only 17 of the more than 100 parliamentary seats in the general election of 1841.[18] To the extent that the movement stayed alive it was the work of

new, young, and more radical idealists associated with a
newspaper called *The Nation,* which began publication in
1842. Its founders were Thomas Davis, a Protestant barrister from Dublin, Charles Gavan Duffy, a Catholic from
County Monaghan, and John Blake Dillon, a graduate of
Trinity College and a scion of a middle-class Catholic family of Mayo. *The Nation* struck a tone of idealistic liberal
nationalism. Like the United Irishmen of the 1790s, it
looked forward to a nonsectarian nation in which sovereignty, self-determination, and independence from British
rule would miraculously heal the scars of centuries, and
end socio-religious strife.

Renewed by the fresh wind from *The Nation,* O'Connell's
Repeal campaign picked up momentum in 1843, but the alliance between the hardened, horse-trading politician and
the idealistic young journalists was improbable and uncertain. The movement reached a climax in the fall of 1843
when O'Connell tried to replay the trump card which had
brought him victory in 1829. Through so-called monster
rallies held around the country, he raised the specter of an
island on the verge of revolution. The Tory government of
Sir Robert Peel called O'Connell's bluff, banned the gigantic rally planned at Clontarf outside Dublin in October, and
arrested O'Connell on charges that were eventually
dropped.[19]

This confrontation with Peel drove a wedge between the
young idealists and the aging "Liberator." O'Connell was
prepared to compromise with the British government and
seek more modest, but more obtainable objectives than repeal. The members of Young Ireland, as the idealists came
to be called, regarded Repeal as a nearly holy cause. Thus
the allies drifted apart despite the fact that O'Connell managed to extract a number of reforms from the Conservative
government. The disaffection of Young Ireland was completed in 1846 when the Whigs came back into office in
Britain, aided by an alliance with the O'Connellites. The
potato failures of 1846–47 and the parsimony of the Whigs
in dealing with the horrors that resulted, completed the

discrediting of the Whig–O'Connell alliance among the Young Irelanders. The Repeal Association was fatally divided, and became "simply irrelevant in a famine-stricken land."[20]

When O'Connell died in May 1847, it was left to Young Ireland to point the future directions of the nationalist movement, but there were latent divisions within Young Ireland itself. Thomas Davis and William Smith O'Brien, a Limerick Protestant landlord and MP who was converted to Repeal in 1843, feared social disorder, preached class harmony, and disavowed the radical principles of the contemporary Chartist movement in Britain.[21] A less traditional view was that of James Fintan Lalor, a member of the group who asserted that "the entire soil of a country belongs of right to the entire people of that country and is the rightful property not of any one class but of the nation at large."[22]

The revolution in France in February 1848 gave the radicals like Lalor and John Mitchel the example and the inspiration they needed. Events in Europe once again appeared to portend the collapse of the old order. The radicals in Young Ireland began to reach out to their counterparts in England, the Chartists, whose objectives were largely constitutional and democratic. The British government responded with arrests on charges of sedition. John Mitchel was convicted and sentenced to fourteen years of "transportation" to the prison colony of Australia. In desperation the Young Irelanders attempted an insurrection on the Tipperary–Kilkenny border in late July, but this was easily suppressed and its leaders were sentenced to join Mitchel in Van Dieman's Land. The hopes of liberal nationalists in Ireland suffered much the same fate as befell them in central Europe where German and Italian nationalist ambitions were crushed. Once again bold enterprise failed, and the ruling power prevailed. Both Repeal and Young Ireland collapsed as viable movements, for neither could implement its vision before its followers, confronted with formidable resistance, lost faith in the immediate struggle.

An instructive fact about nationalism in nineteenth-century Ireland is the bewildering variety and pertinacity with which it recurred. Movements in the direction of unity, independence, or some embryonic form of nationhood were crushed with tedious regularity, and yet the germ of the idea endured and, finding hospitable cultures elsewhere, multiplied anew.

The Catholic Church proved to be one of those cultures. The proscribed Church of the masses had survived its trial of several centuries by an almost self-conscious amorphousness and avoidance of institutionality. Unencumbered by wealth-encrusted shrines and a visibly plump, privileged ecclesiastical hierarchy, the Catholic Church escaped in Ireland the anticlericalism which harried it in revolutionary Europe. But by the same token its presence and influence were modest at the beginning of the nineteenth century, and in many parts of Ireland were virtually negligible. The fact that the Protestant Church of Ireland and the various Protestant sects had made only limited progress among the bulk of the population did not mean that there were millions of disciplined, catechized, observing Catholics.[23]

The founding and endowing by the government of a Catholic seminary at Maynooth in 1795, together with the emancipation of 1829 marked the end of an era of subterfuge, and the beginning of one of re-institutionalization. The hierarchy was conservative and closely identified with the wealthy old Catholic families. Not until after the famine did the Church begin to emerge as a coherent force which, even while it resisted the secular ideology of nationalism, provided an engine to advance Catholic identity and unity. A large part of this accomplishment was the work of Paul Cullen, who was educated on the Continent, and from 1831 to 1849 served as the rector of the Irish College in Rome. In 1849 Cullen returned to Ireland to become archbishop of Armagh. He was translated to the archdiocese of Dublin in 1852, became a cardinal in 1866, played a prominent role in the first Vatican Council of 1870, and exercised great influence over the Irish Church until his death in 1878.

Cullen imposed on the Irish Church much of its modern form. Where it might, like other modern churches, have leaned toward Gallicanism, or independence from Rome, Cullen made it Ultramontane, and highly supportive of the papacy. Where it might have continued a cozy, nepotistic liaison with Catholic families of wealth and status, reserving for them the most comfortable and important ecclesiastical sinecures, Cullen demanded talent and efficiency, and was disposed to reward it wherever in society he found it. Although the Church might have supported nationalist movements, Cullen stoutly opposed the involvement of priests in politics, radicalism, and most nationalistic activities. He struggled to diminish state control over education, insisting not only "on building and maintaining, at enormous cost, a Catholic intermediate and university system," but also "a large diocesan seminary at Clonliffe because he disliked being too dependent for the training of his clergy on Maynooth, which up until 1869, at least, remained a state-subsidized institution."[24]

Cullen was more concerned to separate Church from State than to lay the foundations for a Church-dominated State. His antipathy to political involvement was by no means shared by the rest of the hierarchy or the clergy, some of whom were eager to support nationalist movements, and did so; but Cullen's influential aloofness helps, in retrospect, to explain the secularism of the independent Irish State which emerged in the twentieth century.

Under Cullen the Church acquired an institutional presence and force, symbolized by a great wave of Catholic Church building between 1850 and 1870. Critics of the Church have argued that the immense sums of money gathered for new buildings might have been put to better use in financing industrial development or agricultural improvements, but to the churchmen of the time investment in bricks and mortar was a necessary and logical statement; a declaration of the Church's new and irreversible role in Irish society. Cullen was struggling to divorce the Church from British rule, but at the same time, he was implicitly

23. Color print of Irish soldiers on the continent in battle, represent-
ing regiments of Clare, Dillon, and Lally, c.1750.

These are the "Wild Geese" at their most colorful, but looking little
different, in fact, from other mercenary soldiers of the same period.
Some returned to Ireland, but others founded families with Irish
names and traditions in the territories of the continental monarchies
for which they fought.

Slide from National Library of Ireland.

24. The Lisburn and Lambeg volunteers in the Market Square at Lisburn in honor of the Convention of 1782; color print from an original by John Carey.

The volunteers constitute a colorful chapter in the history of Protestant *Irish nationalism. The concept of military struggle for an autonomous Ireland had been fully elaborated before it was taken over and implemented by Catholic nationalists in the late nineteenth, and twentieth centuries.*

Slide from National Library of Ireland.

25 and 26. Caricatures of the Irish emigrant before and after emigration to the United States: published by Sala at Berlin, mid-nineteenth century. "Outward-Bound" (Dublin). "Homeward-Bound" (New York).

The belief in wealth for every man in the New World was ubiquitous during much of the nineteenth century, and not entirely without factual foundation. Thousands of immigrants from Ireland improved their lot, but many thousands of others did not. Still the powerful westward tide of migration flowed on.

Slides from National Library of Ireland.

27. *Recruiting Poster, 1915, issued by the Central Council for the Organisation of Recruiting.*

The Cunard steamship Lusitania *was sunk by a German submarine in May 1915, just off the Old Head of Kinsale in County Cork. It was carrying British and American passengers from New York to Liverpool, and also, very probably (though secretly), munitions. Many of the victims' remains were washed up on the Cork coast. The Irish, like the British, were horrified by this vicious act of war, and British propaganda took advantage of the situation to enlist Irish support for the war against Germany. This effort, like others before and after it, was only modestly successful, for many Irish were indifferent to Britain's plight, or positively rejoiced in it, believing England, not Germany, was Ireland's historic enemy.*

Slide from the National Library of Ireland.

supporting the social (and also the political) order British rule implied.

The Church had been a revolutionary and seditious force in seventeenth- and eighteenth-century Ireland, but it became, at least officially, a conservative force in nineteenth-century Ireland. That the Church's revival had certain long-term, disruptive effects, can hardly be denied, but these ran counter to the desires of Paul Cullen and his successors, who sought to build a strong church in an island whose subordination to England they were not yet prepared to challenge. The census of 1861 was the first to break down the Irish population by religion and it showed that there were some 4.5 million Catholics and only about 1.3 million Protestants, the majority of whom were located in Ulster. It removed any doubt that Catholicism was the predominant religion of Ireland's inhabitants and that the Catholic Church's posture was critical in any reshaping of Irish society.

From at least the late eighteenth century onward there was a growing sense in Britain of Ireland as "a problem." Serious-minded travelers, mainly English and French, probed the island's recesses and left a rich literature of description, commentary, and criticism.[25] The pre-famine decades saw numerous reforms but the famine dramatized the need for a drastic approach to the turmoil and distress of the island. The one thing lacking was agreement as to the underlying nature of the problem. Its visible symptoms were widespread poverty, massive population decline through famine and emigration, and political instability that frequently gave rise to civil disturbances or even armed uprisings.

But what was the heart of the problem, and what could be done about it? To these simple questions the answers were myriad and diverse. The major British efforts to address "the Irish problem" in the second half of the nineteenth century were clustered around three focal issues or institutions: the Church, the land, and the political framework.

Of these, the Church was probably the least important, and also the first to be dealt with seriously. After emancipation, the Protestant Church of Ireland remained a religious irritant in an island where more than three-quarters of the population was nominally Catholic. In terms of parishioners, the Church of Ireland was an anemic thing, for in the 1830s 425 of its 2,000-odd benefices had less than a hundred Protestants in them, 23 had less than ten, 20 less than five, and 40 had none, though, of course, there were parishes with large Protestant populations in Dublin, Ulster, and elsewhere.[26] *The Edinburgh Review* of 1835 pointed out some of the more disturbing anomalies:

There are 157 benefices in Ireland in which there is no resident clergyman, and no service is performed in a place of worship; and there are 41 in which there is also no member of the Established Church. . . . Few, we think, will now maintain, that it is essential for the religious welfare of Ireland that the Established Church of that country should exhibit in long array 2 archbishops, 10 bishops, 139 dignitaries, 187 prebendaries and canons; or that there should be 1,333 parochial incumbents of benefices and 752 curates.[27]

Nevertheless, this Church which served only 693,000 communicants, according to the census of 1861, had a huge historic endowment of Church lands and took more than half a million pounds annually in tithes from a Catholic peasantry that regarded it, at best, as irrelevant, and at worst, as heretical and damnable. At least some of the tithe burden would have fallen on Protestant landlords if the Irish Parliament had not, by an act of 1735, not reversed until 1832, abolished the tithe on pasture lands.[28]

Thus, the endowed and established religion of a distinct but wealthy minority was heavily supported by exactions upon a generally impoverished and antipathetic majority. Demands for reform arose in Protestant as well as Catholic quarters, and in 1833 the Union Parliament passed an Irish Church Temporalities Act which "suppressed ten sees altogether, reduced the revenues of the remaining twelve, and entrusted the surplus [revenue] to a body of commissioners to be applied to ecclesiastical purposes."[29] It did nothing, however, to ease the grievance of tithes, and a so-called tithe war flared from 1831 to 1838, lead by Maynooth-trained Catholic clergy and some veterans of O'Connell's emancipation campaign. The "war" was more correctly an epidemic of acts of peasant resistance, with consequences that were tragic when they were not farcical. The legislative outcome was the Tithe-Rent Charge Act of 1838, which did not eliminate the exaction of tithes, but changed the manner of their collection. Henceforth the landlords were to be responsible for collecting and remitting the tithe, now to be called a rent charge. The mainly Catholic laity were to be spared disagreeable encounters with the alien Protestant clergy or their hated tithe-proctors and in turn, the Church of Ireland became more openly a creature of the Protestant landlord class. Its always feeble claim to Catholicity was in shreds, and the ideological foundations had been laid for its eventual dethronement. By these modest concessions, the Church of Ireland—though it could hardly know it at the time—purchased no more than twenty-five years of peace.

The issue of the Church was finally grasped by the Liberal English prime minister, William E. Gladstone, during his first ministry from 1868 to 1874. Gladstone virtually created the British perception of "the Irish Problem" as a moral obligation on the English public. Others before him had approached it tentatively, but Gladstone was the first modern British politician to see Ireland as more than a distraction. The famine and the later Fenian outrages of 1867 provoked in this brilliant, religious, and moralistic man a sense of Ireland's dangerous and mishapen condition. He announced this revelation in an important speech of December 1867 and when, shortly thereafter, he formed a Liberal government, he set about dealing with the historic grievances.

By proposing the disestablishment and disendowment of the Church of Ireland Gladstone struck at one such grievance, while rallying political support from the English nonconformists who were an important mainstay of the Liberal party, and whose real target was the established and endowed Church of England. The census figures of 1861 undermined one of the pillars of the Church of Ireland's defense of its privileged position: the argument that it was making progress among the benighted. The revelation that the Protestant population was, on the contrary, falling precipitously in certain "missionary areas" underlined the anachronistic nature of the Church.

Gladstone's Irish Church Act was not popular with either the House of Lords or Queen Victoria, but both came reluctantly to see its necessity. The act severed completely the legal connection between Church and State in Ireland, and from January 1, 1871, the Church of Ireland became a voluntary body. Its ecclesiastical law ceased to be part of the law of the land, and its courts ceased to exercise coercive jurisdiction. Perhaps more important, the Church's property was confiscated and vested in a body of commissioners for Irish church temporalities,[30] entrusted with providing funds for the real needs of the Church, appropriate to its modest modern function as the Church of less than one-fifth of the population. The commissioners were also obliged to satisfy the charges on the Exchequer for the Catholic College at Maynooth, and for the Presbyterian clergy of the north, which had been supported by an annual donation from the Crown since 1672. But it was anticipated that the commissioners would receive income from the former Church property substantially in excess of all those requirements, and this excess was to be applied for the relief of poverty.

None of the excess funds was to be used for the endowment of any form of religion, and this was partly due to the determination of Archbishop Cullen not to allow "dual establishment" in place of "disestablishment." Cullen insisted upon "A Free Catholic Church in a Free State" and bitterly resisted all efforts to make the Catholic Church one of several churches in Ireland officially endowed and established, and thus dependent upon the British government.

As a result of the rigorous Disestablishment and Disendowment of the 1869 act, the Catholic and Presbyterian churches were left to seek financial support from their laity, and between 1871 and 1923 about £13 million of what had formerly been Church of Ireland income was applied to the relief of poverty, the encouragement of agriculture and fisheries, and the endowment of higher education by the commissioners for Irish Church Temporalities.[31] Thus ended the three-hundred-year-long privileges of the Protestant Church of Ireland.

The act of 1869 did not destroy Protestantism nor did it materially relieve the tithe-burdened peasantry. Tithes had already been partly secularized by the act of 1838, and the act of 1869 merely redirected payment from the Church itself to the commissioners. Much of what the act accomplished was symbolic, betokening dismantlement of the elaborate legal structure that protected the Protestant ascendancy. Its wealth still intact, the ascendancy lost after 1869 such legitimacy and moral support as its "official" Church could lend. In material terms it lost numerous sinecures for its sons, and in spiritual terms it lost the sense of righteousness that membership in a state Church had afforded.

The revival of the Roman Catholic Church and the eclipse of the Church of Ireland affected only peripheral aspects of "the Irish Problem," for neither change had much impact upon the distribution of wealth. Materialists like James Fintan Lalor wondered what it would profit the Irish to have religious and political freedom if they remained an impoverished tenantry, dependent upon the charity of rich Protestant landlords. The English and Scottish founders of the "dismal science" of economics were more concerned with the low productivity of Irish land than with the ethical question of who owned it. They assumed that if economic growth could be achieved, landlord and tenant alike would benefit. The first legislative approach to the land question, the Encumbered Estates Act of 1849, aspired to revive the famine-crippled agricultural economy. No land-

lords may have starved in the famine, but the precipitous
decline in rent payments bankrupted more than a tenth of
them.[32] Bankrupt landlords were unable to make the improvements required to increase productivity. Charles Wood,
chancellor of the Exchequer in Lord John Russell's Whig
government reasoned that new owners with capital to invest could take over the estates encumbered with liens and
mortgages, and make them thrive. This turnover of owners
was facilitated by the act of 1849, and indeed nearly one-
seventh of the country changed hands within a decade of
that act.

The new owners, however, were not the eager, improving,
English capitalists envisaged by Wood. Over ninety-five
percent of them were Irish, "mainly younger sons of gentry,
solicitors and shopkeepers who did well out of the famine."[33]
Many of the new owners profited from their new purchases,
but more often because they bought cheaply than because
they improved wisely or generously. Some skeptics found
the new landlords more predatory than the old, and unre-
deemed by the occasional aristocratic virtues of magna-
nimity and graciousness. Like the Church act of 1869 the
major consequences were symbolic.

If title to land could be so simply transferred, why might it not
be transferred to the tenant rather than to a new, frequently far
from noble, purchaser? The Encumbered Estates Act played a
significant role in stimulating tenant thought about the structure
of property rights in land, and contributed to the revolution in
historical consciousness which allowed many farmers to be convinced a generation later that they, as the rightful heirs of the
despoiled Celtic landowners and not the landlords, were the legitimate owners of the land, a revelation granted to few as early
as 1849.[34]

A national Tenant League Association was founded in
1850 to achieve the famous "three F's": fair rent, fixity of
tenure (in effect, freedom from arbitrary eviction), and free
sale (the right of a tenant to recover from his successor the
value of any capital improvements he had made on the

leased land), but most of its early adherents were well-to-do eastern grain-farmers, and not until the 1870s did the land question begin to attract mass participation. By that time, Gladstone had urged through Parliament both the Church Disestablishment Act of 1869, and the Irish Land Act of 1870. The Church Act had actually opened the way by providing the means for tenants of Church lands to buy their holdings, with state support. Some 6,000 farmers took advantage of the provisions of the act, and Gladstone was reluctant to extend the implicit radical principle of "expropriation" at a "just" price, to the much more powerful, wealthy, and numerous lay landlords. Instead, he tried in the act of 1870 to procure for Irish tenants greater security, in effect the three F's demanded by the Tenant League Association.

Though a heroic gesture, the act of 1870 was, in its immediate effects, a failure. Under it, tenants were entitled to "compensation for disturbance" if the landlord evicted them arbitrarily. But nonpayment of rent was the most common cause of eviction, and the act offered few remedies or comforts to those unable to pay. Since the landlord retained the right to raise the rent at his pleasure, he could readily force an eviction where he desired one. The principle accomplishment of the 1870 act was that it pointed the way for legislative intervention in property arrangements. The ascendancy's control of the land was being threatened by forces which had yet to take precise and effective form, but which were perceptibly strengthening.

Bad weather and increased competition from North American cereals helped cause an agricultural crisis that began in 1877, and the resulting distress of tenant farmers inspired an alliance to achieve drastic land reform. Its keystone was the Irish Land League, founded in 1879 by Michael Davitt, the 33-year-old offspring of a poor Catholic family of Mayo. The League's initial objectives were to halt evictions, obtain a reduction of rents, and ultimately make tenant farmers the owners of their land; but it was the breadth and depth of the cause, rather than its specific accomplishments, which allowed it to shake the foundations of the Anglo-Irish state. Davitt succeeded in getting Charles Stewart Parnell, the emerging leader of the Irish Home Rule Party at Westminster, to serve as president of the League. Thus the political movement for greater Irish independence was briefly yoked to the land struggle and lent it an unprecedented legitimacy. This was all the more important in view of the fact that 1879–1882 saw numerous acts of violence on the land (especially in Kerry, Mayo, and Galway), and the support of Parnell and the Home Rulers allowed this "land war" to be described by its leaders as an act of national resistance rather than the outburst of Irish criminality, which many Protestants were disposed to see.

The Catholic Church, following the precept of Cardinal Cullen (who had died in 1878), was opposed to these radical activities, but Thomas William Croke, archbishop of Cashel, enthusiastically supported the Land League, reviving the hope that the Church might eventually smile on radical nationalist causes. Even the American Irish were incorporated into the 'Land War,' with Parnell traveling to the United States in 1879 to raise over $300,000 for famine relief and Land League agitation.[35] The British response to the campaign was a mixture of coercion (special parliamentary acts permitting the establishment of martial law) and conciliation (reform acts intended to ameliorate the situation, or at least defuse it).

When Gladstone came back into office in 1880 he introduced a second land act designed to strengthen the tenant rights that had been adumbrated in the act of 1870. It disappointed the Land Leaguers, including Parnell, who was briefly imprisoned in 1882 for his obstructionism; but eventually a deal was struck by which Gladstone agreed to improve the bill and end coercion, while Parnell agreed to support the revised land act. This defection of Parnell from the die-hard ranks ended the Land League's preeminence, for it had already been outlawed as an organization in 1881, and it needed the respectability which members of Parliament could confer. But if the Land League did not instantly transform the tenantry into proprietors, it laid the foundation for a mass movement which could, over several decades, accomplish that ambitious objective, and eventually be put to political and constitutional uses as well. For the Land League created an improbable alliance of poor tenants, scratching out marginal livings, with large tenants whose substantial incomes made them a virtual rural middle class. It drew together country people with town merchants and Catholic professionals from the big city. The plight of "the land" became a rallying cry for diverse groups of Irish people, and under that banner were mobilized men and women whom the constitutional struggle had not yet affected.

Although it was the Liberals under Gladstone who had first warmed to the cause of land reform as a means of treating "the Irish Problem," the Conservatives proved equally willing to pursue that remedy when it served their political purposes. In 1885, the Conservative leader, Lord Salisbury sponsored the Ashbourne Act, a measure which began the massive return of Irish land to Catholic ownership. The act authorized the government to lend tenants who wished to take advantage of it money at four percent interest, over a forty-nine-year repayment period, in order to purchase their farms.[36] Further funds for the same purpose were provided by an act of 1888, and by 1891 some 25,000 tenants had managed to buy out their landlords and exhaust the £10 million of loan money authorized by the two acts. By contrast, only 731 tenants had chosen to purchase land under the less attractive terms of Gladstone's act of 1881.[37]

By 1903 a total of 70,000 tenants had borrowed £23 million of government-provided funds to purchase lands they had previously rented. But the full flood of land transfer was not unleashed until the Wyndham Act of 1903, with corollary legislation in 1909, offered terms too attractive for either landlords or tenants to turn down. Under this legislation the landlord could sell at a price nearly 28 times the annual rent of his land. Any reinvestment in stocks, bonds, or real estate that yielded more than 3.7 percent an-

nually was an improvement over the previous income in
rent. Although some landlords had strong ties to the country, many were delighted to pull up stakes in a troubled
country where agricultural and political crisis seemed
endemic.

To the tenant the Wyndham Act offered the possibility of
buying his land with no down payment, a 3 percent mort-
gage, and 68 and a half years to pay—a most generous arrangement by modern standards, and one which usually
produced lower annual payments than had previously been
payable as rent. Of course many of the tenants had come to
believe that the lands were rightly theirs in the first place,
and had only become the landlord's by a form of colonial
theft. More than 300,000 tenants availed themselves of the
act, and by 1920 some 10 million acres had changed
hands.[38]

The Land Acts, initiated by the Liberals in 1870, but
brought to their conclusion by the Conservatives in 1885
and 1903, envisaged a material solution to "the Irish Problem." They reversed and undid the Tudor and Cromwellian
settlements of Ireland, and recreated an Irish Catholic pro-
prietary class, not by expropriating the Protestant landowners, but by buying them out on generous terms. In effect, the British Parliament employed the wealth of its
flourishing empire to finance this massive righting of ancient wrongs. By the time of the Anglo-Irish War of 1920–
21, the land issue had been essentially resolved. Everywhere but in Ulster where much of the tenantry, as well as
the landlords, were Protestant, Irish Catholics owned Ireland. What we must struggle to discover and understand is
why this expensive, remarkable, and drastic remedy did
not prevent the conflagration of 1916–1922.

In a work entitled *Oceana* published in 1656, the English
writer James Harrington put forward the simple, but influential, political theory that social upheaval is likely to occur when fundamental changes in the distribution of property in a society are not accompanied by consonant
changes in the distribution of political power. Ireland in

the nineteenth century may be a case in point, for it seems likely that the land acts, rather than reducing friction and discontent, focused it on the political arena where Ireland's Catholic majority, much of it in the process of becoming landed, still lacked a meaningful voice in government.

In any case, the second half of the nineteenth century was animated by intense political activity of two rather different kinds. One was internal, constitutional, and public. The other was external, extra-constitutional, and clandestine. The first took the form of the Home Rule Movement; the second that of the Irish Republican Brotherhoood, called the Fenians after the mythic Celtic hero, Finn. The Brotherhoood was founded simultaneously in Dublin and New York in 1858. Its founders were refugees from the 1848 rebellion of Young Ireland, including John Mitchel, who escaped from Tasmania to North America in 1853, and James Stephen, who returned to Ireland from France in 1856. Exiles and emigrants bulked large in the Fenian movement from its inception. Secrecy and the reiterated necessity for armed resistance were its underlying motifs. Nationalists who operated within the framework of the Union were always susceptible to the charge of collaboration with the British, no matter how vocal their patriotism. The Fenians were proof from such suspicions, and the utter purity and simplicity of their objective of armed resistance to British rule appealed to emigrants impatient with the time-consuming maneuvers of parliamentary politics.

The Fenians burst upon the international scene with an attempted invasion of Canada from the United States at Niagara Falls in 1866, and an attempted insurrection (principally at Tallaght and Kenmare) in Ireland in March 1867. When one of the leaders of the 1867 rising, a Galway-born veteran of the American Civil War, Thomas J. Kelly, was arrested in Manchester the following September, three of his partisans attempted to rescue him from a police van, and killed an English policeman in the process. They were arrested, tried, and hanged, and the furor surrounding the execution of these "Manchester martyrs" and the Fenian bombing of Clerkenwell Prison in London later in the same year contributed to W. E. Gladstone's epiphany in 1868 that Ireland deserved England's serious concern.

Fenianism has been called "the first nationwide lay secular society." No previous movement in Irish history, Catholic or Protestant, relied so little on clerical support. Not only was the leadership completely lay, but it came from a distinctly more plebian level than the leadership of any earlier movement.... [It] was the first political movement to channel the energies of agricultural labourers and small farmers, hitherto expressed in ribbonism and faction fighting, into a national organization.[39]

After its spectacular eruption in the 1860s Fenianism went underground for nearly fifty years. It survived as a style, a tradition, almost a legend, but it ceased to have an impact upon events until the avenues of *political* progress had been utterly exhausted. It was really *there*, in the political arena, that the fulcrum of "the Irish Problem" lay.

In the aftermath of the famine, the land bills, and the parliamentary electoral reform acts of 1832, 1867, and 1884 (all of which widened the franchise by lowering property qualifications, and made more rational the distribution of parliamentary seats) Ireland was slowly becoming a Catholic middle-class country. The superstructure of a colonial ascendancy and a colonial government remained, but there was growing hope that the progress of democracy would eventually result in their being dismantled from within. To that end, two things were necessary. First, nationalists had to be elected to the Irish seats in the Union Parliament. Second, the Irish (nationalist) representation at Westminster had to be bound into a political party, and a strategy had to be found for giving it effective leverage in the affairs of the United Kingdom.

From 1870 to 1890 spectacular progress was made in both of these respects. As late as 1868 only 37 of the 105 Irish MP's were Catholic. The swing toward Home Rule, in effect revision of the Union to provide greater self-government for Ireland, began in 1870 with the foundation by

Isaac Butt, a Protestant lawyer and MP, of the Home Government Association. In 1873 it was superseded, at Butt's lead, by the Home Rule League, and in the elections of 1874, professed home rulers won 59 of the 103 Irish seats (the Conservatives won 32, the Liberals 12). The impact of the Home Rulers at Westminster was moderate at first. Butt was himself a conservative politican, and many of the Home Rulers were British Liberals at heart. Gradually, a left wing of militants emerged including two Fenians, Joseph Biggar and John O'Connor Power, and after his election for Meath in 1875, a Protestant landlord named Charles Stewart Parnell.[40]

When Isaac Butt died in 1879 the radicals had an opportunity to widen their influence over the party, and Parnell's shrewd alliance with the Land League caused him to emerge as the leader of the radical wing. The elections of April 1880 gave a slim majority to Parnell's "New Departure" Home Rulers over the Whig Home Rulers, and the following month Parnell was elected chairman of the party.[41] The ten years that followed were, in many respects, Parnell's decade. By his support of the Land League, his money-raising tour to America in 1879, and his six-month sojourn in Kilmainham jail in 1881–82, Parnell managed to free his partisans at Westminster from the suspicion of truckling to the British. He made obstructionism into a political philosophy and walked a thin line between legal and illegal or, at least, unconstitutional activity. But when he was forced to choose, as in February 1881, whether to remain within the Union Parliament, or be ejected for his obstreperous conduct and continue the struggle elsewhere, he chose to remain a constitutionalist, fighting for reform from inside, rather than from without.

In the elections of November 1885 the Home Rulers won a new record for their party of 85 seats (plus one from an Irish district of Liverpool). Because Gladstone's Liberal party had won 335 seats and the Conservatives 249 it appeared that a Liberal–Home Rule coalition could at long last address the problem of the moribund Union of England and Ireland. On December 17 Gladstone's conversion to the cause of Home Rule was announced, but when the first Home Rule Bill was introduced into the House of Commons in June 1886, it was defeated by a vote of 340 to 311. Gladstone had succeeded in leading his party to water, but not in making it drink. The party's unity had disintegrated over the controversial question of Home Rule, with more than 90 party members voting against their own government's Home Rule bill. Ireland was too emotionally charged an issue for the Liberal rank and file to vote as Gladstone instructed them. The Conservatives had shown some flexibility on Ireland *prior* to 1886, but when Gladstone grasped the nettle of Home Rule, the Conservatives were swift and Machiavellian in their exploitation of the resulting turmoil among their Liberal opponents. Home Rule was readily portrayed as a cowardly surrender of imperial glory, and a betrayal of the loyal, virtuous, industrious Protestants in Ireland, especially Ulster.

When the defeat of the bill forced another election, the Home Rulers retained their 85 seats, but the Conservatives won 316 seats, many at the expense of the Liberals who were divided into 191 pro-Home Rulers and 78 anti-Home Rulers. Clearly the hope of a successful bill had been illusory. Parnell was forced to do business with the new Conservative government of Lord Salisbury from which there was no hope of Home Rule, although it was prepared to consider reform in other areas.

Like O'Connell, Parnell was a hero of gigantic proportions to much of the Irish electorate, while a monstrous villain to much of England. The latter view was given currency when in 1887 the *Times* of London published a letter, supposedly written by Parnell in 1882, which revealed that he had condoned the assassination in that year of Lord Frederick Cavendish, the new chief secretary for Ireland and his undersecretary, T. H. Burke. These were the infamous Phoenix Park murders, carried out by terrorists as the two Englishmen strolled in broad daylight through the beautiful Dublin park surrounding the vice-regal lodge. Parnell denied that the letter was his, or that it expressed his sentiments at the time. A commission appointed to examine the charges against Parnell found in early 1889 that the *Times* letter was almost certainly a forgery, purchased by the *Times* from an unsavoury Dublin character named Richard Pigott. Parnell was vindicated, but his vulnerability to English opprobrium was demonstrated by the affair.

The next such attack upon him was one he could not survive. It turned into a cause célèbre and one of the great set-pieces of Victorian moral drama. Parnell was unmarried, but had been living for some years with Mrs. Katharine O'Shea, the estranged wife of a former member of the Home Rule party, Captain William O'Shea. In an age in which divorce without scandal was almost impossible, the arrangement was one of convenience to all parties, including Captain O'Shea. In December 1889, however, O'Shea sued his wife for divorce and named Parnell as co-respondent. At first it seemed merely another attempt at libel in the manner of the *Times* letter of 1887, but when Parnell was unable to deny the charge, the political climate turned suddenly nasty. Parnell's enemies converged in the offensive against him. The Catholic hierarchy in Ireland, still predominantly conservative, could hardly resist gloating over the clay feet of the Protestant idol. More to the point, Gladstone found the nonconformist (that is, non-Church of England) wing of his party suffering a paroxyism of moral outrage over the professed adulterer with whom it was allied in the cause of Home Rule. To placate this straitlaced element of his own party, Gladstone demanded Parnell's ouster from leadership as the price of continued Liberal support for Home Rule. On December 6, 1890, in a stormy meeting of the Home Rule MPs at Westminster, Parnell's fierce bid to stay on as leader was defeated by a vote of 45 to 27.

Only forty-five years old, a brilliant political career in tatters, Parnell spent the following months struggling to vindicate himself in a series of by-elections. But four of the five candidates he supported went down to defeat, and in October 1891 Parnell died of an illness contracted during the fatiguing campaign. The Home Rule party survived him, but it was divided, lacked a hero, and to some extent, had become Gladstone's creature. The Parnellites, and anti-Parnellites, were bitterly split by the memories of 1890, and in the elections of 1892 Parnellites took only 9 of the 80 Home Rule seats.[42]

Parnell's ghost stalked Ireland for years, as readers of James Joyce know. Gladstone made good on his committment to Home Rule, and after elections which returned him to office in 1892 he introduced a second Home Rule bill in Parliament. This bill differed slightly from that of 1886 in providing mechanisms for Irish representation at Westminster on imperial and Irish matters even after a separate Irish Parliament had been established at Dublin. The bill passed the House of Commons but was decisively defeated in the House of Lords. In an increasingly democratic age the Lords stood out as an unregenerate bastion of privilege. Its members were immune from electoral pressure and, to some extent, from public opinion. Most of them were Conservatives, and since 1886 the Conservative party had virtually married the cause of opposition to Home Rule, or "Unionism," as this opposition came to be called. In 1893 Gladstone was eighty-four years old and his fight for Home Rule had led him into a constitutional cul-de-sac. As long as the House of Lords retained the right to block legislation, the prospects for a Home Rule Act were negligible. Gladstone resigned office and the Conservatives took over for another thirteen years.

This was the twilight, and in some ways the death, of Home Rule as a political movement within the constitution of the United Kingdom. Parnell was dead, his memory tarnished, his party divided into quarrelling factions, his English allies, the Liberals, split and forced out of office. Important elements of English society, elements which still enjoyed great powers under the constitution, were passionately determined to prevent the breakup of the Union and the concommitant submergence of northern Irish Protestants into a state dominated by Catholics. This is to say that Home Rule did not come when it might have been effective in placating the grievances of an emerging people. Like Catholic emancipation, which came twenty-nine years after *its* moment, the chances for the success of the measure when finally implemented dwindled rapidly as circumstances continued to change. Home Rule might have been a solution in 1886 or 1893, but by 1914 when it was finally enacted, it was anachronistic, obsolete and, as events were to indicate, foredoomed.

The period from 1800 to 1893 was one of a more-or-less functioning Union, despite efforts to change it. The period after 1893 was one of crisis. The inadequacy of the political framework had been abundantly demonstrated, but what could take its place? What unyielding elements could be forced or persuaded to change? Might the House of Lords be wooed, or circumvented? Might the bitter opposition of Protestant Ulster be appeased, or overcome? Might the Catholic Irish be fattened with prosperity and "West Britonized"? Or, from the Fenian point of view, might the British simply be thrown out at last, with or without their kinsmen in Ulster? These difficult questions were left for the twentieth century to attempt to answer.

7

A NEW STATE ESTABLISHED: TRIUMPHS AND DILEMMAS

I F ONE were to look at Ireland at the turn of the twentieth century, what would one see? For one thing, an island with its population continuing to decline. Between 1891 and 1901 the population dwindled from 3.47 million to 3.22 million, with an estimated net emigration during that decade of almost 400,000 people.[1] By 1901 the island had substantially less than half the number of inhabitants that it had in 1841, and although the population decline slowed, especially after 1926, it did not reverse until the 1960s. For a second thing, Ireland was still in 1901 a predominantly rural society with only 28 percent of its population living in towns, and 41 percent of this "urban" population living in the teeming city of Dublin, which in that year housed 375,000 people, most of them badly.[2] The urban population was rising while the rural population was continuing to decline. Belfast was in the midst of its remarkable transformation from a town of 80,000 people in 1841 (just a little larger than Cork) to the 360,000 it would hold in 1971.[3]

Certain symbols of the modern age were fairly widespread by 1900. Steamships connected Ireland to England and Scotland with swift and reliable (if not necessarily pleasant) scheduled services. The first railway line, a six-mile stretch from Dublin to Kingstown, had been opened in 1834, and by 1912, more than 3,000 miles of track had been laid within the island.[4] But these and other improvements were more cosmetic than structural in their effects. The economy of the island remained persistently agricultural in the southern three-quarters, while Ulster, and especially the Lagan Valley and Belfast, underwent an industrial transformation very similar to what was happening in parts of Lancashire in England and Clydeside in Scotland during the same period. Belfast had developed as a major port and a linen-marketing town in the eighteenth century. Linen manufacture had become concentrated in the north but it was basically a cottage industry or supplement to the income of Ulster's many small farmers. In the late eighteenth century Belfast saw the growth of a new textile industry, cotton, which was based on the much more elaborate and expensive machinery recently invented. Cotton was processed in factories, and by 1810 2,000 people were engaged in cotton manufacture.[5] After 1815, however, Belfast cotton found itself in stiff competition with the heavily capitalized cotton of Lancashire, and in 1828 a fateful decision was made to adapt the factory system to the manufacture of the older and native textile, linen. Belfast was started down its path as an industrial and factory town.

By 1914 there were 73,000 people employed in Belfast's linen mills, and the peak in exports of linen was reached between 1910 and 1912.[6] Eventually, competition from English cotton, and later synthetic textiles, was to ravage Ulster's linen industry, but by the late nineteenth century, Belfast's major industry had already become shipbuilding. In 1869 the firm of Harland and Wolff signed a contract with the English White Star Line to build transatlantic steamers, and a succession of famous ocean liners including the *Titanic* came off the Belfast ways. In a sense the Belfast shipbuilding industry was an extension of the Scottish industry on the Clyde. The resources it required from Ulster were a convenient harbor, and a pool of skilled and semi-skilled laborers. The raw materials came from abroad, as did much of the capital and entrepreneurial talent.

Dublin was not entirely without industry in the late nineteenth century. Its most prospering enterprise was the Protestant-owned Guinness brewery which, with its nearly sixty acres of operations at St. James Gate, on Dublin's west side, had become one of the largest breweries in the world. Its success was not a tribute to the Irish fondness for drink, for a great part of Guinness' output took the form of exports to Britain and the dominions. Distilling of whiskey was a smaller and more dispersed industry than brewing. The word "whiskey" has a Celtic etymology, and the drink has long been associated with Celtic peoples in northern, grain-growing climates. In 1907 distilling employed some 2,400 people, about a third as many as brewing. A third Dublin industry was that of biscuit (Americans would say cookies and crackers but easily preserved, yeastless cereal products is the point) baking which in 1907 employed 10,000 people, most notably in the firm of W. and R. Jacob.[7] But distilling, brewing, and baking were all forms of agricultural processing, and what was lacking in southern Ireland was so-called heavy industry: metallurgical, mineralogical, or chemical.

Ireland in 1900 was outwardly tranquil. The furors of the Home Rule movement and the Land War were past. But the island was poor, backward, divided, and uncertain. This is not to say that a revolution was necessarily brewing. In retrospect it is all too easy to insist on the relentless movement of a society toward collapse and violence. All that can be said is that Ireland's future in 1900 was clouded and obscure.

Disciples of a dozen different faiths promised a dozen different routes to the promised land. And, as always, there were many who were contentedly smug, and in their comfortable cynicism viewed every threat to the *status quo* as an act of criminal rascality. The smug, the resigned, and the cynical were surely the majority, for along with the squalor of the urban poor and the lingering social and economic inferiority of Catholics, throughout the country there had emerged a petty-bourgeois conventionality. Catholic families, especially middling farmers and merchants, were often keenly aware that they were better off than their fathers and grandfathers. Certain indignities might remain, but it was not necessarily inviting to rock the boat and risk the hard-won advances made since the famine. For every Fenian ready to heave a bomb in the direction of the Union Jack there were a legion of Catholic defenders of the *status quo*, not on the grounds that it was perfect, or even adequate, but from the historically understandable fear that its overthrow would make matters worse.

The quarter of a century between 1890 and 1916 saw numerous efforts to deal with Ireland in ways that were peripheral to politics. Home Rule had been blocked by the House of Lords in 1893. Fenian outrages had not succeed in transforming the constitutional relationship between England and Ireland. The land war and Land League were bearing fruits in the legislation of 1885 and 1903 which enabled peasants to purchase their land. There was a clear attraction to apolitical reform schemes which would not face overwhelming resistance before they were even off the drawing board.

Perhaps the most famous of these was the Gaelic revival. A potential defect in any Irish claim to nationhood was the frailty of the insular culture. In a multitude of ways Ireland, south as well as north, had been anglicized in the hundreds of years since the Norman intervention. In 1851, only 25 percent of the population could speak Irish, and by 1911 that number was cut in half.[8] Without a widely spoken national language the Irish were vulnerable to the argument that they ought to be content as "West Britons," provincial members of the United Kingdom with no cultural excuse for separating themselves from the whole. Irish nationalists could be depicted as frivolous secessionists in much the same way as Southerners were depicted by Northerners in the American Civil War. Furthermore, most English educators and administrators, though by no means all, had for centuries treated the Irish language and the surviving vestiges of Celtic culture as worthless barbarisms.

With the development of modern scholarship, this ignorant prejudice began to recede, at least among educated people. The Royal Irish Academy (founded in Dublin in 1785), the Gaelic Society (founded in 1806), the Irish Archaeological Society, the Celtic Society, and the Ossianic Society (which flourished in the 1840s and 50s) all sponsored and encouraged studies which began to uncover the unmistakable evidence of a rich and splendid history.

But it was one thing for a handful of scholars to become aware of the cultural wealth of Irish antiquity, and quite another to translate this knowledge into effective support for the dying vernacular language. A group of young enthusiasts made this leap in July 1893 when they founded the Gaelic League with a Protestant, Douglas Hyde, as its first president. The league's aims were "first, the preservation of Irish as the national language of the country, and the extension of its use as the spoken tongue; and second, the study and publication of existing Gaelic literature, and the cultivation of a modern literature in Irish."[9] As evidence of the way English culture had undermined and corrupted Irish culture Douglas Hyde cited numerous Irish names which had strayed from their origins into muddled English versions. The Gillespies, he wrote in *The Necessity for De-Anglicizing Ireland* derived their names from the name Giolla-Easbuig, or "Bishop's servant" which at least one of their ancestors must have been. But in nineteenth century Ireland many Gillespies had been transmuted into "Bishops" and Gahagans into "Goggins."

By 1908 there were 600 registered branches of the Gaelic League and the introduction of the Irish language into the primary education system had been largely achieved.[10] Progress was also made in secondary schools and in 1909 Irish was established as a prerequisite for matriculation in the new National University.[11] The league sought to maintain an apolitical "neutrality," but this proved increasingly difficult as its membership swelled with political nationalists. Hyde resigned the presidency in 1915 over the League's drift to militancy, but by then the league had accomplished a large part of its objective. It could not stop the decay of Irish as a native spoken language, and the number of native speakers has relentlessly continued to dwindle down to the present day. But the league made the language—which had been a kind of embarrassment or stigma—into a rallying point, a legacy of importance and pride.

Another organization with a similar objective was the Gaelic Athletic Association, founded in County Tipperary by Michael Cusack in 1884. Cusack himself was a controversial and unlovable figure, but the association provided another avenue for attacking English culture. The late nineteenth century saw, all over the world, a revival of organized sports which culminated in the revival of the Olympics. A fierce appetite for national assertion and competition was a prominent part of the movement. Games like cricket, rugby, and polo could all be depicted as peculiarly English—and hence alien—forms of recreation in Ireland. Hurling and Gaelic football were vigorously boosted as both more manly (sports for women were not yet thought appropriate) and faithful to native tradition. The association attracted Fenians and other radicals from the start, including the nationalist Catholic Archbishop Croke of Cashel, who was the association's first patron. Though nominally apolitical, the association served a proto-nationalist function. It vehemently attacked and derided even the most peripheral elements of English culture while glorifying those elements' counterparts in Gaelic culture, even where it was necessary to exhume them from centuries of neglect. The G.A.A. provided a channel for radical nationalism before a political movement existed to tap it. Organizations like the G.A.A. and the Gaelic League nursed and shaped Catholic Ireland's growing identity in a period when political and constitutional progress was at a standstill.

Although the quarter of a century between the collapse of Parnell's Home Rule movement and the outburst of nationalist violence at Easter 1916 appeared one of quietude and relative stability, we are forced to conclude that it was, on the contrary, a period of tension and fermentation. Catholic expectations were rising. The sense of outrage at an enduring and anachronistic colonial relationship was being sharpened and disseminated. Sensitive Protestants were increasingly subject to feelings of guilt over the privileges to which they were entitled in Ireland by the mere accident of birth. They confronted the difficult choices of either leaving their native land, adamantly and contemptuously defending their inherited privileges, or of defecting from the self-interested defense of their class to support various Catholic and/or nationalist causes. Protestants like Yeats, Synge, Douglas Hyde, Erskine Childers, and Lady Gregory were a critical, probably an indispensable, component of the rising tide of nationalist feeling, from which the political movement would eventually draw so much support.

Not all of the reforming Protestants aimed at cultural or political separatism. Sir Horace Plunkett, a descendant of one of the prominent Norman families of the Pale, came to believe that poverty and inefficiency were the chief maladies from which Ireland suffered, rather than the inequities of colonial subjugation. After an English education at Eton and Oxford and a stint of cattle ranching in Wyoming, Plunkett returned to Ireland in 1889 and threw himself into the improvement of Irish agriculture. Like the rest of Europe, Ireland faced, from the 1880s onward, the powerful competition of North American agriculture, particularly cereals, which faster and cheaper shipping could bring to European markets. But in the dairy sector, where perishability limited competition from far-flung producers in the era before refrigeration, Ireland also faced intense competition from the closer Dutch and the Danish who were gaining in the important English market a reputation for reliably high quality products, especially butter.

Plunkett wanted Irish agriculture to meet this challenge and believed it could do so only if farmers acquired an incentive to improve the quality of their produce. He believed they were frequently denied this incentive by the middlemen who bought and marketed the products of the farms. To remove the middleman Plunkett took a leaf from the book of the English Cooperative Movement of the mid-nineteenth century and began a campaign for rural cooperative societies and rural cooperative dairies, or "creameries" as they were called in Ireland. With farmers pooling their resources to finance and operate cooperative dairies, better equipment could be obtained and quality control was more easily achieved. Furthermore, the farmers acquired a share of the profits of marketing which had formerly gone to the middlemen. They also acquired some of the risks, but these, like the profits, were shared with the other members of the cooperative. By 1894 33 creameries and cooperative societies had come into existence, mainly in Cork, Tipperary, and Kilkenny; by 1904 there were 876, spread throughout the country.[12]

Politically, Plunkett was a Unionist. He was elected to the Union Parliament for south Dublin in 1891 and 1895 and his agricultural improvement schemes were congenial to the Unionist governments of the 1890s, committed as they were to "killing Home Rule with kindness." In 1899 a Department of Agriculture and Technical Instruction was created for Ireland, and Plunkett was made its vice-president. By 1914 it had a staff of several hundred and was engaged in a great deal of useful work. Nevertheless, Plunkett's vision proved defective, partly because there was a limit to how much economic productivity could be increased without major political reforms, and partly because such improved productivity as occurred did not placate historic and ancient grievances. Perhaps "cooperation," in agriculture, as elsewhere, is impossible without pre-existing "community," and the deep fissures in Irish society, between Protestant and Catholic, great landlord and small farmer or tenant, were not easily papered over. Plunkett was not wrong in his emphasis upon agricultural improvement. He erred only in his optimistic belief that it could be a substitute for the redistribution of political power.

The question of power relentlessly reasserts itself in modern Irish history. Parnell's fall, the split among his followers, the unbudging resistance to Gladstone's Second Home Rule bill in the House of Lords in 1893, and the immense electoral popularity of the Conservative (Unionist) party for two decades after 1886 all seemed to seal the fate of Irish independence, barring an almost unimaginable revolution. The return of the Liberals to power in the elections of 1906 ended that illusion of hopelessness at a stroke, and set in train momentous events. The Irish Nationalists won 83 seats in the Parliament elected that year, but the Liberals, alone, with 400 seats easily dominated a House of Commons in which there were only 157 Conservatives. Thus the new prime minister, Henry Campell-Bannerman, owed the Irish Nationalists nothing, and showed no inclination to offer more than he owed. When ill health forced his retirement in 1908 he was succeeded as Liberal prime minister by Herbert Henry Asquith, who promptly and gratuitously reasserted the Liberal party's former committment to Home Rule.

The real remaining obstacle was the House of Lords, of whose 600 members, all privileged to sit in that chamber for life, 480 were professed Unionists, opposed to the dismemberment of the United Kingdom, which they took Home Rule to be. The Liberal government found the Lords disobliging for other reasons as well, and a predictable, almost intentional, crisis blew up when the Lords rejected the Liberal budget of 1909. The chancellor of the Exchequer was the agile Welshman David Lloyd George, and he had loaded the budget with provocative taxes aimed at the rich. The Lords swatted it impulsively like a noisome fly, with a vote of 350 against to 75 for. Such a vote ran counter to an unwritten tradition that money bills were the prerogative of the House of Commons, and Asquith, adopting the role of an injured party, called for new parliamentary elections in the hope of vindication by the electorate. Instead, in the elections of January 1910, Liberal strength slipped materially, but was offset by the Irish Nationalists, some 70 of whom behind John Redmond were prepared to support the controversial "People's Budget" because they saw it as a club for beating the House of Lords into constitutional impotence.

In effect, a deal was struck in which the Redmondite Nationalists offered Asquith and Lloyd George Irish support for the budget in return for a promise that the veto power of the Lords would be abolished and a Home Rule bill brought in forthwith. King Edward VII died in May 1910 and in an effort to ease the burdens of his successor, George V, Unionists and Liberals agreed to take the issue to the people once more, in elections to be held in December. The results were almost identical to those of January. A bill to curtail the obstructive powers of the House of Lords ("The Parliament Bill") was introduced into the Commons where it passed amid scenes of unprecedented anger and vituperation. In order to get it through the Lords, Asquith drew up a list of 249 men whom he would ask the king to create as new (Liberal) peers if the Lords rejected the bill. Such a technique had been threatened only twice before: once in 1713, and again in 1832. In August 1911 the Lords had the choice between accepting their own constitutional emasculation or suffering inundation by new peers. After heated debate and massive abstentions, the bill passed by 131 votes to 114, and became law when it received the assent of George V. Henceforth the Lords' power of obstruction was limited to two years.

Asquith introduced the third Home Rule bill into the House of Commons in April 1914. The bill did not envisage restoration of the Irish Parliament as it had existed in the late eighteenth century, but instead adumbrated a federalist principle in which purely local affairs would be handled by a new Irish Parliament of two houses, one popularly elected and one appointed, and imperial matters such as defense, foreign policy, trade, customs, and excise would continue to be the province of the Union Parliament. Forty-two representatives of Ireland would be at Westminster. This plan was more on the order of devolution, or gradual decentralization of political authority, than a means of granting complete independence. It was denounced on exactly those grounds by the embryonic separatist movement called Sinn Fein. Thirty years earlier even Parnell might have disdained the 1914 bill as an insipid gesture. Now the times had changed. Whatever Home Rule bill passed the House of Commons would almost surely become law, for the veto of the House of Lords was no longer a threat. But if the potential for actual passage was greater, so was the alarm of those who felt threatened by the resulting legislation.

The Irish Nationalist MP's, led by John Redmond, enthusiastically endorsed the bill, overlooking its many defects. The Unionists rose up in fury, perceiving in the bill the condemnation of Irish Protestants to minority status in a nascent Catholic Irish state. Unionism was not confined to Protestants, but it was predominantly Protestant, and Ulster was the only one of Ireland's four traditional provinces in which Protestants came even close to constituting a majority of the population.[13] This demographic fact dictated that the only amendment of Home Rule capable of saving a substantial number of Protestants was the exclusion of Ulster. This amendment, of course, would do little or nothing for those Protestants situated in the other three provinces, but it would at least establish one part of Ireland as a sort of sanctuary. From the Home Rule point of view, and from the view of the Catholic Nationalists in general, any exclusion of Ulster from the bill amounted to dismemberment, partition, and betrayal of the native land for whose separation from British rule generations of Irish patriots had been struggling, suffering, and sometimes dying. Thus Asquith's modest Home Rule bill, the twenty-seven-year old child of W. E. Gladstone's 1885 conversion to the cause, unexpectedly rekindled violent sectarian passions.

The initiative lay with the Unionists, for the Home Rulers could wait for Asquith and the Liberals to fight the bill through Parliament. The real question was how much trouble could the Ulster Unionists make? And events were to prove that they could make a great deal. Catholic Nationalists have often underestimated the strength and endurance of Ulster Protestant determination *not* to be part of a Catholic Ireland. The social structure of modern Ulster and the fact that Protestant small farmers and workingmen grew accustomed to reassuring themselves with notions of racial, cultural, and religious superiority, clearly contributed to this phenomenon. Ulster proved to be packed with the kind of tinder demagogues could turn into conflagrations. The organizing of resistance to Home Rule had begun in the 1880s, but it was powerfully accelerated by the Parliament Act of 1911 and the introduction of the third Home Rule bill of 1912.

This mobilization of Ulster feeling was orchestrated by members of the formerly aloof upper classes, and produced three great leaders. The first was Sir Edward Carson, a Dublin-born (1854) Protestant of Scottish Presbyterian background who rose to prominence as a lawyer, first in Dublin and later in London. Carson believed that Ulster intransigence could block Home Rule altogether, as the reformed House of Lords was no longer able to do. He was the spellbinding rhetorician of the movement. The second leader was Captain James Craig, the son of a millionaire whiskey distiller from Belfast. Craig organized the resistance to Home Rule, and the preparation of an independent, refractory state of "Northern Ireland" prepared to fight, if necessary, to avoid inclusion in virtually any form of Irish state. The third member of the Ulster triumvirate was Bonar Law, a Canadian of Ulster-Scottish origin who, in November 1911, succeeded Arthur Balfour as leader of the out-of-power Conservative party, and by his pro-Ulster sympathies formed a powerful link between the party and the Unionist cause.

The obstructionist potential of Ulster Unionism would have been limited had it not possessed wide and deep support in Britain. The issue of Home Rule split Britain as it split Ireland, and millions of English voters regarded it as a lamentable step backward, a surrender of power and prestige to lawless and uncivilized Celts. Unionism is not an easy cause to understand today, but in the late nineteenth and early twentieth centuries it was a gospel of compelling force. The Unionist's world view equated "civilization" in the British Isles and much of the overseas world with the progress and triumph of Protestant Anglo-Saxon peoples and those others with the wisdom to follow their ways. Catholic Ireland appeared, accordingly, an impoverished, priest- and superstition-ridden land inhabited by indolent, uncultured, and sometimes savage natives. The only exception was the industrialized north, but that anomaly was easily explained by the heavy concentration of Protestant Scots and English in that region. In such a world view Home Rule meant turning the clock back by centuries; it meant reversing the historic centralization of the British Isles under English leadership, and worse than that, surrendering Ireland's most worthwhile, productive, and civilized inhabitants—the Protestant northerners—to barbarous domination by southern Catholics. In this Manichean view of the world as a ceaseless struggle between goodness and evil, Home Rule would amount to the triumph of Satan. Hence the passionate resistance of the Ulster Protestants and some of their brethren in England and Scotland.

Profound revolutions are often initiated by conservatives who perceive that time is working against them and determine to bring matters to a sudden head. By a dramatic demonstration of their remaining powers and privileges they hope to forestall gradual defeat. At the parliamentary level the Unionists sought to amend into nullity Asquith's Home Rule bill. But at another level they were preparing to resist by force implementation of the bill if it ever became law. An Ulster Volunteer Force was formed in 1912, and in April 1914, it succeeded in procuring substantial armaments purchased in Germany and smuggled into Ulster through the small, northeastern ports of Bangor, Larne, and Donaghadee. The predictable consequence was the formation of paramilitary Catholic counterparts in the south, and gunrunning there as well. Ireland was threatening to split in two under the fissiparous effect of Home Rule. But Europe was splitting even faster than Ireland, and by August 1914 had blundered into what would prove the most devastating war in its history.

The first world war put immediate pressure upon Britain

to find a solution to the Irish problem—any solution—which would allow Britain to concentrate its forces against Germany. John Redmond, the leader of the Irish Nationalists at Westminster, chose to take advantage of this pressure rather than gamble that the adversities of war would eventually force Britain into more generous concessions of independence to Ireland. On August 3d, 1914, Redmond pledged Irish support for the British war effort, fully expecting that Asquith would force the Home Rule bill through Parliament. This, Asquith apprehensively did in the following month, but not before two provisoes had been introduced in what was renamed the "Government of Ireland Act." The two provisoes were meant to prevent the disaffection of Ulster and a resulting Irish war which would have been disastrous for Britain's war against Germany. One stated that the act would not come into force until the conclusion of the war; the other prevented it from coming into force until Parliament had had "the opportunity of making provision for Ulster by special amending legislation."[14]

The triumph for Home Rule, after thirty years of struggle, was thus a hollow one. The issue had, in effect, been shelved again, this time, for the duration of the war, however long that might be. Because Home Rule meant little to the Nationalists if not Home Rule for *all* of Ireland, and because Ulster would participate only in an Irish state governed by British Protestants, the result was a tragic impasse. The first world war, and its requirements, obtruded. There was a calm which was, in fact, a lull. In retrospect it appears that the political and nationalistic momentum which had built up since the famine could not now be switched off. On the surface, however, Irish quarrels were subordinated. Redmond's Irish Volunteers, formed originally to guard the Catholic south against Carson's Ulster Volunteers, were transformed into the National Volunteers, some 170,000 strong with the avowed purpose of defending the island against Germany, thus releasing English and empire troops for duty elsewhere. Only some 11,000 Irish volunteers refused to follow Redmond's lead, and constituted

themselves as the *New* Irish Volunteers under the leadership of a Catholic professor and Gaelic scholar, Eoin
MacNeill.

In the course of the war over 200,000 Irishmen either
served in or volunteered for the British Army.[15] Many of
these, of course, were Protestants. Ulstermen, with their
long and proud military tradition, were formed up into
provincial divisions. The 36th Ulster Division participated
in the disastrous battle of the Somme in 1916. The first day
of that battle, July 1, coincided with the date (as calculated
prior to the eighteenth century) of William of Orange's
great seventeenth-century victory at the Battle of the
Boyne. As the men of the 36th went "over the top" to face
withering German fire, they were wearing orange ribbons
and shouting "Remember 1690," their "tunes of glory"
sounding sadly discordant notes. But the British forces also
included southern Protestants, and Catholics both high-
born and low. A haunting 1916 poem of W. B. Yeats, "An
Irish Airman Forsees His Death," sketches the thoughts of
a southerner with strong ties to his country:

> I know that I shall meet my fate
> Somewhere among the clouds above;
> Those that I fight I do not hate,
> Those that I guard I do not love;
> My country is Kiltartan cross,
> My countrymen Kiltartan's poor,
> No likely end could bring them loss
> Or leave them happier than before

Many who fought were Catholic Nationalists who believed,
along with John Redmond, that their sacrifice for Britain
would eventually be repaid with magnanimous British
concessions of Home Rule. A final, and less happy, class of
combatants were the Catholic poor who had been a mainstay of the British army throughout the nineteenth century.
They had fought in the Crimean War, and in the Boer War,
and unscrupulous recruiting methods, together with the
lure of "the king's shilling" no doubt played a large part in

calling them to the colors.[16] Unlike the Ulster Protestants, most of them were dispersed among the forces. When they were gathered into regiments such as the Connaught Rangers or the Dublin Fusiliers, their officers were generally Protestants.

To John Redmond fell the thankless task of keeping Ireland loyal to a Britain which barely tolerated it and could scarcely conceal its scorn. If he was successful in the main, the cost was his own reputation as a Nationalist leader worthy of succession to Parnell. Discontent with Redmond's policy swelled the ranks of the New Irish Volunteers, which despite the moderation of its leader, MacNeill, came under the influence of the Irish Republican Brotherhood. Radical fringe movements, though small in numbers of adherents, flourished in the vacuum created by Redmond's cooperation with Britain. As the war dragged on, and Britain's peril grew, Redmond's path seemed less defensible. If Germany was going to win the war, or push England to the wall, the moment was propitious to srike for Irish freedom, to reject British authority entirely, to seize and subdue a refractory Ulster, and to ally with Germany if necessary.

No single group of men had a monopoly of such thoughts, and on other matters there was much divergence. The Volunteers, under MacNeill, were the most substantial of these dissidents, but MacNeill was unwilling to commit them to a hopeless battle, another doomed gesture in the name of Irish independence. Others, most notably Roger Casement, trod the bitter footsteps of Wolfe Tone, the patriot of the 1790s, in laboring to persuade Germany to furnish significant support for an Irish insurrection. Germany, like France and Spain before it, feared to beard the British lion in its Irish den. With the royal navy dominating the surrounding waters, chances of success were thought by German planners to be slim. The Germans were as doubting and niggling as had been their continental predecessors. But the slender possibility of their intervention nourished hopes of a triumphant rising.

In addition to MacNeill's Volunteers, a paramilitary or-

ganization called the Irish Citizen Army was being trained
and drilled by a Catholic socialist, James Connolly. Much
smaller than the Volunteers, probably never more than a
few hundred stalwarts, the I.C.A. emerged from an entirely
different tradition. Socialism and trade unionism had little
opportunity to develop in a predominantly agrarian Ireland. Such activity as there was centered in Belfast and
Dublin. In the northern city the labor leader James Larkin
built a powerful union of carters and dockers, and in 1908
founded the Irish Transport and General Workers Union,
soon one of the most militant unions in the British Isles.
Larkin expanded his activity to the ports of Cork and Dublin, and by 1913 membership in the I.T.G.W.U. had risen to
something over 10,000. The summit of Larkin's career arrived in August 1913 when he led a long, bitter, and ultimately unsuccessful strike against William Martin Murphy's Dublin United Tramway Company. Admitting defeat
(and blaming English trade unions for their lack of support) Larkin went to America in 1914, and a different kind
of laboring man, James Connolly, succeeded to the leadership of the movement.

Connolly was a socialist theoretician rather than a trade
union organizer. He believed that the wealth of the world
belonged by right to its inhabitants and not to an exclusive
capitalist class. His preoccupation with a just distribution
of wealth was at variance with the Fenians, whose principal concern was the destruction of British political power
over Ireland. Yet there was at least one point of intersec-
tion. Connolly believed that the wealth of Ireland belonged
to the Irish. Socialism in Ireland must, therefore, entail the
expropriation of Ireland's wealth from foreign (or capitalist) interests, but it would subsequently have to be divided
among the Irish in such a way as not to reestablish capitalist inequities in the new Irish state. With the first part of
such a philosophy many Fenians could agree. The second
part was irrelevant until the wealth of Ireland was within
the power of an independent Irish state, something Connolly would not live to see.

The Irish Citizen Army (I.C.A.) was founded by Larkin

and Connolly in November 1913, initially to provide some protection for workers threatened by the hired toughs of Dublin employers. But after Larkin's departure for America, the I.C.A. became Connolly's personal instrument, arming and drilling in preparation for some unspecified and almost unimaginable revolutionary situation. The British army maintained a garrison of 20,000 troops in Ireland, and in any extended struggle it would be supported by the Royal Irish Constabulary and possibly some of Redmond's National Volunteers. The only hope for success was an alliance of MacNeill's Volunteers with Connolly's I.C.A., coupled with substantial support from Germany and the advantage of surprise.[17]

To achieve such a concatenation became, as early as August 1914, the design of the Irish Republican Brotherhood, the lingering, sputtering remnant of the Fenian movement of the 1860s. The brotherhood was short on political philosophy, but it was usually itching to fight. Under the sway of three romantic revolutionaries, Patrick Pearse, Thomas MacDonagh, and Joseph Plunkett, the Supreme Council of the I.R.B. planned and coordinated an attempt to overthrow British rule in Ireland. They infiltrated MacNeill's Volunteers and made overtures to Connolly. But the key to success lay in foreign intervention. An eminent Protestant civil servant, Roger Casement spent a year and a half in Germany trying to procure the vital assistance needed. The fruit of his labors, and of representations from American Irish, was the grudging dispatch in April 1916 of 20,000 rifles, 10 machine guns, and ammunition in the steamer *Aud*. Disguised as a Norwegian freighter, the *Aud* was to unload its precious cargo near Tralee in County Kerry, but British Intelligence had learned of its mission and the ship was intercepted on the Friday before Easter 1916. It was scuttled by its captain while being escorted into Cork Harbor. On the same day, Roger Casement had been landed near Tralee by a German submarine. The Germans expected him to help lead the insurrection, but he had secretly determined to try to call it off, because of what he regarded as the inadequacy of German aid. Instead he was captured by the Royal Irish Constabulary within hours of his landing, and was executed for treason after a still controversial trial.

The I.R.B. had scheduled the insurrection to begin on Easter Sunday, but it had done this without informing MacNeill, commander of the Volunteers. The Easter weekend was spent in chronic confusion. MacNeill would not authorize a military action which seemed hopeless, *unless* there was firm evidence that the Dublin government intended to suppress his organization, something it had heretofore been extremely reluctant to do. Whether or not a rising was hopeless depended upon aid from Germany. Was it imminent? Had it already arrived? Was it substantial? The leaders in Dublin were groping in the dark, uncertain of what was happening, what the Dublin government knew, or what it intended. MacNeill attempted to countermand the I.R.B. orders for a rising on Easter Sunday, and the I.R.B. went along with this, though neglecting to inform him that it was merely postponing the event until the following day, Easter Monday. Pearse and the I.R.B. were determined that their months of preparation should not be wasted. They accepted that, without some miraculous and unpredictable occurrence, their insurrection would be suppressed. Nevertheless they went forward, convinced that they were striking a blow for the freedom of Ireland, and forcing the hands of many who could not hold back, despite their doubts, once the battle was joined.[18]

On Easter Monday, April 24, a force of some 200 men from the I.C.A. and 1,400 from the Irish Volunteers took over a series of strongpoints in Dublin City on both banks of the Liffey. At noon, in front of the general post office in Sackville (now O'Connell) Street, Pearse proclaimed the establishment of a provisional government of the Irish Republic. The insurrection lasted six days, ending on Saturday afternoon, April 29, with Pearse's formal surrender. British military superiority had left no alternative. The rising had been witnessed by a largely frightened and apathetic civilian population. It triggered no massive uprising and no miracle occurred. Several hundred people had been killed and several thousand wounded, many of them non-combatant Dubliners. A rigorous military government was imposed upon the island by Major General Sir John Maxwell who saw the uprising as proof of the civilian government's softness and incompetence. The leaders of the uprising were arrested, imprisoned, court-martialed and, one by one, fourteen of them were executed before firing squads, between May 3d and 12. The impact of the executions was crucial in the future development of the Nationalist movement.

In death Pearse, Connolly, and their brethren became martyr-heroes to a population which had first regarded their adventure as hare-brained, if not positively mad. A mere 1,600 Irishmen had risen and the proportion of the population that shared their extremist views must have been small indeed. But in the weeks and months which followed, a new mood infected the south. It was nationalistic, anti-British, and embittered. This new mood made unlikely that the Home Rule bill as passed in 1914 would satisfy the growing appetite for separatism and independence when it finally came into effect after the war.

The political movement which exploited that mood was called Sinn Fein (or simply, "Ourselves"). Its origins were modest, and by the standards of the Easter Rising, not very radical. Founded by a Dublin journalist, Arthur Griffith, in 1908, Sinn Fein advocated passive, rather than violent, resistance to British authority. Griffith had declined to join the Supreme Council of the I.R.B. and did not take part in the Rising, though some Sinn Fein members did. The British, however, were in no mood after Easter 1916 to make nice distinctions between Nationalists. All of them were tarred with the brush of treason. Griffith was arrested and imprisoned for several months, and the press, as well as certain English politicians, took to referring casually to Irish revolutionaries as Sinn Feiners, whether they were or not, in fact. This imprecision allowed Sinn Fein to take credit (in Nationalist Irish opinion) for a role in the Easter Rising which it did not, strictly speaking, deserve.

Sinn Fein became, after the fact, the political party dedicated to the Rising and the realization of the Rising's objectives. In a by-election in North Roscommon in February 1917, Sinn Fein backed Count Plunkett, father of the executed Rising leader, Joseph Plunkett, in his race against a Redmondite candidate. Plunkett won and declined to take his seat at Westminster. Sinn Fein candidates won three successive by-elections in the months which followed, and like Plunkett, refused to take their seats. The old party of Isaac Butt and Charles Stewart Parnell was coming apart. A party which had staked its reputation on participation in the British political process, however abhorrent, was being toppled by a party which refused to countenance or acknowledge British authority and British institutions. This was the fruit of the Rising and it made possible, or even inevitable, a war of national resistance supported from diverse quarters.

The rise of Sinn Fein and the collapse of Redmond's party occurred against a backdrop of continued crisis in the European war. The United States joined the Allies in 1917, but Russia withdrew into its inner turmoil of revolution and civil war. Early 1918 saw a major German offensive which caused another massive effusion of English and Commonwealth lives. The armed services reached deeper into the manpower pool, conscripting older men and those with dependents, who had heretofore been spared. Pressure grew to extend conscription to Ireland where, by now, it would almost certainly have provoked determined resistance. Sinn Fein exploited the widespread resentment and apprehension which attended the threat. Lloyd George, who had replaced Asquith as prime minister in December 1916, convened an ad hoc Irish Convention in July 1917, and it vainly groped for some solution to the worsening Irish problem until it was dissolved in April 1918. The German offensive of early 1918 was eventually checked and followed by a successful Allied offensive in the fall, and an exhausted Germany finally agreed to an armistice in November.

The war was over. Ireland had been spared conscription,

but it now faced an England free to redeploy its military forces, war-weary though they were. The wartime Parliament was dissolved on November 25 and elections were scheduled for December. Despite the growing strength and unity of Sinn Fein, which swelled in memberhsip from 66,000 to 112,000 in 1918, the outcome of the parliamentary elections in Ireland was unpredictable. An important electoral reform, the Representation of the People Act in 1918, had made the vote universal for men and extended it for the first time to women over thirty. The Irish electorate was nearly triple what it had been in the previous election, that of 1910. In any event, Sinn Fein candidates captured the election, winning 73 of 105 seats, 25 of them uncontested. Redmond had died in March at the age of sixty-one, and his parliamentary party clung to a pathetic 6 seats while the remaining 26 went to Unionists, all but three of them from northeast Ulster.[19]

When the new Westminster Parliament convened in January 1919 the newly elected Sinn Fein MP's refused to take their seats and 27 of them—the rest were in jail, or in hiding—gathered instead in Dublin where they constituted themselves as the Dail Eireann, or Assembly of Ireland. By inviting the other newly elected Irish MP's (Unionist and Nationalist) to join them, they signified their intention to establish a new de facto government of a united Ireland. Naturally, the Unionists would not touch such an assembly, regarding it as illegal and pernicious. The Dail acted as if it were simply the logical political outgrowth or sequel of the republic which had been proclaimed at Easter 1916. It appointed various officers of state and sent a delegation to Paris in the hope of being admitted to the peace talks with which the first world war was concluding. Every effort was made to symbolize Ireland's independence of Britain, even though there were deep divisions within Sinn Fein as to the form and principles the new Irish state should adopt.

English response to this situation was ambiguous, but it was crystallized by an outbreak of violence. On January 21, 1919, a cartload of explosives was being escorted from one

rock quarry to another in Tipperary by two policemen of
the Royal Irish Constabulary (R.I.C.) when the procession
was held up by a group of Volunteers at Soloheadbeg.
Whether by intention or accident, the two constables were
killed and the Volunteers made off with the explosives,
which they wanted for making grenades. It was the first
killing of a policeman or British soldier in Ireland in the
two years and eight months since the Easter rising, but it
initiated a spate of violence directed particularly at the
R.I.C.[20] More embarrassing for the British than the recru-
descence of violence was the approach of the Dail's delegation to the Peace Conference at Paris and the support
drummed up for this effort among the Irish in America.
These activities served to externalize the struggle, undermining the British claim that the difficulties in Ireland
were of a criminal nature rather than a legitimate struggle
for national independence. Ultimately, the Dail's delegation was rebuffed at Paris as Britain, France, and America
closed ranks. President Woodrow Wilson was affronted by
what he saw as the meddling of Irish-Americans, even
though he was reluctant to lose their votes.

In June 1919 the newly elected president of the Dail, Eamon De Valera, came to America in the hope of marshaling
Irish-American influence behind the nascent state. Finan-
cially, the mission was successful in selling $5 million of
the new state's bonds, but it did *not* serve to unify Irish-
Americans, for bitter divisions over tactics emerged. Neither did the mission succeed in obtaining U.S. recognition
for the Irish Republic. The Dail and its supporters, thousands of whom were now in arms either as Volunteers, Irish
Republican Brethren, or members of the Irish Republican
Army, were left to wrestle painfully with the British for the
control of the institutions by which the island was governed.

In early 1920 this struggle took on the aspect of guerilla
warfare. The responsibility for preserving the status quo
fell mainly on the Royal Irish Constabulary, a kind of national police force which had been organized in the 1830s.
As tension increased between the government and the citi-

zenry, the R.I.C. experienced growing numbers of resignations as constables, many of whom were Catholic, found themselves torn between their official responsibilities and a sense of loyalty to their kinsmen and countrymen. With R.I.C. units coming under attack and morale crumbling, the British decided to send reinforcements to Ireland in the form of the "Black and Tans"—named after the contrasting colors of their irregular uniforms—and the "auxilliaries." Eventually these supplemental forces numbered 40,000 men.[21] Both groups were officially "police," but were recruited from hardened veterans of the British army and soon gained a reputation for cruelty which made the R.I.C. seem humane by comparison.

Martial law replaced civil procedures. Superficially, life went on as usual, subject to terrible interruption by ambush, raid, assassination, and reprisal. The guerrillas took cover in a civilian population which looked upon them with sentiments ranging from idolatry to terror, and which absorbed hundreds of casualties through nothing more than the bad luck of being in the wrong place at the wrong time. Much of the anti-British violence was independently initiated and lacked the sanction of either the Dail, its ministers, or its official commanders. It was an "open season" on the British and their functionaries, and it provoked repayment in kind. On November 21, 1920, for instance, the I.R.A., with the approval of the Dail's minister of defense, assassinated in Dublin eleven English civilians who were believed to be intelligence agents. That afternoon in reprisal the Black and Tans invaded a Gaelic football match at Croke Park in Dublin, and firing indiscriminately on the players and the crowd killed twelve people and wounded sixty.

Such a conflict does not easily produce heroes, nor is it measureably "won" or "lost." The British possessed the resources to repress dissidence in Ireland, but at what cost, and to what purpose? Local election results in January 1920 suggested that Sinn Fein was a political force with which to reckon, and not merely a flash in the pan. Even in

Ulster it captured 23 out of 43 local government councils.[22] Late in 1920 the British Parliament passed the Better Government of Ireland Act, the effect of which was to amalgamate the Ulster demand for partition with the now-senescent concept of Home Rule. Two local parliaments were to be established: one for six of the nine counties of Ulster, an area comprising approximately 820,000 of the 890,000 Protestants then in Ulster, and another for the twenty-six southern counties.[23] In the elections of May 1921, held under the act, Unionists captured 40 of the 52 seats in the new northern Parliament, but in the south Sinn Fein candidates again swept to victory and again constituted themselves as a Dail Eireann (the second one) thus undermining the intent of the British act. In June, King George V struck a conciliatory note in the speech with which he opened the first session of the new Parliament of Northern Ireland, and on July 11, 1921, a truce was achieved between the forces of the British Crown and those of the Irish Dail. A peace conference met between October 11 and December 6 and resulted in the initialing of a treaty by the members of the Irish delegation.

The Anglo-Irish treaty that resulted has been a subject of unending controversy. The president of the Dail, Eamon De Valera, was not a member of the Irish delegation, and it is clear that in the final stages of negotiation, the British prime minister, David Lloyd George, put great pressure on the Irish delegates to accept his proposals. The treaty to which they agreed established an Irish Free State with dominion status comparable to that of Canada, Australia, South Africa, and New Zealand. The members of the Free State's Parliament were to take an oath which subordinated their loyalty to the British Crown to their loyalty to the new state. The Free State was to make certain military, especially naval, facilities available to Britain both in war and peace. The treaty permitted Northern Ireland to reject the jurisdiction of the new Free State, but in the event that it did so, called for a three-man commission to establish the appropriate boundaries between the two states. Inasmuch as neither side had clearly defeated the other, neither side anticipated giving up its most cherished objectives. The Irish delegation believed it had obtained all that was possible under the circumstances, even though total independence had not been achieved and partition had not been definitively prevented. They believed dominion status was a valuable stepping-stone toward complete independence and that partition might become much less palatable to the north once the boundary commission lopped off some of its territory, as it was confidently expected to do. After all, the six-county area contained more than 500,000 Catholics who had no wish to remain in union with Britain. The opponents of the treaty, including President De Valera, who had elected to stay in Dublin in order to restrain his party's extremists, denounced the treaty as a sellout, an unworthy and dishonorable surrender of the principles for which generations of Irish patriots had struggled and died.

Thus the treaty split Sinn Fein as nothing previously had done. When the final vote was taken in the Dail on January 7, 1922, the division was 64 in favor of the treaty, 57 against. The minority feared that they were witnessing the dissolution of the Republic and the substitution for it of the so-called Free State. Gradually they withdrew into opposition, and in April 1922 a group of anti-treaty army officers challenged the government of the new Free State by occupying the landmark set of government buildings on the north bank of the Liffey called the Four Courts. After two months of attempting to conciliate the rebel officers, the government forces bombarded the Four Courts with artillery, destroying them in the process and forcing the survivors' surrender. A ten-month-long civil war was ignited in which more Irish lives were lost than in all the fighting between Easter 1916 and the signing of the treaty.

Previously there had been a high degree of unity in the struggle against the British, but now families and friends were divided and the new state came close to being torn apart from within. At the outset Republican forces held Cork and Kerry, but by August the provisional government had broken their hold on Munster, and the war degenerated into the kind of a guerrilla struggle which had been waged against the British. Against terrorism, such as the ambush of the pro-treaty commander Michael Collins in County Cork in August, the provisional government replied with stern measures. Some 77 captured Republicans were put to death during the struggle, as proof of the Free State's determination to impose order. In May 1923 the Republican forces surrendered their arms, and the military triumph of the pro-treatyites was complete.

It remained to be seen what kind of polity could be established on so fractured a base. In December 1922 the Dail had passed the Irish Free State constitution bill, and the provisional government, which had ruled since the Anglo-Irish Treaty, gave way to the first regular government. But the lingering strength of Republican sentiment was revealed in August 1923 by the first elections to the Dail held under the new constitution. Republicans won 44 out of 153 seats and gained nearly 28 percent of the popular vote.[24] The Republicans kept, or more accurately, revived, the name of Sinn Fein for their party, but refused to recognize the Dail or take their seats in it. The pro-Treatyites, with 63 seats, organized themselves as the Cumann na nGaedheal party and faced only token opposition in the Dail from the Farmers' Union and Labour parties. But the defenders of the treaty suffered a setback when the Boundary Commission convened in 1924 and failed to revise the border with Northern Ireland. The treaty had purposely obscured the partition issue, leaving all parties to believe what they wished. The action, or inaction, of the Boundary Commission shattered the hope, or illusion that Northern Ireland would be left with too little territory to endure as a separate state. Partition became an inescapable legacy of the treaty and thus another rod with which to beat the backs of the Treatyites.

Sinn Fein, however, had its own difficulties. Boycotting the Dail had symbolic potential, but as a long-term policy it was sterile and without political effect against a viable government. Sinn Fein began to separate on the one hand into those diehards (many of them I.R.A.) who were prepared for eternal defiance, and on the other hand into more moderate, politically inclined Republicans who were ready to work from within the constitution rather than rail at it from the wilderness. The leader of this latter group, Eamon de Valera, formed a new political party in 1926 and called it Fianna Fail. In the elections of 1927 Fianna Fail won an impressive 44 seats against Cumann na nGaedheal's 46, but its members still refused to take the prescribed oath to the Free State and were thus prevented from taking their seats in the Dail.

After the government passed an electoral amendment bill declaring parliamentary seats to be vacant which were not occupied by the candidates elected to them, Fianna Fail members finally accepted the oath in August 1927 and thus returned to the constitutional arena. Participation in the Free State was made less bitter for Republicans in 1931 when the British Parliament's Statute of Westminster significantly enlarged the independence of all the Commonwealth nations. Proponents of the treaty had been right to forsee the loosening of Commonwealth ties to Britain, but enemies of the treaty can hardly be blamed for lacking confidence that such would be the case. Dominion status in 1921 had still meant subordination to a British imperial authority that could not be taken lightly.

De Valera's Fianna Fail party slowly acquired the respectability of an official opposition, the natural beneficiary of all the mistakes of the party in power. In the election of 1932 Fianna Fail won 72 seats to C.N.G.'s 57, and formed a government for the first time. When elections were called the following year, Fianna Fail widened its lead and achieved a simple majority of the Dail. The pro-treaty party, Cumann na nGaedheal, was now in the minority and in opposition for the first time, and it underwent a certain change in character. Social and economic issues began to vie with the purely national ones that had dominated the century's first decades. C.N.G. became, to some extent, the party of the middle class—not necessarily the rich, but the propertied. It stood on guard against the incipient socialism of which radical nationalism was always capable. It was only a short step from asserting that the island's wealth belonged to "Ireland" to asserting that the *State,* or "Ireland," incarnate, had a right to dictate its distribution.

Such tendencies had been successfully restrained in the past, most notably in the first Dail of January 1919, but the world depression of the 1930s created new pressures to revive them. C.N.G. feared reprisal from Fianna Fail and created what was, in effect, a private army known at first as the Army Comrades Association, and from mid-1933, misleadingly, as the National Guard. When De Valera fired the commissioner of the Gardai or national police, General Eoin O'Duffy, the Army Comrades Association appointed him its commander. Under O'Duffy the association adopted practices inspired by the fascist parties of Italy and Germany: ostentatious military ritual, mass marches, and addiction to military uniforms, which in this case took the form of blue shirts. The government tried to curb the National Guard's activities, but in September 1933 the Guard merged into C.N.G. which now acquired a new name, Fine Gael, or United Ireland, and a new leader in the person of O'Duffy. Apologists for O'Duffy stress that his movement was not really antidemocratic, though it was unquestionably antisocialist, and that it borrowed the trappings of continental fascism without its characteristic venom. Nevertheless O'Duffy's Blue Shirts soon became an embarrassment. O'Duffy was forced to resign from Fine Gael in August 1934, and in 1936 he formed an Irish Brigade to fight in the Spanish Civil War, on the side of General Franco.

Once in power in 1932 Fianna Fail abolished the detested oath of allegiance contained in the treaty and, by cutting off the annuities due to the British Exchequer under the pre-World War I land purchase acts, triggered a costly trade war with Britain. But even these gestures of defiance did not satisfy the I.R.A., which regarded De Valera as a turncoat. There had been an uneasy truce as long as both

Fianna Fail and the I.R.A. faced the common threat of
O'Duffy's Blue Shirts, but once O'Duffy made his exit, De
Valera could dispense with the I.R.A. He had it proclaimed
an illegal body and imprisoned its chief of staff. The organization had already, in 1934, split into traditionalist and
socialist wings, the latter of which sent a brigade to Spain
to fight *against* Franco. The I.R.A. refused to die, although
it has, since 1936, experienced long periods of dormancy.
Inasmuch as it draws so much of its spiritual sustenance
from the flawed dream of Irish unity, perhaps its final demise must await the eventual end of partition.

Starting with its accession to power in 1932 Fianna Fail
under De Valera created a Republic *within* what had been
constituted in 1922 as a Dominion, the Irish Free State. In
the winter of 1936–37 this remodeled state was given a formal constitution, and it is that constitution which remains
the foundation of the Irish State today. The legislature was
bicameral and consisted of an upper house, or Seanad, and
a lower house, the Dail. A popularly elected president was
to perform largely formal duties, but real political power
was to lie in the hands of the prime minister or taoiseach.
Article 44 of the constitution recognized the "special position" of Roman Catholicism, but the linkage between
Church and State was purposely made vague and informal,
though perhaps no less effective for that. The constitution
was submitted to a popular vote and was endorsed by 57
percent of those voting. In 1938 Douglas Hyde, the Protestant founder of the Gaelic League, was elected first president under the new constitution. A set of Anglo-Irish agree-
ments concluded in April 1938 ended the trade war, and
British claims to the naval bases in Cork Harbor and elsewhere. Irish autonomy had been achieved, for all practical
purposes.

What had not been achieved was Irish unity. The Unionists of the north had availed themselves of the provisions of
the Better Government of Ireland Act (1920) to establish a
separate Parliament of Northern Ireland, and Unionists
dominated this body from its inception in 1921. When the

Anglo-Irish Treaty ended warfare in the south later that
year, Northern Ireland was already functioning as a separate entity, and all attempts to involve it in negotiations
aimed at eventual unification proved to be futile. From almost any point of view the six counties constituted an odd
assemblage. Strictly speaking they did not comprise "Ulster," for the excluded counties of Donegal, Monaghan, and
Cavan were part of the traditional province. It was "Northern Ireland" only if one overlooked that the Free State's
County Donegal extended further northward than any of
the six counties. But most crucially, although two-thirds of
the inhabitants of the six counties were Protestants and
Unionists, substantial areas were dominated by Catholics
who tended to be Nationalists opposed to the separate
northern state. Counties Down and Antrim were comfortably Protestant, but elsewhere the sides were more nearly
equal, or even predominantly Catholic, as in the town of
Derry or the County Tyrone. The six counties were, in es-
sence, as large an area as the Unionists of the north could
claim, while retaining a relatively safe overall Protestant
majority. The Catholic inhabitants of the area were, however, virtually a captive minority, and their instinct was to
ignore the new state which contained them, and its alien
political institutions.

The withdrawal of Catholics from political life in the
north accorded well with Unionist desires to govern Northern Ireland with a free hand. In jobs, education, housing,
and local government, the state devised ways—some ingenious, some crude—of favoring Protestants over Catholics.
By 1932 northern Catholics reluctantly acknowledged the
durability of the resultant state and began to take their
seats in its parliament, located in that year in an elaborate
edifice at Stormont, outside of Belfast. By then, however,
the foundations of the Protestant state had been solidly
laid, and Nationalists could rarely capture more than 12 of
the 52 Stormont seats, or 2 of the 12 seats by which Northern Ireland was represented in the Westminster Parliament. It is ironic that the only place in the British Isles

where Home Rule truly succeeded was in Northern Ireland, and there its effect was to enable a Protestant majority to tyrannize over a Catholic minority.

Sectarian strife had largely disappeared from the rest of Ireland, partly because the Protestant population in the south shrank to negligible proportions and partly because the Free State made a determined effort to appear tolerant. In Northern Ireland it reached new heights of savagery, with Belfast an open sore where ghettoes of Protestants and Catholics chafed against one another, and not infrequently went to war in the streets. The national festivals of Northern Ireland—the July 12 celebration of the anniversary of the seventeenth-century Battle of the Boyne or the relief of the Siege of Londonderry—were not reminiscences of triumph over a foreign power, but triumph over the native Catholic population. They were an assertion of Protestant superiority and of the determination to maintain it. An auxiliary Protestant police force, the B Specials, was created to supplement the Royal Ulster Constabulary when Catholic dissidence got out of hand. The Orange Order, a secret society closed to Catholics, paralleled constitutional government, much as political parties parallel and inform official government in totalitarian states. Northern Ireland institutionalized and perpetuated inequities based on religion and culture. It became increasingly anachronistic in a post-World-War-II West which at least paid lip service to democratic and humanitarian ideals.

The Catholic population of the north was the chief sufferer, but Nationalists in the south sympathized and grieved for the division of Ireland that had resulted from the partial achievement of independence. After 1945, however, northern Catholics enjoyed certain benefits of the British welfare state which would not have been available to them in, or under, the Republic, and this may explain why more of them did not "vote with their feet" by moving south, something which they were always free to do. By the same token, southern governments, rhetoric to the contrary, have found their hands full with the problems of the twenty-six counties. The prospects of administering six more, including a hornets' nest of northern Protestants, has not been altogether appealing. Thus, the I.R.A. has found considerable room in which to operate, and grounds on which to charge a succession of Irish governments with lassitude, indifference, or "truckling to Britain." But the I.R.A. has remained fissiparous itself, one wing inclined to blame capitalism for the smug, materialistic inactivity of the southern politicians; the other less interested in ideology and more disposed to fight the Protestants of Northern Ireland, and the British, at every opportunity.

In a work of this breadth it would be disproportionate to attempt a chronicle of the course of Irish history since the second world war. For such subjects as De Valera's policy of neutrality, the struggle over social policy in the republic, and the development of the civil rights struggle in Ulster, readers will have to consult works devoted more specifically to modern and contemporary Ireland.[25] The object of this chapter has been to show the dynamics that produced the modern Irish state, and its imperfections. Any denouement (or exacerbation) of the crisis which began in 1969 with the civil rights movement in the north will only be intelligible against this background; but no outcome can be predicted upon the basis of this knowledge. Unless one of the contending parties manages to destroy the other, or expel it from the island, Ireland will have to continue to accommodate two traditionally inimical populations whether in two states, or one. The tenacity of northern Protestants should not be underestimated any more than should the determination of some Nationalists to continue fighting for a united Ireland, until it is achieved.

If there is any miracle drug in the political apothecary, perhaps it is "prosperity." Much of the sectarian bitterness in Ireland has been exacerbated, even if it has not been created, by generations of poverty, insecurity on the land, low wages and high unemployment in the cities. If Ireland were to prosper, might any of this rancor abate? In eighteenth- and nineteenth-century Ireland wealth was concentrated in a few hands and the island as a whole was poor. But the twentieth-century has caught glimpses of a future Ireland with comfort and security for many. Efficient modern farming and dairying can turn Irish land into a chief granary and grocery of the European Economic Community, which Ireland joined formally in 1973. Capital, technology, and management skills can provide employment for Irish workers in light industry such as pharmaceuticals and electronics, or even heavy industry such as chemicals and automobile assembly. Mineralogists have located valuable deposits of metals such as zinc and copper of which Ireland was previously thought barren, or hold out the dream of possible oil and gas treasures beneath the Celtic Sea.

Not all of these visions may come to pass, and each has at least some undesirable consequences. Traditionalists may abhor them altogether, but it is beyond doubting that a great deal of progress has already been made, and that year by year Ireland more nearly approximates the standard of living attained by the rest of Western Europe. A world depression might end all of this, but until or unless it does, it seems reasonable to expect Ireland to continue to diverge from the Ireland of the famine or the land war, to become increasingly urbanized, industrialized, cosmopolitan, and even secular. If such a transmogrification does occur perhaps it will overtake and evacuate of their force the passions inherited from the past. On the other hand, one cannot count on that fickle fate, prosperity. No less likely is it that the ghosts of the past will sabotage the future, keeping the dream of a tranquil, prosperous Ireland out of reach. History can show the path by which one has come. It can connect the present with the past. It can see *where* the future will be, but not *what* it will be. Such are its limits.

8

THE IRISH ABROAD:
EXAMPLES AND
CONCLUSIONS

For the early part of its long history Ireland was a receptacle, a catchment area for Celts, Vikings, Normans, English, Welsh, and Scots. Much of the story of that period concerns the conflict with, or assimilation of, these immigrants. There were always, of course, some emigrants, none more famous than St. Brendan and the peripatetic Irish saints of the sixth and seventh centuries. But emigration of a more profound sort came to be a hallmark of the modern era, and it remains one of the least easily assessed aspects of Irish history. That dramatic population movement created one Ireland at home and a host of Irelands abroad. Unlike the Jewish diaspora, it did not drain its Palestine entirely, but depleted it sufficiently to end the earlier identity of all things Irish with the island of Ireland. For an observer of Irish history and culture, the problem is how to follow this diaspora, and how to relate it to developments within the island home.

For some, emigration is the single most important fact of modern Irish history. One scholar stated the case extravagantly when he wrote:

... all prominent personalities in Irish politics over the past century or so would not have been heard of but for emigration.... The reason is that, without emigration, which for 150 years has removed permanently from Ireland every second person born in Cork and the other twenty-five counties of the Irish Republic, the course of Irish history would have been totally different. In an Ireland not bled by emigration of every ounce of radicalism there would have been no place for people like Parnell, Pearse, De Valera, and the others, all of heterogeneous racial origin and with tenuous Irish connections.[1]

This view is not so much in error, as unverifiable. One cannot say with certainty what the effect of no emigration would have been, nor can one imagine what other factors would also have had to be different in order to diminish the pressure to leave.

The very breadth of the diaspora also complicates its assessment. Although by far the greatest part of the emigration was to Britain, Canada, the United States, Australia, and New Zealand, the *early* emigrants went principally to France, Spain, Austria, and the Netherlands, and a good many of the *later* ones wound up in exotic places like India, South Africa, or Latin America. No short chapter in a short book could hope to comprehend, or do justice to, the extent and color of the dispersion. What is intended, instead, is to chronicle the origins of modern Irish emigration and then offer as case studies several brief descriptions of the experience of the Irish abroad.

Early emigration from Ireland was aristocratic and scholarly in nature. Irish students, particularly from the Pale, were relatively common at Oxford in the late Middle Ages. This was partly the result of the growth of interest in university education, and the absence of any such institution in Ireland until the late sixteenth-century. A small number of Irish students sought educations on the European continent, and this number grew dramatically after 1570 when the doctrines of the Church of England were proclaimed by the papacy to be heretical. Irish and Anglo-Irish families that wanted their sons reared in Roman orthodoxy could, if they had the means, send them to the universities and seminaries of Catholic Europe. By the middle of the seventeenth century there were some twenty

"Irish colleges" scattered across Europe, with the heaviest concentration in France and the southern Netherlands. Some, like the two at Paris and Nantes, were sizable, and might have had as many as a hundred Irish students at a time. Others, like those at Santiago, or Seville, in Spain, seldom attracted more than a dozen. Few of these colleges lasted as long as a century and a half, and their heyday, as a class, was the early eighteenth century. Their collective purpose was to sustain and nourish Roman orthodoxy among the Irish, and to this end they made a significant contribution. The colleges helped to sustain a Catholic culture, church, and hierarchy, among the Irish outside of Ireland, but the exact impact of this activity upon Catholicism *within* Ireland is not clear. The Church faced profound obstacles to maintaining or expanding the faith within the island, and its success should not be exaggerated.

The seminarians did not necessarily intend to remain abroad; many hoped to return at the earliest opportunity. But they were followed from the early seventeenth century onward by a class of emigrants whose departure was more permanent. These were the "Wild Geese," the warriors who despaired of their own, and Ireland's future in the aftermath of the Elizabethan conquest of Ulster. From the late sixteenth century onward Irish soldiers found that they could sell their services profitably to the Catholic monarchs of Europe, particularly Spain with its far-flung empire and constant crises. By the eighteenth century Irish soldiers and brigades were a familiar institution of Continental military life, and were serving in the armies of Austria, Spain, and especially France.

The Wild Geese did not produce a concentrated Irish colony in any single place. On the contrary, they left flashes of a Celtic presence across Europe; an outstanding French cognac named Hennessy; a Celtic Cross at Fontenoy, in Belgium (erected in 1907), to mark the spot where, in 1745, the Irish played a major role in a French defeat of the English during the War of the Austrian Succession. Fontenoy was, in some ways, the symbolic climax of this military exodus.

Six regiments of Irish foot soldiers, and one of cavalry, took part in the battle, some 4,000 men in a French force of roughly 30,000. The Irish foot soldiers played a distinguished part, and suffered heavy casualties. Among the opposing English force were several thousand of their countrymen: coreligionists who had sold their services to the nearer, Protestant bidder, rather than the further, Catholic one.[2]

The Wild Geese may have been driven out of their native land by the constraints placed upon them there, but their departure was more volitional than that of thousands of poor Catholic Irish who were forceably carried to the West Indies and Middle American colonies in the middle years of the seventeenth century. From the 1630s onward Irish men and women were a major component of the immigration to the Leeward Islands and Barbados, and after the British capture of Jamaica from Spain in 1655 they were a mainstay of that settlement. At many points, the Irish Catholic populations of these colonies outnumbered the Protestant British, giving rise to grave concern about their long-term stability. Introduced to the West Indies and Virginia as indentured servants, Irish immigrants were, for the most part, overwhelmed and displaced by the tide of black African labor the slave merchants introduced.[3] Few, if any, Irish Catholic families survived this process to rise to prominence *in situ*, although Irish surnames remain common in Jamaica among yet another group of "black Irish."[4]

The first wave of Irish emigrants to make a lasting mark in American locations were Protestants. Some would deny that they were "Irish," and it is by the term "Scots-Irish" that they have generally been known in the United States. Ulster received in the course of the seventeenth century by far the largest migration of Britons to occur in Irish history. Exactly why this immigration was not adequately absorbed, but was partially disgorged to North America in the eighteenth century, is not easy to explain. One can merely recite on the one hand the grievances of Ulster farmers: high rents, low prices, religious constraints, and the vagaries of the linen trade; and on the other hand, the historical allurements of North America: cheap land, religious freedom, and prospects of economic opportunity.[5] Whatever the reasons, thousands of Ulster Protestants crossed the Atlantic in the middle decades of the eighteenth century and established themselves along the Appalachian frontier, especially in Pennsylvania, Virginia, and North Carolina.

There was *some* Irish Catholic migration to North America in the eighteenth century, but it was numerically insignificant prior to 1815. From the end of the Napoleonic Wars, annual emigration of Catholics from Ireland was substantial, and it has remained such almost down to the present day, with the most dramatic surge occurring in the years immediately following the Great Famine. It is basically this exodus of the last century and a half which has resulted in the Irish diaspora as we know it. The United States, Britain, Australia, and Canada were the principal, but by no means the exclusive, destinations. Between 1841 and 1851 the number of Irish-born inhabitants of Great Britain rose from 49,000 to nearly 734,000.[6] Between 1841 and 1925 some 70,000 Irish migrated to Canada, 370,000 to Australia; and nearly 4.75 million to the United States.[7] Smaller numbers found their way to South Africa, South America, and New Zealand.

Emigration occurred in different ways, from different places, and for different reasons. The most obvious variation is in volume, which changed, sometimes dramatically, from year to year or decade to decade. But the emigrant flow itself also changed in its composition, in its proportion of males to females, of landholders to landless laborers, of better-off to worse-off, of literate to illiterate, of individuals to families, and of countrymen of one area to countrymen of another. To give but one example, the places in Ireland from which emigrants tended to come showed striking variation over the course of the nineteenth century. Between 1821 and 1841 Ulster and its neighboring counties in Leinster and Connacht suffered by far the heaviest losses of pop-

ulation through emigration, a phenomenon which has been
ascribed to the contraction of the textile industry in that
area.[8] Only very gradually did the emigrant stream come to
be dominated by refugees from the subsistence farming
areas of the south and west, and even then a complex of
factors (including the ability to raise the needed passage
money) underlay the change.

BRITAIN

Britain was the first, closest, and cheapest refuge, and it
has continued to be one of the most important. As recently
as 1946–51, eight out of ten Irish emigrants were relocating
in England, Scotland, or Wales, and the census of 1971 revealed that nearly 9 percent of the inhabitants of the English Midlands industrial county of Lancashire were Irish-
born, as were nearly 15 percent of the inhabitants of the
Scottish counties surrounding Glasgow.[9] The geography of
the British Isles has always permitted a two-way flow of
populations between Britain and Ireland, but whereas this
flow was predominantly westward, to Ireland, in the early
period, it reversed, toward Britain, in the modern period.
The inauguration of cross-channel steam packet service in
1818 from Glasgow to Belfast facilitated, rather than
caused, this phenomenon.[10]

The peak of Irish emigration to Britain was reached in
1861, by which time the census counted 601,634 Irish-born
in England and Wales (approximately 3 percent of the population) and 204,083 in Scotland (6.7 percent of the population).[11] From that point the Irish-born population stabilized at the level of about 700,000 persons, while the
population of Britain as a whole continued to expand. By
1951 the Irish-born constituted only 1.4 percent of the population of England and Wales, and 1.7 percent of that of
Scotland, but these percentages neglect a very sizable number of people who were not born in Ireland, but were of
Irish descent and identity. A British sociologist could write
with justification in 1963: "Britain is now the main desti-

nation for Irish emigrants, and whereas in 1890 the number of Irish-born in Great Britain was only one-third the number in the United States, today there are considerably more Irish-born than in the United States."[12] United States immigration restrictions in 1920, 1924, 1929, and 1930 drastically reduced the number of immigrants from Ireland (and elsewhere), but Britain facilitated immigration from the newly independent Irish state, partially as a means of stressing the benefits of the Commonwealth tie. Some of the migration to Britain was merely seasonal, and represented the search for work by laborers who would return to Ireland within a matter of months, or years. Other migrants tarried only briefly in Britain before taking shipping from there to a more permanent destination overseas. Thus the place of Britain in the story of Irish emigration is considerably more complicated than that of the more distant lands in which the Irish settled.

By and large, emigrants seem to go the shortest distance necessary to accomplish their purpose. Thus, intending emigrants from Ulster gravitated to Belfast, from where they took shipping to Glasgow. Midlanders gravitated to Dublin *en route* to Liverpool and the English Midlands; and southerners followed a similar path via Cork to Bristol, or eventually London. For the most part they were bound for the cities and major towns. Only in rare areas, such as Wigtownshire in Scotland, did sizable numbers of Irish immigrants find work as agricultural laborers.[13] It was urban and industrial life which awaited most of the immigrants. Glasgow is thought to have had 31,000 Irish Catholics by 1831, Manchester, 35,000 by 1825, and Liverpool, 24,000 by the same date.[14] The census of 1841 showed the greatest concentration of Irish (above 5 percent of the population) in those English and Scottish counties adjacent to the ports of arrival. The areas least affected were the northern counties of Scotland, the central counties of Wales, the southwesternmost English county of Cornwall, and the eastern region of East Anglia.

For centuries there had been small Irish colonies in the

major towns. The London Irish were roughly estimated at
14,000 in 1814.[15] By 1841 the number had climbed to nearly
80,000, and with the passage of another decade it rose to
109,000.[16] Because the census from which these figures are
taken measured only the Irish-born, and not subsequent
generations of Irish descent, the mid-century Irish community in London was probably much larger, perhaps over
200,000. Certainly it was sufficiently large to justify a recent statement by a student of the subject: "The Irish were
easily the biggest and indeed the only large foreign group
in London until the last quarter of the nineteenth century,
when migration from eastern Europe and Russia created a
substantial Jewish community."[17]

London had an infamous Irish quarter as early as the
eighteenth century, the so-called rookery of St. Giles, now
completely effaced by the tangle of streets just to the southwest of the British Museum. Near it, in 1792, was built St.
Patrick's, Soho, the first church in England dedicated to the
patron saint of Ireland. As the London Irish became more
numerous, they settled in numerous districts rather than
concentrating in any one. By the end of the nineteenth century "they had created not a ghetto but a string of settlements tucked into the tumbledown corners of working-
class London."[18]

The Irish in London tended not to take over whole districts but rather the poorest dwellings and shops in a variety of areas, thus constituting a kind of web rather than a
compact settlement. The 1851 census clearly revealed the
London Irish concentrated "in occupations that placed
most of them among the lowest social and economic
groups."[19] The only skilled trades in which they established
themselves were shoemaking and tailoring "both depressed
industries where conditions were slowly deteriorating with
the influx of child and female labor."[20] Irish men tended to
be general laborers. Women found work in domestic service
and the clothing trades. Henry Mayhew, the century's most
celebrated investigator of London's poor, estimated that
around 1851 there were some 10,000 Irish hawkers and

street vendors, most of them selling fruit.[21] By the next census, in 1861, matters had improved very little, and even at the end of the century, the Irish were a prominent part of London's poor, long after they had been joined by more recent Jewish and Italian immigrants, most of whom lacked a knowledge of English.

The Irish underwent various changes in their urban English environment, even if they were not at first upwardly mobile. They were country people, small farmers and rural laborers, forced to adapt to a rapidly expanding industrial and urban society. The patterns of their lives came slowly to approximate those of the host population among whom they were dwelling. Thus, for instance, average family size declined among the Irish in both London and Liverpool, and average age at marriage tended to decline as well.[22] Smaller and less fecund families became the rule. The diminished role of the Catholic Church may have played a part in this process, for the Catholic Church in England had a much less immediate and powerful impact upon the lives of its parishioners than did the mid- and late nineteenth-century Church in Ireland. On the other hand, the Irish immigration created a crisis for the slowly reviving English Catholic Church. Whereas the Catholic Church in the United States was largely formed and molded by immigrant Catholics, particularly Irish and German, a relatively small elite of English Catholics fought vigorously, and ultimately successfully, to retain control of the Church in their country. The tide of Irish coreligionists was both an embarrassment and a challenge. It impeded the painfully slow ascent to social respectability and influence, and it created a pressing need for more clergy, more churches, and more funds.[23]

It has often been asserted that the Irish became less religiously observant in their English setting, and this falling away from the Church has sometimes been blamed on the inadequate response of English Catholics to the challenge of so many immigrant Irish in their midst. Neither part of the hypothesis is easily verified, due to the difficulty of measuring the levels of observance in different times and places. One scholar has estimated that at mid-century, whereas attendance at mass may have included some 75 percent of the population in Ireland, the figure was closer to 50 percent among the Irish in England, almost irrespective of the part of the country in which they lived.[24] Thus, the falling away, although measurable, was probably less than catastrophic, and was part of the larger process of adaptation to a new environment itself in the midst of dramatic change.

Irish immigration to Britain was more than a flash in the pan. It was a sustained population movement which continues to the present day and has resulted in connections between the two islands that Americans of Irish background have sometimes failed to understand. Although there remain city districts with high concentrations of Irish, such as the borough of Paddington in London (with 8.4 percent of the population recorded as Irish in 1951), the area in Glasgow called "the Gorbals," or "Scotland Road" in Liverpool, the Irish population has tended to disperse throughout the country. By 1951 not one British county had more than 5 percent Irish born, compared with a maximum of 11 percent in 1861; and only one county—Warwickshire, with its large Irish population in Birmingham—had more than 2.5 percent. The Irish constituted less than 2 percent of the population of England, Scotland, and Wales, and about 3.3 percent of the population of London. As in the United States, people of Irish descent have become a substantial, abiding, and ubiquitous component of society at large.

The Irish in Britain are overwhelmingly (five-sevenths) from the twenty-six counties which became the Irish Free State.[25] The south and the west have been particularly strongly represented. Between 1851 and 1900 the six counties of Cork, Kerry, Galway, Tipperary, Mayo, and Limerick accounted for 48 percent of the emigration to Britain from the twenty-six counties, and between 1900 and 1921, Cork, Mayo, Galway, Kerry, Donegal and Clare accounted for 55 percent of the emigration.[26] Since 1921 there has been an increase in the relative number of emigrants from Dublin and other towns, but this is a reflection of the tendency toward urbanization within Ireland itself. For the most part the rural Irish arrived in large numbers on the British scene just in time to participate in much of the trauma, and little of the triumph, of industrialization. Gangs of them won the appellation of "navvies" (for navigators) when they were employed to dig the eighteenth- and early-nineteenth century canals that revolutionized and cheapened England's inland transportation system. They went on to be prominent parts of the work force which built the tunnels, bridges, and railways devised by a generation of bold Victorian engineers and entrepreneurs.

Gradually Irish laborers gravitated to certain occupations. In Liverpool, for instance, by 1830 all the bricklayers' laborers were said to be Irish, whereas they had all been English thirty years earlier.[27] The Irish tended to find work in unskilled sectors where there was little trade or union organization to resist them. Many worked on the docks, or in the coalfields of south Wales or west Scotland, and sometimes English employers consciously used them in those locales to break up strikes of native workers. On the London docks many Irish rose to be stevedores. Although by the end of the century there were some remarkable tales of individual financial success, Irish immigrants were still concentrated on the lowest rungs of the work force. The census of 1911 showed that of 63,408 Irish-born, employed males, nearly 12,000 were in mining, and nearly 25,000 in manufacture of iron and metals.[28]

Politically, the Irish in Britain came in the early twentieth century to be closely identified with the emerging Labour party. Despite the Catholic Church's opposition to trade unionism, Irish immigrants and their descendants played an important role in numerous radical causes. Even as early as the 1840s three of the leading Chartists were John Doherty, Bronterre O'Brien, and Fergus O'Connor (although the Irish were not prominent in the lower ranks of

the movement). Later in the century Irish labor leaders
were active in the great dock strike of 1889. Disraeli's Reform Act of 1867, together with the Ballot Act of 1872, gave
the power of the vote to perhaps as many as 150,000 male
Irish by 1885.[29] This voice, if mobilized and concerted,
could make an impact on either an internal, British question, or a matter bearing upon the independence of Ireland.

Numerous Irish nationalist organizations developed among
the Irish in Britain. The Home Rule Confederation of Great
Britain was formed in Manchester in 1875, and in 1882
changed its name to the Irish National League of Great
Britain. One of its leaders, T. P. O'Connor, was elected in
1885 as "the first, and only, Irish nationalist candidate in
an English constituency" and held that seat, the "Scotland
Division" of Liverpool, until 1929.[30] The League effectively
mobilized the Irish vote in Britain behind Parnell, but with
the great leader's disgrace in 1890, the movement was left
leaderless in Britain as well as Ireland. Reborn as the
United Irish League, the movement attached itself to John
Redmond, Parnell's harried successor, and the Irish vote in
Britain remained strongly organized until the outbreak of
the first world war.

The emergence of the Labour party in the elections of
1918, and the outbreak of serious fighting in Ireland in
1920–21 dissolved the relative unanimity of the Irish in
Britain. Thereafter the community began to reflect the
same vigorous divisions of opinion that were fragmenting
Ireland itself. Furthermore, second and third generation
Irish experienced some assimilation into British society.
After 1922 the establishment of an independent Irish state
freed these "British-Irish," to some extent, from the burden
of constantly demonstrating support for the Irish cause.
Their primary concerns could become their own lives in
Britain and the imperfections of the state in which they
lived and worked.

While undergoing a measure of assimilation, the Irish
community in Britain remained large and diverse enough

to harbor extreme nationalists in its midst. Both in 1937 and 1973–74 the I.R.A. mounted terrorist campaigns in Britain which authorities found it almost impossible to combat, even if their political impact was ultimately very small. A large part of the terrorists' success resulted from their ability to merge into a large and, for the most part, law-abiding population of Irish background. The presence of the Irish in Britain has not failed to elicit a nativist, or xenophobic response, especially in periods of Anglo-Irish tension. By 1835 there were three hundred lodges of the Catholophobic Orange Order in Britain, and the industrial cities of the north and Scotland have proved particularly fertile breeding grounds for anti-Irish and anti-Catholic movements.[31] Thus the removal of the Irish from Ireland to England has not necessarily resolved "the Irish problem," but merely refashioned and relocated it. On the whole, however, it has contributed to a more cosmopolitan and less provincial attitude within the British Isles and, perhaps, it has laid the groundwork for a less antagonistic and more equitable relationship between the political states established there.

THE UNITED STATES

The Irish migration to North America has had a very different result. It was so heavy for so long, and its effects were so enduring, that it rapidly created an Irish population far larger than the one left behind in Ireland. Perhaps some five million Irish Catholics, in all, have removed to the United States in the last two centuries, but they have proliferated to the point that the Irish-American community is reckoned to contain some twenty-five million people, or more than five times the number of Catholics in present-day Ireland, north and south. The United States was by far the largest recipient of Irish immigration. Between 1876 and 1921, for instance, the United States received 84 percent of the emigrants from the twenty-six counties of the current Irish Free State. In contrast, 8 percent went to England, Wales, and Scotland; 7 percent went to Australia, and 1 percent went to all other countries combined.[32]

The effect of so massive an immigration was to create in the United States a veritable "Ireland Abroad," and yet the dispersion of these five million Irish over so spacious a land resulted in their encountering dissimilar, sometimes antipodal, circumstances. Imagine the difference between the life of a domestic servant in Boston, and that of a sheep farmer in eastern Oregon, one of the comparatively rare areas where Irish immigrants found rural vocations. Or the difference between the difficulty of professing Catholicism (and observing its rituals) in Puritan New England, and the relative ease of joining an already established Catholic community, albeit largely French, in New Orleans. Over the migratory period as a whole, rural areas were neglected, and Irish settlement was most pronounced in the growing cities of the east and midwest: Boston, the New England mill towns, New York, Philadelphia, Chicago, Milwaukee, Minneapolis, and St. Louis. In 1940, nine out of ten Irish immigrants (from the southern twenty-six counties) were living in major cities, more than half of them in New York, Chicago, Philadelphia, Boston, and San Francisco.[33] The descendants of these immigrants are still to be found in the largest numbers around those urban centers, but by now there must be very few sections or towns in the United States where Irish names are rare or unknown.

The rate of immigration to the United States was most intense in the late 1840s and early 1850s, a direct consequence of the famine, but it again reached the dramatic level of 655,000 per decade in the 1880s, before diminishing gradually and erratically in the twentieth century. In the 1920s it was still some 220,000, but dropped to a mere 13,000 in the 1930s. For the 1960s it was 37,461.[34] The cities of the eastern seaboard were inundated by the post-famine tide, with resulting strains on the social fabric. In Boston, for instance, between 1856 and 1863, at least half of the inmates of the House of Correction were Irish, as in 1864 were three-fourths of all persons arrested and detained by the police.[35] The violent antidraft riots in New York City in 1863 drew in large part on the bitter frustrations of the city's growing population of poor Irish. Northern abolitionists seemed more sensitive to the sufferings of the South's slaves than to the poverty and misery of the immigrants in their very midst.

It is not easy to generalize about the immigrants, although certain tendencies have been observed in the surviving records. Most of the immigrants were young and unmarried at the time of their disembarkation, but they were not *all* males, and indeed, in some years the number of female immigrants outnumbered males. "In contrast to the overwhelming preponderance of males in the immigrant populations of most other ethnic groups, the Irish had the greatest percentage of female immigrants."[36] Only a very small percentage of the male immigrants claimed before immigration authorities that they were, or had been, "farmers," and that fact, together with the relatively high cost of starting an agricultural enterprise (estimated at $1,000 in 1860) may help to explain the rareness of Irish involvement in American agriculture.[37]

A good deal has been written about Irish family structure, both in Ireland and abroad, by sociologists, social anthropologists and, more recently, social historians. The anthropologists, particularly Conrad Arensberg, have created a highly detailed and influential model of post-famine family structure.[38] It remains to be seen how well this model corresponded to localities other than that of County Clare, from which a great deal of it was derived by Arensberg in the 1920s. For instance, how accurate was it for Wicklow in the 1850s, or Armagh in the 1880s? Was it a model which adequately described the Irish family overseas? Was it in any sense enduring and widespread, or was it time- and place-specific in ways which the anthropologists did not discover?

The basic feature of this model was the so-called stem family, an extended household usually clustered around a moderately sized (more than fifteen acres) piece of country property. The post-famine disinclination to divide property meant that the heir to this unit of wealth owned little or nothing until his father's death. He married late, if at all, and might well bring his bride into his parents' household. Controversy still surrounds this model, though it is doubtless correct in substance. Abroad, however, new pressures and circumstances gradually reshaped Irish families until no single pattern, or model, remained.

Language facility is another vexing question concerning the immigrants. By 1841 probably no more than 20 percent of the population of Ireland spoke Irish exclusively (i.e., knew no English). Literacy in English spread rapidly throughout the remainder of the nineteenth century, speared on by the educational efforts of the Catholic Church. It would be possible—but almost certainly wrong—to assume that immigration occurred predominantly among the exclusively Irish-speaking. In fact, many Irish-speakers came to America, and Irish-language newspapers (for the literate among them) appeared in New York and other major cities. But English was the language of the majority, and knowledge of the Irish language died out even faster among the Irish in America than it was doing among the Irish in Ireland. Irish immigrants were discriminated against on social and religious grounds in many parts of the United States, but it is correct to distinguish the Irish from other European immigrants who faced an acute language barrier.

The propensity of Irish immigrants to settle in urban areas has already been mentioned, and this has often been explained in terms of the lack of opportunity on the land. The reasons may be deeper rooted and more complex. In the 1890s Archbishop John Ireland of St. Paul contrived to purchase a large tract of fertile Minnesota land and settle it with both Irish and Belgian farmers. The Belgians prospered, but the Irish "quickly abandoned their fields to work in factories or on the railroad."[39] If this was a fair test case, it may reveal that there were other than economic reasons for Irish immigrants to settle in the cities. Or perhaps we simply do not yet understand well enough the circumstances they faced on the land in general, on Archbishop Ireland's tract in particular, or elsewhere.

The history of the development of the Catholic Church in the United States is a subject much larger than that of Irish immigration, but it is one in which the Irish play a central part. Between 1850 and 1900 the Roman Catholic population of the United States increased from 1.5 to over 12 million. In effect, the Irish were in on the ground floor of the Church's dramatic expansion. Although today they constitute only 20 percent of the nation's Catholics, in 1861 they were reckoned to constitute 80 percent.[40] Only German Catholic immigrants were numerous enough to vie with the Irish for domination of the Church, and the Irish won by almost every test. "Of 464 bishops appointed in the American Catholic Church from 1789 to 1935, 268, or 58 percent were the sons of Irish fathers."[41] Of the 69 bishops in the American Church in 1886, 35 were of Irish ancestry or birth, 15 were German (including Swiss and Austrian), 11 French, 5 English, 1 Dutch, and 1 Spanish.[42]

How should one assess the Irish contribution to the Catholic Church in America? On the one hand, as the first numerous wave of Catholic immigrants the Irish gave a vulgar image to a faith which had previously been identified with a small, generally privileged minority. Catholicism was no real threat to American Protestantism before the Irish. On the other hand, the Irish dominated the hierarchy and are said to have imparted to the American church a strength and discipline that made it a major force in American life. This is easy to illustrate, but difficult to prove. Perhaps the ascetic and puritanical quality of Irish Catholicism needs itself to be better understood, before we can speak confidently of its impact on a new and polyglot church in America.

BOSTON

The experience of the Irish in America has varied considerably with the regions in which they settled. The best known of these is, ironically, the region in which they probably fared worst—New England. Boston was the closest major United States port to the British Isles. By 1840 it was a city two hundred years old, not much younger, in fact, than the Protestant ascendancy in Ireland. For the middle and latter part of the nineteenth century, Boston was a city in relative decline, as the center of entrepreneurial activity shifted to New York, Philadelphia, Baltimore, and the newer cities of the midwest. In social terms, no part of the United States was more similar to the Ireland the immigrants had left. Protestant families of mainly English extraction controlled the economy of the region, owning the land, the factories, and most of the investment capital.[43] Through sheer force of numbers the Irish were gradually able to dislodge these Yankees politically, but with remarkably little impact upon the social and economic structure of the region. An Irishman was elected mayor of Boston for the first time in 1886, and in 1889 the Irish won a majority of seats on the City Council. A second Irish mayor, Patrick Collins, was elected in 1901, and was succeeded in 1905 by John F. ("Honey-Fitz") Fitzgerald, maternal grandfather of President John F. Kennedy. Boston was politically dominated by the Irish almost continuously thereafter, most flamboyantly and unapologetically under James Michael Curley, mayor from 1921 to 1925, 1929 to 1933, and governor of Massachusetts from 1934 to 1936.

Politics gave the Irish access to patronage, and patronage eventually provided thousands of secure, though generally low-paid, jobs in the various branches of government. The influence of Irish politicians also eased the way for Irish entrepreneurs to win contracts for construction, provisioning, or numerous other services required by government. But the rapid ascent of Irish leaders to political power did *not* have a dramatic effect upon the Irish population of Boston as a whole, or upon its level of education, accumulation of wealth, or attainment of professional or highly salaried vocations. The census of 1890 recorded that a negligible percentage of Irish immigrants were members of the professions (.013 percent), that 10 percent were in white-collar work, 25 percent in skilled manual labor, and 65 percent in unskilled work. This put the immigrant Irish at the bottom of the labor ladder. By contrast, of American-born Protestants in Boston, 4 percent were in the professions, 43 percent were white collar workers, 29 percent were skilled laborers, and only 24 percent were in unskilled labor. Even the Scandinavian immigrants, who vied with the Irish for last place, made a far better showing.[44] On the other hand, the 1890 census figures suggest that *second* generation Irish were faring considerably better than their immigrant parents, but not so well as the second generations of the other immigrant groups.[45]

In contrast to the evidence of slow occupational advancement among the Irish in Boston, a study of the Massachusetts textile town of Newburyport has suggested that "the Irish working class families were especially successful in accumulating property."[46] This has been explained in terms of "land hunger" and the "older peasant values," on the assumption that one lesson of the famine was the indispensability of the land, and that the Irish in America, despite their urban settings, struggled desperately to purchase the land they lived on and the houses which sheltered them. Investment in property, however humble, may even have taken precedence over investment in the younger generation's education, although such a theory neglects the way in which Irish immigrants *did* invest in education through the Catholic Church. The Catholic educational system purposely turned its back on science and the professions, until well into the twentieth century, with some probable restraint on upward mobility. This is not to criticize the Church (though many commentators have proceeded to that conclusion), for our own age is eccentric in the high economic value it has set on scientific and secular knowledge, and churchmen could hardly have foreseen that in vigorously upholding traditional moral values they were restricting the avenues of wordly advancement for their students.

In any case, social and economic advancement was to come eventually for a large number of Irish immigrants and their descendants. By 1969 the median income of "Irish" families in the United States was slightly above the national median, and by that year, "the employment status of Irish males over 16 showed 29.6 percent in high-level white collar jobs (managerial and professional) compared with 28.2 percent nationally."[47]

In Boston the Irish rose in the Church, politics, and the entertainment world, including athletics. Limitations on social and economic opportunity have a way of breeding fighters, and out of Boston emerged John L. Sullivan, the most legendary of American prizefighters. Sullivan's great decade was the 1880s, and in the course of it he became the idol of the Irish and much of the nation. Until about 1890 boxers fought bare-fisted and hit, kicked, or gouged one another until there was an indisputable victor. Sullivan's last bare-knuckled defense of his heavyweight title in 1889 went for seventy-five rounds.[48] His fame was an important contribution to the stereotype of "the fighting Irish" which had at least as much of America in it, as of Ireland. The Irish prizefighters fought for their own gain and glory, not for Ireland's, but an unintended side effect was to touch with a reputation for strength and courage every American of Irish descent.

PHILADELPHIA

Boston was a hard town, but at the end of the nineteenth century, only 17 percent of Irish-Americans lived in Massachusetts, Rhode Island, or Connecticut, the southern New England region of which Boston was more-or-less typical;[49] 15.5 percent were in Illinois, Iowa, and Missouri, while 35 percent were in the two mid-Atlantic states of New York and Pennsylvania.[50] In Philadelphia especially they seem to have prospered, at least relatively. Compared with Boston, Philadelphia in the second half of the nineteenth century was a flourishing metropolis with a relative abundance of

land, jobs, and housing. Old Boston was geographically wa-
terlocked, a peninsula jutting into the harbor. Philadelphia
had ample room to spread up the widening triangle of land
above the convergence of the Schuylkill and Delaware rivers. Compared to Boston's four, and Manhattan's twenty-
two square miles, Philadelphia comprised an expansive 130
square miles.[51]

Although, as in Boston, there were areas of wretched
slum housing, the Irish appear to have become owner-
occupiers at a much earlier point in Philadelphia. In the
Moyamensing district, for instance, more than half the
property owners were Irish, by name, in 1851.[52] Some of
the slum tenements were Irish-owned as well, and it seems
likely that an Irish middle class had established itself in
Philadelphia prior to the post-famine tide of immigrants.
The superior housing conditions in Philadelphia were reflected in the death rates recorded in the cholera epidemic
of 1849. While New York lost 35 citizens per 1,000, and
Boston 26.5, better sanitary conditions contributed to Philadelphia's low rate of 20.9. Among the Irish-born the death
rate in Boston was 37.7 per 1,000; 21.2 in New York, and
only 12.2 in Philadelphia.[53]

The anachronistic Philadelphia custom of ground rent
meant that immigrants could rent building lots at a nominal sum for long periods, rather than having to accumulate
the sum necessary to buy them. The row houses for which
the city became famous further reduced the cost of accom-
modations through economies of construction. Small houses
could be purchased in the 1870s for $1,000 to $2,500, or
rented for $8 to $15 per month.[54] A survey of 1869 found
rents in Philadelphia to be approximately half those in
New York, and Boston was even more expensive.[55] A European visitor in the 1860s observed that "there is certainly
not a city in the world where the working population lives
with the comfort they enjoy in Philadelphia."[56] The growth
of more than six hundred building and loan associations by
1875 helped to provide the capital for the proliferation of
immigrants' homes. Home ownership on a modest but com-

fortable scale was apparently an achievable goal for most of the Irish who settled in the Quaker City.[57]

Not only was housing relatively cheap, but jobs were abundant. The economy of Philadelphia flourished in the decades after 1850, and there was employment in the manufacture of iron, machinery, textiles, shoes, and clothing, as well as in transportation and construction. By 1850, it has been estimated, only one-third of the Irish in Philadelphia were still classified as laborers. Many were drifting into retail trades or small manufacturing concerns. In 1857 one-fifth of the grocers listed in the city directory had Irish names, a far larger proportion than in Boston.[58] It may be that the differences between the Irish situation in Boston and Philadelphia have been exaggerated, but there should be little doubt that Philadelphia, far more than Boston, lived up to the immigrants' dream of a new world, a new life, and a land of opportunity.

As if to illustrate the almost reciprocal relationship between the private and public sectors, the Philadelphia Irish were slow to enter politics, the police, and the civil service. Even when they became active, they failed to dominate city government in the way of the Boston Irish. This was partially due to the fact that their early Democratic proclivities left them an impotent minority in a staunchly Republican city and state.[59] Not until the 1960s was an Irish Catholic elected mayor of Philadelphia.

Boston's best-known figure of Irish extraction is President John F. Kennedy, in whose parentage was combined the political legacy of his maternal grandfather, John F. Fitzgerald, mayor of Boston, and the business fortune of his father, Joseph P. Kennedy. The colorful and dramatic ascent of the Boston Kennedys elicits awe and admiration from some and vigorous censure from others. Philadelphia's nearest counterpart, perhaps, is Princess Grace Grimaldi of Monaco, a one-time movie star of rare beauty, born as Grace Kelly. Her father, John B. Kelly, was one of ten children of an immigrant from County Mayo. From a bricklayer's apprentice he rose to be the owner of the largest brickworks in the country.[60] John B. made a fortune in contracting, switched his political support from the Republicans to the Democrats in 1933, and ran unsuccessfully for mayor in 1935. His family fame was furthered thereafter by his daughter, whose cultivated manner and well-publicized adventures in high society symbolized the gentility achieved in the twentieth century by some Irish Catholics in Philadelphia.

As a site of Irish settlement, New York has been much less well investigated than either Boston or Philadelphia. It had the largest Irish population of the three, but in a much more fluid setting. In 1850 26 percent of the population of New York City consisted of persons born in Ireland: some 133,000 out of 513,000. The census of 1890 showed 190,000 Irish born, plus 409,000 children of Irish immigrants.[61] At that date they may well have constituted a majority of the citizenry, but thereafter the relative size of the Irish constituency declined, as central and south European immigrants thronged the city. Crudely speaking, New York resembled Philadelphia in its relative abundance of jobs, but also resembled Boston in the prominent part played by the Irish in politics. New York's first Irish Catholic mayor, William R. Grace, was elected in 1880. Born in County Cork, Grace had run away to sea, settled in Peru, and made his first fortune dealing in supplies for ocean-going vessels. After the Civil War he moved to New York and prospered further, founding the huge shipping and chemical company which still bears his name.

Grace was by no means unique among Irish Catholics in achieving great wealth in New York. The Murrays, McDonnells, and Buckleys were, perhaps, the best known of a handful of families which challenged and sometimes rivaled, or even joined in marriage, America's Protestant aristocrats.[62] But even though New York had its first Irish Catholic mayor, in the person of Grace, six years before Boston, New York never became, politically, an Irish town like Boston. For every St. Patrick's Day parade, New York was to provide a Columbus Day festival of rival proportions, not to mention a host of other ethnic occasions. When a great Irish politician, Alfred E. Smith, did emerge from New York, his appeal was not simply as an Irishman to Irishmen, but as a spokesman for urban immigrants from numerous different backgrounds. Smith was the Democratic candidate for President in 1928 and was beaten by the Republican candidate, Herbert Hoover. Many people, Smith among them, viewed the defeat as a triumph of prejudice and nativist bigotry. One modern commentator has appraised the election less gloomily:

Smith's losing campaign was actually rich with meaning for the future. He stimulated and focused the political power of the millions of city voters of immigrant background. They voted in heavier numbers than ever before, and they voted Democratic. The revolutionary political pattern of 1928 made clear for the first time what was to be the power structure of the New Deal. In the nation's twelve largest cities . . . the Republicans in 1920 polled an overall majority of 1,638,000 votes. This GOP majority declined slightly in 1924. In 1928 Smith converted it into a majority of 38,000 for the Democrats. He carried New York, Boston, Cleveland, St. Louis, and Milwaukee, and ran neck-and-neck in all the others except Los Angeles.[63]

The political muscle of New York's Irish was thus expressed less in the government of New York City (or New York State where it was balanced by a powerful Republican upstate vote) than in the formation of a national Democratic majority in the Roosevelt years.

The difficulty of coming to any summary conclusion about the Irish in the United States is, first, that they are so numerous, and second, that there is no precise system for identifying them in the general population. The distortion of patrilineal genealogy is that we classify as "Irish" a large number of people who may be only half, a quarter, or an eighth Irish due to having maternal ancestors with other than Irish backgrounds. At the same time we classify as "not-Irish" a large number of Irish descent who happen not to have had Irish fathers (or fathers with Irish names). But beyond those problems of classification, how is it possible to sum up an experience that has been so diverse and which, in the long run, has tended toward assimilation? There were Irish sheep farmers in eastern Oregon, gold-miners in California and the Klondike, shopkeepers in Vermont, ranchers in Texas, and plantation owners in the antebellum South. If there were major barriers to their economic and social advancement in American society, most of those that mattered have yielded with time. If there are still a few exclusive clubs without Catholic members (Irish or otherwise), the slight can probably be borne by a people who have established themselves so solidly in the firmament of American society.

As for the impact of the American Irish on events within Ireland itself, the story is equally tangled and complex. The American Irish contributed men and money to a motley variety of causes—some as purely charitable as the Irish Hospitals' Sweepstakes, others as wholeheartedly political as Jerome Collins' and John Devoy's Clan na Gael. In general, the American Irish have been more willing to support militancy than have their counterparts in Ireland. At a distance of three thousand miles the complexities of "the Irish problem" have been less visible than the historic verities of Irish suffering and British oppression. Irish-American contributions to the diplomatic scene have usually taken the form of anti-British pressure, and there have been times, especially 1919–1922, when these pressures helped to produce the desired result of greater independence for Ireland. Although anti-British sentiment is likely to be a continuing part of the Irish-American outlook, the prevailing attitude might become less rancorous and more cosmopolitan. Ireland, after all, is no longer a fragile, embattled nation; and Britain is no longer a world-shaking imperial force. As those realities are slowly incorporated into Irish-American opinion, there should be more interest in good-faith mediation in dealing with Anglo-Irish problems, and less enthusiasm for the violent and military solutions so frequently popular in the past.

THE COMMONWEALTH

It would be desirable to include in this discussion of the Irish abroad sections concerning their experience in the two major dominions of Canada and Australia, for in both cases Irish immigrants found themselves still under the influence of Great Britain and participated in the national struggle for independence. Unfortunately, the literature on both communities is scant, and more local studies are needed before the history of the Irish in those two commonwealth nations can be written on other than a conjectural and impressionistic basis. A few general remarks will have to suffice.

Although a large number of Irish were forcibly sent to Australia, their status as convicts tended to eclipse their identity as Irish. They stood out less from the early settlers, because they *were*, in many cases, the early settlers. Thus the distinction between "poor immigrants" and prospering "first families," which was so sharp in nineteenth-century America, was much less acute in the South Pacific. In Canada, the distinction was more evident, for an upper class of Scottish and English Protestants was a prominent feature of British North America in the nineteenth century. The only mitigating circumstance was the large French-speaking population of Quebec. After their acquisition of French Canada in 1763 the British were more or less obliged to take a tolerant attitude toward the practice of Catholicism in Quebec in order not to drive the Quebecois into the waiting arms of the Americans to the south. But the Irish probably benefited less from the toleration of Catholicism in Quebec than from the existence of the Quebec Catholics as an underclass. The ethnic challenge of the Francophones gave rise, to some degree, to an ethnic accommodation between the English and Scots Protestants on the one hand, and the Irish Catholics, on the other. Religious differences diminished under these circumstances, at least compared to the situation in England and the United States. Yet a report of 1864 that the Irish Catholics of Toronto constituted

27 percent of the city's population and accounted for 59 percent of the city's crime sounds disconcertingly similar to Boston and other American cities in the same period.[64]

The reason for treating the Irish diaspora in a book devoted to Ireland and the Irish is perhaps self-evident. The seawall around the island has proved increasingly porous with the passage of time. Invaders and settlers have arrived; emigrants by the millions have departed. This demographic respiration has been a critical—even a dominant—part of the island's life. No other small modern nation has disgorged so large a part of itself, disseminating so widely its culture. My contention has been that "Ireland and the Irish" can be intelligible only within this broad context. At home, modern Ireland developed under the watchful, often emotional, eye of the emigrant population abroad. Those who left the island carried with them many marks of their birth and upbringing: customs, habits, attitudes, and tastes which, even though they tended gradually to change abroad, nevertheless connected them with the Ireland they had left behind. Ireland and the Irish are by no means coterminous subjects, but the interrelationships between them are so numerous and consequential that neither is adequately understood alone.

9

LITERATURE AND THE IRISH

Ireland has two languages and two literatures, and therefore two literary traditions. The first is rooted in the Irish language, which remained preponderantly oral until the later Middle Ages, and which has suffered in the modern period from the dramatic shrinkage of the Irish-speaking and Irish-reading population. Though Irish is today an official language of Ireland, taught in the schools, broadcast on radio and television (along with English), and required for many government jobs, it is probably understood by less than a million people, and the glories of its literature are available to a larger audience only through the imperfect medium of translation. In the second chapter of this book, we glimpsed the heroic Irish literature of the Middle Ages, but by the sixteenth and seventeenth centuries, if not before, the bardic tradition was on the defensive. The sagas and song cycles, the tales and poetry of Irish, were incomprehensible savagery to the new masters of the land. As the seventeenth-century poet O'Bruadair (1625–1698) lamented:

> Sad for those without sweet Anglo-Saxon
> Now that Ormonde has come to Erin;
> For the rest of my life in the land of Conn
> I'll do better with English than a poem.[1]

Irish became the language and literature of the dispossessed, and it erupted in modes which could be angry, ingenious, melancholy, or irreverently bawdy. An example is "The Lament for Art O Laoghaire," by Eibhlin Dhubh Ni Chonaill, one of the O'Connells of Derrynane, County

Kerry, from whom Daniel O'Connell, "the Liberator" traced
his descent. In 1767 Eibhlin married a hot-blooded young
captain of the Hungarian Hussars, back from service on the
continent. In 1773 O Laoghaire got into a bitter quarrel
with Abraham Morris, high sheriff of Cork, and on May 4,
set out to kill him. Instead he was himself killed by one of
Morris' bodyguards.

My steadfast love!
When I saw you one day
by the market-house gable
my eye gave a look
my heart shone out
I fled with you far
from friends and home.

And never was sorry:
you had parlours painted
rooms decked out
the oven reddened
and loaves made up
roasts on spits
and cattle slaughtered;
I slept in duck-down
till noontime came
or later if I liked.

My steadfast friend!
It comes to my mind
that fine Spring day
how well your hat looked
with the drawn gold band,
the sword silver-hilted,
your fine brave hand
and menacing prance,
and the fearful tremble
of treacherous enemies.
You were set to ride
your slim white-faced steed
and Saxons saluted
down to the ground

not from good will
but by dint of fear
though you died at their hands,
my soul's beloved . . . .[2]

Here is the tradition of the "keen" with its piercing tone of unrestrained grief, and in some ways it is the heroic tradition turned inside out to memorialize suffering rather than triumph.

Irish could also be put to outlandishly secular purposes, as in the famous long poem by Brian Merriman (1749?–1803), "The Midnight Court." In one section, the poet dreams the celibacy of the Catholic clergy is denounced by a court of angry women.

What is the use of the rule insane
That marriage has closed to the clerical clan
In the church of our fathers since first it began.
It's a melancholy sight to a needy maid
Their comely faces and forms displayed,
Their hips and thighs so broad and round,
Their buttocks and breasts that in flesh abound,
Their lustrous looks and their lusty limbs,
Their fair fresh features, their smooth soft skins,
Their strength and stature, their force and fire,
Their craving curbed and uncooled desire.
They eat and drink of the fat of the land,
They've wealth and comfort at their command,
They sleep on beds of the softest down,
They've ease and leisure their lot to crown,
They commence in manhood's prime and flood,
And well we know that they're flesh and blood!
If I thought that sexless saints they were
Or holy angels, I would not care,
But they're lusty lads with a crave unsated
In slothful sleep, and the maids unmated.[3]

Secularism may well be the key to modern literature in Irish, for with a rapidly diminishing reading public, the language went to ground, surviving in songs, humorous tales, proverbs, and folk tales, and generally eschewing high and serious literary flights. Like Yiddish, Irish became a patois in which art forms such as the short story, novel, and theater were entirely possible but immensely difficult, because the audience for them was so restricted and scattered.

The history of the other literary tradition in Ireland, that in English, is exactly the converse. Irishmen (of whatever background) who wrote in English had by the twentieth century a world audience of several hundred million people to appreciate and subsidize their work. This hardly explains why so many of the most accomplished craftsmen of English literature had Irish connections, but the list is an astonishingly long and eminent one. It begins in the early eighteenth century with Jonathan Swift (1667–1745) and includes Laurence Sterne (1713–1768), the author of *Tristram Shandy;* William Congreve (1670–1729) and George Farquhar (1678–1707), two of the cleverest Restoration dramatists; Oliver Goldsmith (1728–1774); Edmund Burke (1729–1797); and Richard Brinsley Sheridan (1751–1816), who created the memorable caricature of a hot-blooded Irishman, Sir Lucius O'Trigger, in his great comedy *The Rivals.*

The nineteenth and twentieth centuries provide a list no less distinguished, with names such as Oscar Wilde, George Bernard Shaw, John Millington Synge, William Butler Yeats, James Joyce, Sean O'Casey, and Samuel Beckett. Some of these can be dismissed as having had so little to do with Ireland that it is scarcely relevant to an understanding of their work. This could be said of Sterne, Congreve, Farquhar, and Sheridan, on none of whom Ireland made any substantial imprint. It is true to a lesser degree of Goldsmith, Shaw, and Wilde, all of whom shared the colonial and Protestant background of the first group, lived their adult lives principally in England, and wrote principally about English subjects. Yet one feels misgivings with all three. Goldsmith's famous poem of social criticism, "The Deserted Village" was based on observations in Ireland, not England. Shaw wrote a whole long-winded (even for him!) play about Ireland *(John Bull's Other Island)* and returned to the subject in numerous places. Wilde (1856–1900), the most supremely "English" writer of his—and perhaps any—generation, never gave a thought to Ireland in his most famous works, but his credentials are so impeccable that one is tempted to see his fateful immersion in English society as the very product of his Irishness.

So many tangled threads come together in Oscar Wilde that he is worth a pause even in a note as brief as this. His father's family were descendants of a Dutch Colonel De Wilde who settled in Ireland after serving there with William III. Oscar Wilde's father, Sir William, was a physician, a collector of Irish folklore, and a genuine Dublin eccentric. He married Jane Francesca Elgee, the daughter of a Wexford lawyer, who nearly went to jail in 1848 for her inflammatory nationalist writings. She gave her son Oscar the middle names Fingal O'Flahertie Wills, which he saw fit to drop when he settled as a young man in England. He said on one occasion "I am Irish by birth, and English by adoption." It is hard to know which island's claim on him is the stronger.

The remaining figures, Swift, Synge, Yeats, Joyce, and O'Casey, belong together because—like many less well-known authors whom they exemplify—they wrote in English about Ireland. Swift is *sui generis* because he made memorable literature out of Ireland in an era in which Irishmen regarded the island as unfit for that purpose. But it was basically as a tractarian and polemicist that Swift did this. Not until the early nineteenth century did an English-writing novelist, Maria Edgeworth of County Longford, make Ireland and Irish life the focus of fiction, and a succession of novels published between 1800 and 1817—*Castle Rackrent* the best-known of them—established a pattern to be followed by others throughout the remainder of the century.

This momentous change in literary focus paralleled—even though it differed from—the emerging interest in Irish antiquities, culture, and language that gave rise to the Royal Irish Academy, the county historical and archaeological societies, and eventually the Gaelic League. Maria Edgeworth was a dyed-in-the-wool product of the Protestant ascendancy and her humane, astute view of life in rural Ireland was limited by what could be perceived from the elevated, blinkered "Big House." But by the end of the century, English writers from similar backgrounds were venturing beyond chats with the Irish servants in the pantry, and a writer like Synge (1871–1909) could banish himself to the Gaelic fastness of the Aran Islands (in 1898 and afterwards) to steep himself in Irish culture where it was least spoiled and corrupted by English landowners.

In a sense the two paths of interest in Irish (qua Gaelic) antiquity and in Ireland as a fit subject for literature *per se* converged in the plays of Synge (*Riders to the Sea* and *The Playboy of the Western World* are the best known) and in the work of his longer lived, more brilliant, and more prolific contemporary, W. B. Yeats (1865–1939). What gives coherence, then, to so much of the best literature in English written by Irishmen in the modern period is that it reflects Ireland, something which was emphatically not true of the earlier period. This coherence eclipses and effaces considerations such as the culture, religion, or place of residence of the author. Yeats was a Protestant and lived much of his life in England. Joyce (1882–1941) was a Catholic, but he left Ireland at the age of 22 in 1904 and spent the rest of his life on the continent. Neither could be expunged from the pantheon of Anglo-Irish literature without the structure's collapsing, for each, in very different ways, immortalized Ireland and the struggle of its people.

It is not at all surprising that this centrality of Ireland should continue in the writings of younger generations of Irish writers. Austin Clarke (1896–) was born not so long after Joyce, but survived to record the less heroic Ireland of post World War II, as in his short poem, "Irish-American Dignitary":

> Glanced down at Shannon from the sky-way
> With his attendant clergy, stayed night
> In Dublin, but whole day with us

To find his father's cot, now dust
And rubble, bless new church, school buildings
At Glantworth, drive to Spangle Hill
And cut first sod, hear, answer, fine speeches,
Accept a learned gown, freedom
Of ancient city, so many kissing
His ring—God love him!—almost missed
The waiting liner: that day in Cork
Had scarcely time for knife and fork.[4]

Seamus Heaney (born 1939), probably the most celebrated of Ireland's late twentieth-century poets, has reflected the grim struggle in Northern Ireland which re-
emerged in 1969 and poisoned so many of the years which
followed. "The Toome Road" is an example:

One morning early I met armoured cars
In convoy, warbling along on powerful tyres,
All camouflaged with broken alder branches,
And headphoned soldiers standing up in turrets.
How long were they approaching down my roads
As if they owned them? The whole country was sleeping.
I had rights-of-way, fields, cattle in my keeping,
Tractors hitched to buckrakes in open sheds,
Silos, chill gates, wet slates, the greens and reds
Of outhouse roofs. Whom should I run to tell
Among all of those with their back doors on the latch
For the bringer of bad news, that small-hours visitant
Who, by being expected, might be kept distant?
Sowers of seed, erectors of headstones . . .
O charioteers, above your dormant guns,
It stands here still, stands vibrant as you pass,
The invisible, untoppled omphalos.[5]

Literature may focus temporarily on "the State" and its
problems, but it is contrary to its nature to remain fixed
there. It is to be expected that the fertile Irish literary tradition (in English) will seek new themes and new subject
matter—as indeed, its greatest practitioners have done all
along. There will again come a day when what Irish writers
have in common is that they were born or have lived in Ire-

land, rather than that they write about it. Samuel Beckett (1906–), long a resident of France, may prove the progenitor of a new race of literary assimilationists who, like Congreve, Sheridan, and Wilde have their beginnings in Ireland, but for whom it is neither the be-all nor the end-all.

NOTES

1. THE INSULAR CONDITION AND EARLY INHABITANTS

1. Thomas W. Freeman, *Ireland: A General and Regional Geography* (London: Methuen, 1972), p. 8.

2. *Ibid.*, p. 59.

3. Eileen McCracken, *The Irish Woods Since Tudor Times* (Newton Abbot, England: David and Charles, 1971), p. 15.

4. *The Readers Digest Complete Atlas of the British Isles* (London: Readers Digest Association, 1965), p. 138.

5. Freeman, p. 67.

6. McCracken, *The Irish Woods Since Tudor Times*, p. 15.

7. *Ibid.*, p. 35.

8. *Ibid.*

9. Peter Harbison, *The Archaeology of Ireland* (New York: Scribner's, 1976), p. 18.

10. *Ibid.*, p. 21.

11. *Ibid.*, p. 26.

12. *Ibid.*, p. 60.

13. Joseph Raftery, ed., *The Celts* (Cork: Mercier Press, 1969), p. 19.

14. *Ibid.*, p. 29.

15. *The Conquest of Gaul* (Penguin ed.), I.1.31.

16. Quoted by Anne Ross, *Everyday Life of the Pagan Celts* (New York: Putnam, 1970), p. 106.

17. Harbison, *The Archaeology of Ireland*, p. 42.

18. See D. B. Quinn, *The Elizabethans and the Irish*, plate XII, for an illustration of the use of a skin cauldron from John Derricke, *The Image of Irelande*, 1581.

19. *Agricola*, para. 24, Penguin translation. Tacitus had ambivalent feelings about the expansion of Roman arms and the resulting subjugation of 'barbarous' peoples.

20. Raftery, ed., *The Celts*, p. 11. Similarly the "Q" celts kept the "Q" sound in the Latin word for horse, *equus*, while the "P" Celts transformed it into the word, *Epos*.

21. Quoted in Maire de Paor and Liam de Paor, *Early Christian Ireland* (London: Thames and Hudson, 1967), pp. 47–48.

22. Kathleen Hughes, *The Church in Early Irish Society*, p. 35.

23. *Ibid.*, p. 50.

24. *Ibid.*, p. 65.

25. *Ibid.*, p. 75 and pp. 73–74.

26. *Ibid.*, p. 77.

27. S. E. Morison writes: "We are not straining the evidence to conclude that Brendan sailed . . . on the circuit Hebrides-Shetlands-Faroes-Iceland, possibly as far as the Azores . . . . But discovery of America—no!" *The European Discovery of America: The Northern Voyages* (New York: Oxford University Press, 1971), p. 25.

28. *Bede*, III, 25 (Penguin edition).

29. Cited by Kathleen Hughes, *The Church in Early Irish Society*, p. 108.

30. Michael Ryan, Keeper of Antiquities, National Museum of Ireland, in *Ireland Today* (Bulletin of the Irish Department of Foreign Affairs) (April 1980), no. 965.

31. Henry, *Irish Art in the Early Christian Period to 800 A.D.*, p. 96.

32. *Ibid.*, p. 97.

33. *Ibid.*, p. 161.

2. A HEROIC AGE: THE CELTIC, VIKING, AND NORMAN INHERITANCE

1. Maire de Paor and Liam de Paor, *Early Christian Ireland* (London: Thames Hudson, 1967), pp. 61–62.

2. Thomas Kinsella translation, London, 1969, p. 120.

3. Liam de Paor in T. W. Moody and F. X. Martin, *The Course of Irish History*, p. 93. The translation is by de Paor from W. Stokes and J. Strachan, eds., *Thesaurus Palaeohibernicus*, ii (1903), p. 290.

4. In my treatment of the Vikings I am indebted to Donncha O Corrain, whose account in *Ireland before the Normans* I follow closely.

5. This interpretation closely follows that of James Lydon, *The Lordship of Ireland in the Middle Ages*, pp. 120–49.

6. *Ibid.*, p. 143.

7. Kathleen Hughes, *The Church in Early Irish Society*, p. 274.

8. Cited in John Watt, *The Church in Medieval Ireland*, p. 37.

9. James Lydon, *Ireland in the Later Middle Ages*, p. 33.

10. *Ibid.*, pp. 94–95.

11. Watt, *The Church in Medieval Ireland*, p. 50.

12. *Ibid.*, pp. 60, 84.

13. James Lydon, *Ireland in the Later Middle Ages*, p. 118.

3. LATE MEDIEVAL IRELAND AND THE TUDOR CONQUEST

1. James Lydon, *Ireland in the Later Middle Ages*, p. 139.

2. *Ibid.*, p. 34.

3. Kenneth Nicholls, *Gaelic and Gaelicised Ireland*, p. 21.

4. Brendan Bradshaw, *The Dissolution of the Religious Orders in Ireland Under Henry VIII*, p. 206.

5. Margaret MacCurtain, *Tudor and Stuart Ireland*, p. 35.

6. Bradshaw, *The Dissolution*, Appendix I, p. 232.

7. 33 Hen. VIII, c. I, *Stat. Irel, Hen. VII & VIII*, p. 176.

8. The Vocation of John Bale, *Harleian Miscellany*, vi (1745), pp. 416–7.

9. Moody, Martin, and Byrne, eds., *A New History of Ireland*, 3:78.
10. *Ibid.*, p. 85.
11. *Ibid.*, p. 89.
12. *Ibid.*, p. 90.
13. W. L. Renwick, ed., *A View of the Present State of Ireland* (Oxford: Oxford University Press, 1970), p. 19.
14. Moody, Martin, and Byrne, eds., *A New History of Ireland*, 3:110.

4. THE MAKING OF THE PROTESTANT ASCENDANCY

1. Aidan Clarke, in Moody, Martin, and Byrne, eds., *A New History of Ireland*, 3:197.
2. *Ibid.*
3. Aidan Clarke, *The Old English in Ireland*, appendix 3.
4. Cited by J. G. Simms, *A New History of Ireland*, 3:495.
5. *Ibid.*, p. 506.

5. IRELAND AS A PROTESTANT NATION: THE EIGHTEENTH CENTURY

1. Brian De Breffny and Rosemary ffolliott, *The Houses of Ireland*, p. 84.
2. Receiving £60,000 out of £4 million. Maureen Wall in Moody and Martin, eds., *The Course of Irish History*, p. 220.
3. W. E. H. Lecky, *A History of Ireland in the Eighteenth Century*, ed. and abridged by L. P. Curtis, Jr. (Chicago: University of Chicago Press, 1972), p. 188.
4. J. C. Beckett, *The Making of Modern Ireland, 1603–1923*, p. 230.
5. *Ibid.*, pp. 250–51.
6. Remarkably, one of the boldest and clearest anticipations of this antisectarianism is to be found in the late 1640s where it grew out of the hearty disinclination of English soldiers to be dispatched for service in Ireland. One of the radical English "Levelers," William Walwyn allegedly complained "that the sending over forces to Ireland is nothing else but to make way by the blood of the army to enlarge their [the commonwealth government's] territories of power and tryanny; that it is an unlawful war, a cruel and bloody work to go to destroy the Irish natives for their consciences and to drive them from their proper natural and native rights." Moody, Martin, and Byrne, eds. *A New History of Ireland*, 3:lxii, citing *Walwins wiles* (London, 1649), an anti-Walwyn pamphlet reprinted in William Haller and Godfrey Davies, eds., *The Leveller Tracts, 1647–1653* (Gloucester, Mass.: Peter Smith, 1964), pp. 288–9.
7. Frank MacDermot, *Tone and His Times* (Tralee: Anvil Books, 1968), p. 193.
8. There are notable exceptions to this assertion, the most important being the work of Sir William Petty, the Cromwellian polymath who executed a sweeping survey of the lands of Ireland, the so-called Down Survey, in the 1650s, and published some of his many calculations in 1691 in a volume entitled *The Political Anatomy of Ireland*.
9. Edith Johnston, *Ireland in the Eighteenth Century*, p. 14, citing K. H. Connell, *The Population of Ireland, 1750–1845* (Oxford: Oxford University Press, 1950), p. 25.

10. Raymond D. Crotty, *Irish Agricultural Production*, pp. 294–307, as cited in F. S. L. Lyons, *Ireland Since the Famine*, p. 782.

11. All figures from L. M. Cullen, *An Economic History of Ireland Since 1660*, p. 54.

12. A mechanized cotton industry did develop in many parts of Ireland from the 1780s onward, but by the 1830s most of these operations were defunct, or working linen. *Ibid.*, pp. 93–94, and 106–7.

13. De Breffny and Rosemary ffolliott, *The Houses of Ireland*, p. 123.

14. *Ibid.*, p. 178.

15. L. M. Cullen, *An Economic History of Ireland Since 1660*, pp. 45–47.

16. *Ibid.*, p. 83.

17. E. M. Johnston, *Ireland in the Eighteenth Century*, p. 84.

18. De Breffny and ffolliott, *The Houses of Ireland*, p. 59.

6. CATHOLIC IRELAND RESURGENT: THE NINETEENTH CENTURY

1. James Carty, *Ireland, 1783–1850* (Dublin: C. J. Fallon, 1966), p. 97.

2. *Ibid.*, p. 98.

3. J. C. Beckett, *The Making of Modern Ireland*, p. 285.

4. Gearoid O'Tuathaigh, *Ireland Before the Famine, 1798–1848*, p. 50.

5. *Ibid.*, pp. 60 and 62.

6. *Ibid.*, p. 70.

7. Under the Act of Union Ireland was nominally administered by the lord lieutenant, as representative of the Crown, but the real decisions were made by the government in power in England, one crucial member of which was the Chief Secretary for Ireland. The undersecretary, a permanent (later, civil service) official not subject to the vagaries of electoral politics, was normally resident in Ireland and acted as liaison between lord lieutenant and chief secretary.

8. Gearoid O'Tuathaigh, *Ireland Before the Famine*, pp. 88–89, 94–95.

9. *Ibid.*, pp. 101, 104.

10. *Ibid.*, p. 106.

11. F. S. L. Lyons, *Ireland Since the Famine*, p. 38.

12. *Ibid.*, p. 38, citing R. N. Salaman, *The History and Social Influence of the Potato* (Cambridge: Cambridge University Press, 1949), pp. 603–8. The failure of 1822 produced a government enquiry which accurately described the perilous conditions created by the increasing dependence of Irish cottiers on a subsistence crop. R. D. Edwards and T. D. Williams, eds., *The Great Famine* (Dublin: Browne and Nolan, 1956), p. 122.

13. T. W. Moody and F. X. Martin, eds., *The Course of Irish History*, p. 268.

14. R. D. Edwards and T. D. Williams, eds., *The Great Famine* (New York: New York University Press, 1957), pp. 123, 125.

15. *Ibid.*, pp. 123–127.

16. *Ibid.*, p. 128.

17. Joseph Lee, *The Modernisation of Irish Society*, p. 3.

18. Gearoid O'Tuathaigh, *Ireland Before the Famine*, p. 185.

19. *Ibid.*, p. 190.

20. *Ibid.*, pp. 196, 197.

21. *Ibid.*, p. 197. Many Irish, especially Feargus O'Connor and James Bronterre O'Brien were prominent leaders of the Chartist movement. See Lynn H. Lees, *Exiles of Erin*, pp. 226–31.

22. O'Tuathaigh, *Ireland Before the Famine*, p. 198.

23. See in general the growing body of work by Emmet Larkin on the history of the Church in nineteenth-century Ireland, and his articles "The Devotional Revolution in Ireland, 1850–70," *A.H.R.* (1972), vol. 67 and 'Economic Growth, Capital Investment, and the Roman Catholic Church in Nineteenth-Century Ireland," *A.H.R.* (1967), vol. 62.

24. Emmet Larkin, "Church, State, and Nation in Modern Ireland," *A.H.R.* (1975), 70:1260.

25. Irish travel literature is a large subject in its own right, and shades imperceptibly into the writing of observers who were sometimes resident Anglo-Irish, like Sir Jonah Barrington or Maria Edgeworth. The best known of the visitors, however, were the English agriculturalist Arthur Young (1776–1779), the French writers Alexis de Toqueville and Gustave de Beaumont (1835), and the English novelist William Makepeace Thackeray (1842). A convenient introduction to the subject in general is Constantia Maxwell, *The Stranger in Ireland.*

26. Desmond Bowen, *The Protestant Crusade in Ireland, 1800–1870*, (Dublin: Gill and Macmillan, 1978), p. 160, citing James Godkin, *Ireland and Her Churches* (1867), p. 141.

27. Quoted *Ibid.*, p. 298.

28. *Ibid.*, pp. 156, 160.

29. F. S. L. Lyons, *Ireland Since the Famine*, p. 22.

30. J. C. Beckett, *The Making of Modern Ireland*, p. 367.

31. *Ibid.*, p. 369.

32. Joseph Lee, *The Modernisation of Irish Society*, p. 36.

33. *Ibid.*

34. *Ibid.*, p. 39.

35. Thomas Hachey, *Britain and Irish Separatism*, p. 21.

36. *Ibid.*, p. 25.

37. Joseph Lee, *The Modernisation of Irish Society*, pp. 102–3.

38. F. S. L. Lyons, *Ireland Since the Famine*, p. 219. Joseph Lee, *The Modernisation of Irish Society*, p. 103.

39. Joseph Lee, *The Modernisation of Irish Society*, p. 57.

40. *Ibid.*, pp. 62, 63, 64.

41. *Ibid.*, p. 78.

42. *Ibid.*, p. 117.

7. A NEW STATE ESTABLISHED: TRIUMPHS AND DILEMMAS

1. Robert E. Kennedy, *The Irish*, p. 212.

2. *Ibid.*, p. 214.

3. Ruth Dudley Edwards, *An Atlas of Irish History*, pp. 214–5.

4. F. S. L. Lyons, *Ireland Since the Famine*, p. 58.

5. *Ibid.*, p. 61.

6. *Ibid.*, p. 63.

7. *Ibid.*, p. 67.

8. Ruth Dudley Edwards, *An Atlas of Irish History*, p. 229.

9. F. S. L. Lyons, *Ireland Since the Famine*, p. 229.

10. *Ibid.*

11. *Ibid.*

12. *Ibid.*, p. 211.

13. In the elections of 1885 Ulster elected 17 Irish Nationalists and 16 Conservatives—the only ones elected anywhere in Ireland, except for Trinity College, Dublin. Thomas Hachey, *Britain and Irish Separatism*, p. 69.

14. F. S. L. Lyons, *Ireland Since the Famine*, p. 311.

15. T. D. Williams in F. X. Martin, ed. *Leaders and Men of the Easter Rising: Dublin 1916* (Ithaca, N.Y.: Cornell University Press, 1967), p. 145.

16. According to the census of 1871, 23 percent of all British army officers, and 25 percent of British army soldiers had been born in one of Ireland's 32 counties. It is not known what percentage were Protestant or Catholic. Robert E. Kennedy, *The Irish*, p. 78.

17. Thomas Hachey, *Britain and Irish Separatism*, p. 154.

18. Michael Joseph Rahilly, called "The O'Rahilly," was one such, *Ibid.*, p. 160, n.62.

19. John Murphy, *Ireland in the Twentieth Century*, p. 5.

20. Thomas Hachey, *Britain and Irish Separatism*, p. 210.

21. F. S. L. Lyons, *Ireland Since the Famine*, p. 416.

22. John Murphy, *Ireland in the Twentieth Century*, p. 22.

23. *Ibid.*, p. 24.

24. *Ibid.*, p. 59.

25. New works in this area are constantly appearing. In addition to the works cited in this chapter, it would be well to consult the semi-annual journal, *Irish Historical Studies* (Dublin) for notices and reviews of more recent scholarly works devoted to Irish history since 1939.

8. THE IRISH ABROAD: EXAMPLES AND CONCLUSIONS

1. Raymond Crotty, reviewing James Donnelly, Jr.'s *The Land and the People of Nineteenth-Century Cork*, *Journal of Modern History* (September 1976), V. 48(3):543.

2. See Maurice N. Hennessy, *The Wild Geese* (Old Greenwich, Conn.: Devin-Adair, 1973), for a comprehensive, if popular, account.

3. For a scholarly account and analysis of the process in Virginia see Edmund Morgan, *American Freedom, American Slavery* (New York: Norton, 1975).

4. The most celebrated "black Irish" are, of course, the dark skinned, dark-haired people of the west who are alleged to be descendants of various survivors of the Spanish Armada of 1588, so many vessels of which were wrecked upon the Irish coasts.

5. The best treatment of the subject to date is R. J. Dickson, *Ulster Emigration to Colonial America, 1718–1775*.

6. Ruth Dudley Edwards, *An Atlas of Irish History*, p. 148.

7. F. S. L. Lyons, *Ireland Since the Famine*, p. 45.

8. Lynn Hollen Lees, *Exiles of Erin*, p. 38, citing the work of S. H. Cousens, "The Regional Variations in Emigration from Ireland between 1821 and 1841," *Transactions and Papers of the Institute of British Geographers* (1965), 37:22–29.

9. Robert E. Kennedy, *The Irish*, p. 75.

10. John Archer Jackson, *The Irish in Britain*, pp. xv, and 7.

11. *Ibid.*, p. 11.

12. *Ibid.*, p. 21.

13. *Ibid.*, p. 81.

14. *Ibid.*, p. 7.

15. Lynn Hollen Lees, *Exiles of Erin*, p. 44.

16. *Ibid.*

17. *Ibid.*, p. 48.

18. *Ibid.*, p. 56.

19. *Ibid.*, p. 92.

20. *Ibid.*, p. 94.

21. *Ibid.*, p. 96.

22. *Ibid.*, pp. 136–39.

23. This subject is explored thoughtfully by John Bossy, *The English Catholic Community, 1570–1850*, (London: Darton, Longman and Todd, 1975) pp. 313–16 especially.

24. *Ibid.*, p. 314.

25. John Archer Jackson, *The Irish in Britain*, p. 19. The reference is to the 716,028 Irish-born found in Britain by the 1951 census.

26. *Ibid.*, p. 26.

27. *Ibid.*, p. 85.

28. *Ibid.*, p. 94.

29. *Ibid.*, p. 120.

30. *Ibid.*, p. 122.

31. *Ibid.*, p. 155.

32. Robert E. Kennedy, *The Irish*, p. 74.

33. *Ibid.*, p. 75.

34. Norman R. Yetman, "The Irish Experience in America" in Harold Orel, ed., *Irish History and Culture* (Lawrence: University of Kansas Press, 1976).

35. Lawrence McCaffrey, *The Irish Diaspora in America*, p. 68.

36. Norman R. Yetman, "The Irish Experience in America," p. 352.

37. *Ibid.*, footnote 5, p. 373.

38. See *The Irish Countryman*, New York, 1937 and subsequent editions.

39. Lawrence McCaffrey, *The Irish Diaspora in America*, p. 65.

40. Norman R. Yetman, "The Irish Experience in America," p. 360.

41. *Ibid.*, p. 360.

42. William V. Shannon, *The American Irish* (New York: Macmillan, 1963), p. 136.

43. The resulting barrier to the Irish—even the Irish of "gentle" birth—is brilliantly treated in Eugene O'Neill's play, *A Touch of the Poet*.

44. Figures from Stephan Thernstrom, *The Other Bostonians* (Cambridge: Harvard University Press, 1973), p. 131.

45. *Ibid.*, p. 133.

46. Stephan Thernstrom, *Poverty and Progress* (New York: Atheneum, 1978), p. 156.

47. Marjorie R. Fallows, *Irish Americans*, p. 63.

48. William V. Shannon, *The American Irish*, pp. 98–99.

49. Lawrence McCaffrey, *The Irish Diaspora in America*, p. 78.

50. *Ibid.*

51. Dennis Clark, *The Irish in Philadelphia*, p. 51.

52. *Ibid.*, p. 41.

53. *Ibid.*, p. 49.

54. *Ibid.*, p. 50.

55. *Ibid.*, p. 53.

56. *Ibid.*, p. 74.

57. *Ibid.*, p. 60.

58. *Ibid.*, p. 84.

59. *Ibid.*, p. 140.

60. *Ibid.*, p. 156.

61. William V. Shannon, *The American Irish*, pp. 28 and 76.

62. See Stephen Birmingham's popular, informative *Real Lace: America's Irish Rich* (New York: Harper & Row, 1973).

63. William V. Shannon, *The American Irish*, p. 180.

64. Murray W. Nicolson, "The Irish Catholics and Social Action in Toronto, 1850–1900," *Studies in History and Politics* (1980), 1:48.

9. LITERATURE AND THE IRISH

1. Translation by John Montague. *The Faber Book of Irish Verse* (London: Faber, 1974).

2. Translation by Thomas Kinsella. *An Duanaire: An Irish Anthology, 1600–1900* (Philadelphia: University of Pennsylvania Press, 1981), pp. 200–3.

3. Translation by Arland Ussher. *The Faber Book of Irish Verse*, p. 169.

4. *Faber Book of Irish Verse*, p. 268.

5. From *Field Work* (New York: Farrar, Straus, & Giroux, 1979).

BIBLIOGRAPHY

The purpose of this bibliography is to guide readers to the most important, informative, and authoritative work currently being written about Ireland and the Irish. Though small in area and population, the subject is vast, and no bibliography of a hundred titles could hope to be definitive. The result is that many works of relevance and merit have been left out. Some of the decisions have been *ad hoc*, or personal, though I hope, not frivolous. I have inclined *toward* monographs, and *away* from articles, collections of essays or articles, general histories, and primary sources of all kinds. Very few works published before 1960 have been included, although thousands of such works have enduring value for the researcher with a highly defined interest. The books listed below should be relatively easy to find in American college and university libraries, or in bookstores that deal in scholarly and historical materials. Anyone seriously interested in Ireland and the Irish will be speedily led beyond the "history" bookshelves to the reaches of fiction, poetry, archaeology, geography, sociology, anthropology, art history, and economic history, in each of which important aspects of the subject reside.

Aalen, F. H. A. *Man and the Landscape in Ireland*. London, New York, and San Francisco: Academic Press, 1978.

Akenson, Donald H. *The Irish Education Experiment*. London: Routledge & Kegan Paul, 1970.

Arensberg, C. M. and S. T. Kimball. *Family and Community in Ireland*. Cambridge, Mass.: Harvard University Press, 1968. A pioneering work of anthropology which describes Irish society in the 1920s.

Barnard, T. C. *Cromwellian Ireland: English Government and Reform in Ireland, 1649–60.* Oxford: Oxford University Press, 1975.

Beckett, J. C. *The Making of Modern Ireland, 1603–1923.* New York: Knopf, 1966, 1969.

Beckett, J. C. *The Anglo-Irish Tradition.* Ithaca, N.Y. and London: Cornell University Press, 1976.

Bolton, G. C. *The Passing of the Irish Act of Union.* Oxford: Oxford University Press, 1966.

Bottigheimer, Karl S. *English Money and Irish Land: The "Adventurers" in the Cromwellian Settlement of Ireland.* Oxford: Oxford University Press, 1971.

Bradshaw, Brendan. *The Irish Constitutional Revolution of the Sixteenth Century.* Cambridge: Cambridge University Press, 1979.

Bradshaw, Brendan. *The Dissolution of the Religious Orders in Ireland under Henry VIII.* Cambridge: Cambridge University Press, 1974.

de Breffny, Brian, and Rosemary ffolliott. *The Houses of Ireland.* New York and London: Viking, 1975.

Brody, Hugh. *Inishkillane: Change and Decline in the West of Ireland.* Harmondsworth (England): Penguin, 1974.

Brown, Thomas N. *Irish-American Nationalism.* Philadelphia: Greenwood, 1966.

Canny, Nicholas P. *The Elizabethan Conquest of Ireland: A Pattern Established, 1565–76.* New York: Barnes and Noble, 1976.

Clark, Dennis. *The Irish in Philadelphia.* Philadelphia: Temple University Press, 1974.

Clark, Samuel. *Social Origins of the Irish Land War.* Princeton, N.J.: Princeton University Press, 1979. A sociological analysis.

Clarke, Aidan. *The Old English in Ireland, 1625–1642.* Ithaca: Cornell University Press, 1966.

Connell, K. H. *Irish Peasant Society.* Oxford: Oxford University Press, 1968. Provocative essays on illicit distilling, illegitimacy, etherdrinking, and Catholicism and marriage.

Connell, K. H. *The Population of Ireland, 1750–1845.* Oxford: Oxford University Press, 1950.

Crotty, Raymond D. *Irish Agricultural Production: Its Volume and Structure.* Cork: Cork University Press, 1966.

Cullen, L. M. *An Economic History of Ireland since 1660.* London: David and Charles, 1972.

Curtis, L. P. *Apes and Angels: The Irishman in Victorian Caricature.* Washington, D.C.: Smithsonian, 1971.

Dickson, R. J. *Ulster Emigration to Colonial America 1718–1775.* New York: Humanities Press, 1966.

Dolley, Michael. *Anglo-Norman Ireland.* Dublin: Gill & Macmillan, 1972. Gill History of Ireland, Irish paperback.

Donnelly, James S. *The Land and the People of Nineteenth-Century Cork.* London: Routledge and Kegan Paul, 1975.

Edwards, Ruth Dudley. *An Atlas of Irish History.* London: Methuen, 1973. Interesting and useful, but sometimes misleading or confusing.

Evans, E. Estyn. *The Personality of Ireland.* Cambridge: Cambridge University Press, 1973.

Fallows, Marjorie R. *Irish Americans: Identity and Assimilation.* Englewood Cliffs, N.J.: Prentice-Hall, 1979.

Flanagan, Thomas. *The Year of the French.* New York: Holt, Rinehart, & Winston, 1979. A best-selling novel which provides a sensitive, learned, and memorable portrait of "the West" in 1798.

Green, E. R. R. *The Lagan Valley, 1800–1850.* London: Hillary, 1949. Linen, cotton, and industrialization in eastern Ulster.

Green, E. R. R., ed. *Essays in Scotch-Irish History.* London: Routledge & Kegan Paul, 1969.

Hachey, Thomas E. *Britain and Irish Separatism from the Fenians to the Free State, 1867–1922.* Chicago: Rand-McNalley, 1977. American paperback. A clear and comprehensible survey of a crucial period.

Harbison, Peter. *The Archaeology of Ireland.* New York: Scribner, 1976.

Henry, Françoise. *Irish Art in the Early Christian Period to A.D. 800.* Ithaca, N.Y.: Cornell University Press, 1965.

Henry, Françoise. *Irish Art during the Viking Invasions, 800–1020.* Ithaca, N.Y.: Cornell University Press, 1967.

Henry, Françoise. *Irish Art in the Romanesque Period, 1020–1170.* Ithaca, N.Y.: Cornell University Press, 1970.

Herity, M. and G. Eogan. *Ireland in Prehistory.* London: Routledge & Kegan Paul, 1977.

Hughes, Kathleen. *The Church in Early Irish Society.* Ithaca, N.Y.: Cornell University Press, 1966.

Hughes, Kathleen. *Early Christian Ireland: Introduction to the Sources.* London: Hodder and Stoughton, 1972. English paperback.

Jackson, John Archer. *The Irish in Britain.* London and Cleveland: Press of Case Western Reserve, 1963.

Johnston, Edith Mary. *Ireland in the Eighteenth Century.* Dublin: Gill and Macmillan 1974. Gill History of Ireland, Irish paperback.

Jones, Emrys. *A Social Geography of Belfast.* London: Oxford University Press, 1960.

Kearney, Hugh F. *Strafford in Ireland, 1633–1641.* Manchester: Manchester University Press, 1959.

Kennedy, Robert E. Jr. *The Irish: Emigration, Marriage and Fertility.* Berkeley: University of California Press, 1973.

Larkin, Emmet. *The Roman Catholic Church and the Creation of the Modern Irish State, 1878–1886.* Philadelphia: American Philosophical Society, 1975.

Larkin, Emmet. *The Roman Catholic Church and the Plan of Campaign, 1886–1888*. Cork: Cork University Press, 1978.

Larkin, Emmet. *The Roman Catholic Church in Ireland and the Fall of Parnell, 1888–1891*. Chapel Hill and Liverpool: University of North Carolina Press, 1979.

Lee, Joseph J. *The Modernisation of Irish Society, 1848–1918*. Dublin: Gill and Macmillan 1973. Gill History of Ireland, Irish paperback.

Lee, Joseph J., ed. *Ireland, 1945–1970*. Dublin: Macmillan, 1979.

Lees, Lynn Hollen. *Exiles of Erin: Irish Migrants in Victorian London*. Ithaca, N.Y.: Cornell University Press, 1979.

Lydon, James. *Ireland in the Later Middle Ages*. Dublin: Gill and Macmillan 1973. Gill History of Ireland, Irish paperback.

Lydon, James. *The Lordship of Ireland in the Middle Ages*. Toronto: Toronto University Press, 1972.

Lynch, Patrick and John Vaizey. *Guinness's Brewery in the Irish Economy, 1759–1876*. Cambridge: Cambridge University Press, 1960. Includes an analysis of the Irish economy which extends far beyond brewing.

Lyons, F. S. L. *Charles Stewart Parnell*. Oxford: Oxford University Press, 1977.

Lyons, F. S. L. *Culture and Anarchy in Ireland, 1890–1939*. Oxford: Oxford University Press, 1979. The Ford Lectures delivered at Oxford in 1978.

Lyons, F. S. L. *Ireland Since the Famine*. London: Fontana, 1973. The most authoritative and detailed one-volume (850 pages) history of modern Ireland. English paperback.

McCaffrey, Lawrence J. *The Irish Diaspora in America*. Bloomington: Indiana University Press, 1976.

MacCurtain, Margaret. *Tudor and Stuart Ireland*. Dublin: Gill and Macmillan 1972. Gill History of Ireland, Irish paperback.

MacCurtain, Margaret and Donncha O'Corrain, eds. *Women in Irish Society: The Historical Dimension*. Dublin: Women's Press, 1978. A hard-to-get paperback containing ten essays on a neglected subject.

McDowell, R. B. *Ireland in the Age of Imperialism and Revolution, 1760–1801*. Oxford: Oxford University Press, 1980.

MacLysaght, Edward. *Irish Life in the Seventeenth Century*. Cork: Irish Academic Press, 1939 and 1950; New York: Barnes & Noble, 1969.

Mac Niocaill, Gearoid. *Ireland Before the Vikings*. Dublin: Gill and Macmillan 1972. Gill History of Ireland, Irish paperback.

Maguire, W. A. *The Downshire Estates in Ireland, 1801–1845*. Oxford: Oxford University Press, 1972.

Mansergh, Nicholas. *The Irish Question, 1840–1921*. Toronto: University of Toronto Press, 1965.

Maxwell, Constantia. *The Stranger in Ireland from the Reign of Elizabeth to the Great Famine*. London: Cape, 1954; reprinted Dublin: Gill and Macmillan, 1979.

Miller, David W. *Queen's Rebels: Ulster Loyalism in Historical Perspective.* New York: Harper & Row, 1978.

Mitchell, Frank. *The Irish Landscape.* London: Collins, 1976.

Montague, John, ed. *The Faber Book of Irish Verse.* London: Macmillan, 1974. The best one-volume anthology.

Moody, T. W. and F. X. Martin, eds., *The Course of Irish History.* Cork: Mercier Press, 1967. Irish paperback. An excellent one-volume survey from the Celts to the twentieth century, well-illustrated.

Moody, T. W., F. X. Martin, and F. J. Byrne, eds. *A New History of Ireland.* Vol. 3, *Early Modern Ireland, 1534–1691.* Oxford: Oxford University Press, 1976. And other volumes of the nine projected, as they appear.

Murphy, John A. *Ireland in the Twentieth Century.* Dublin: Gill and Macmillan 1975. Gill History of Ireland, Irish paperback.

Nicholls, Kenneth. *Gaelic and Gaelicised Ireland in the Middle Ages.* Dublin: Gill and Macmillan 1972. Gill History of Ireland, Irish paperback.

O'Corrain, Donncha. *Ireland Before the Normans.* Dublin: Gill and Macmillan 1972. Gill History of Ireland, Irish paperback.

O'Cuiv, Brian, ed. *A View of the Irish Language.* Dublin: Stationery Office, 1969.

O'Farrell, P. J. *England's Irish Question.* New York: Shocken, 1971.

Orel, Harold, ed. *Irish History and Culture.* Lawrence: University of Kansas Press, 1976. Sixteen essays by members of the faculty of the University of Kansas.

O'Tuama, S., ed. *The Gaelic League Idea.* Cork and Dublin: Mercier Press, 1972.

O'Tuathaigh, Gearoid. *Ireland Before the Famine, 1798–1848.* Dublin: Gill and Macmillan, 1972. Gill History of Ireland, Irish paperback.

Otway-Ruthven, A. J. *A History of Medieval Ireland.* London and New York: Barnes & Noble 1968.

Perceval-Maxwell, M. *The Scottish Migration to Ulster in the Reign of James I.* London: Routledge and Kegan Paul, 1973.

Quinn, D. B. *The Elizabethans and the Irish.* Ithaca, N.Y.: Cornell University Press, 1966.

Senior, Hereward. *The Fenians and Canada.* Toronto: Toronto University Press, 1978.

Senior, Hereward. *Orangeism in Ireland and Britain, 1795–1836.* London: Routledge and Kegan Paul, 1966.

Simms, John G. *Jacobite Ireland, 1685–1691.* London: Routledge and Kegan Paul, 1969.

Solow, Barbara Lewis. *The Land Question and the Irish Economy, 1870–1903.* Cambridge, Mass.: Harvard University Press, 1971. A hard-nosed, but astute view of the land question from an economic historian.

Stewart, A. T. Q. *The Narrow Ground.* London: Faber & Faber, 1977. A recent study of the Ulster question.

Thompson, William Irwin. *The Imagination of an Insurrection: Dublin, Easter 1916.* Oxford: Oxford University Press, 1967;

Treasures of Early Irish Art, 1600 B.C. to 1500 A. D. New York: Metropolitan Museum of Art, 1977. The catalogue of a peripatetic exhibition, lushly illustrated, containing several essays of substance.

Watt, John. *The Church in Medieval Ireland.* Dublin: Gill and Macmillan 1972. Gill History of Ireland, Irish paperback.

Whyte, J. H. *Church and State in Modern Ireland, 1923–70.* New York: Barnes and Noble, 1971.

Woodham-Smith, Cecil. *The Great Hunger.* New York: Dutton, 1962.

INDEX